♦ FIRST EDITION ♦

Englefield & Arnold Publishing

Show What You Know™

On Ohio's Sixth Grade Proficiency Test

PARENT AND TEACHER EDITION

Written by: Jolie S. Brams, Ph.D., Patricia Nay,
Joan Schrader, M.S. Ed., and Deborah Tong

Illustrations by: Cynthia Kerr   Graphic Design by: Cindi Englefield Arnold

Published by: Englefield & Arnold, Inc.
2121 Bethel Road, Suite D • Columbus, Ohio 43220-1804
1-800-225-PASS (7277) Ohio only • www.eapublishing.com

Publisher: Cindi Englefield Arnold
Production Editor: Eloise M. Sasala
Printer: McNaughton & Gunn, Inc.
Distributor: Partners Distributing, Inc.

Send inquiries to Englefield & Arnold Publishing, 2121 Bethel Road, Suite D, Columbus, Ohio 43220-1804 or call (614) 459-3994 (local), 1-800-225-PASS(7277) Ohio only, or FAX to (614) 459-3995. Email: EAPublishg@aol.com, Internet: www.eapublishing.com

02 01 00 99 98   -96Aug- 15 14 13 12 11 10 9 8 7 6 5 4

ISBN 1884183-04-2

Publishing

Printed in the U.S.A.

Table of Contents

Reading

Mathematics

Citizenship

Science

Introduction

Five, Four, Three, Two, One, Lift Off!
Prepare your students for take off!

Show What You Know® On Ohio's Sixth Grade Proficiency Test provides the necessary information about the sixth-grade proficiency test. The book includes some of the most important information that the Ohio Department of Education has made available in the *Ohio Proficiency Tests for Grade 6 Practice Test Booklet, Practice Test Answer Booklet,* and *Sixth-grade Proficiency Tests: Information Guide.* Our team of writers have taken the Strands and Learning Outcomes, one by one, and expanded on them to help you review the material with your students. Each learning outcome is followed by example problems formatted as simulated proficiency test items with an analysis of how the problem is solved, and the correct answers. The two book set is designed to help prepare students to achieve high performance on the Ohio Sixth Grade Proficiency Test. The set includes this teacher's edition and a student workbook which has the same simulated proficiency test practice problems that correlate with the teacher's edition.

The *Show What You Know®* proficiency test preparation materials are successful because they are designed to increase the students' test performance. Test-taking skills are taught throughout, with one chapter dedicated to learning the skills. Students are given information on test anxiety, increasing their understanding and reducing the amount of test anxiety the student has about the test. Practice items are provided so that the student gains confidence in their skills and their knowledge. When students combine knowledge, test-taking skills, and confidence they are empowered with the three most important ingredients for test success. These are the three things that the *Show What You Know®* program is based on.

Recommended Use of the Materials

Classroom sets are available to schools, which include one teacher's edition, 30 student workbooks, and one answer key booklet for use as a grading tool. We have talked to teachers and school administrators about the different ways they use the materials to prepare students for the tests. Here are some ideas on how to use the material:

- **How To Prepare Students For High Performance** - Use the teacher's edition to review the Test-Taking Strategies chapter with the class, going over the test-taking tips, and the strategies for the three different types of test questions; multiple-choice, short-answer, and extended-response. Review the concept of Test Anxiety and let students do the short exercises that are found in their student booklet.

- **How To Use The Student Workbook** - The Writing, Reading, Citizenship, Mathematics, and Science chapters of the student workbook are covered by:
  - teacher presents the question and the class participates in analyzing the question and finding the correct answer.
  - students have a designated time set aside each day to work on the practice items independently or by small groups.
  - teachers can administer a mock proficiency test with each chapter, with one section per day. Teachers can use the answer key booklet to grade the work books or the teacher can present the correct answers while students follow along and grade their own booklets.

- **Discovering Your Students' Weak Areas** - The Answer Key Booklet can be used to grade the student workbooks. Since the practice items in the workbook are in order of learning outcome, the teacher can analyze which learning outcome the class is weak in and cover that content area in the classroom.

- **How To Review Your Students' Weak Areas** - The teacher's edition is used to review areas needed by the class by going over the practice items. Teachers go over the analysis of why the correct answer is correct AND why the incorrect answer is incorrect. There are boxes of information in each chapter that give teaching tips, ideas, and classroom activities for each of the learning outcomes.

Our goal in publishing this book is to help the parents, teachers, and students in Ohio to prepare for their opportunity to: *Show What They Know*!

Test-Taking Strategies

Test-Taking Strategies for The Sixth Grade Proficiency Test

Helping Your Students Perform Their Best

Strategies that help students do well on tests are not "tricks" in a negative sense. Their purpose is not to suggest to students that knowledge is unimportant, nor to encourage getting away with anything. Quite to the contrary, teaching students methods to approach test-taking situations allows them to perform optimally, gives them a sense of confidence, and teaches them problem-solving skills that can be applied to a variety of other situations.

The test-taking methods and skills throughout this book are proven techniques that increase test performance. The material used to teach is based on Ohio's Learning Outcomes for the six-th grade proficiency tests and the State Model Curriculums.

The test-taking strategies covered in this chapter come from two major areas:

1) How to approach tests in general, and
2) How to approach specific types of questions
   (ie. multiple-choice, short-answer, extended-response).

Note that the Writing portion of the Ohio Sixth Grade Proficiency Test has the same format as the fourth grade proficiency test, and therefore similar strategies are suggested for both tests.

Test-taking strategies can be taught in several ways. Information can be presented as a separate learning module, integrated with specific preparation for each section of the Proficiency Test, or integrated as part of the general curriculum, focusing on how these and similar strategies can be used in situations beyond this particular test.

This chapter provides information to you as teachers as well as examples to use with your students. Portions of this chapter are also found in the *Show What You Know* sixth grade student workbook. The material from the student workbook is shown in a box. The chapters on test-taking skills have been written to assist in teaching or reinforcing test-taking strategies specifically for the Ohio Sixth Grade Proficiency Test.

A child's confidence and competence in taking tests is also influenced by their level of anxiety. You may also want to use the information from the "Test Anxiety" chapter to assist your students.

General Test-Taking Strategies

All of us have taken many tests to reach our professional goals. Because test-taking is so familiar to us, the skills that have made us perform successfully seem natural to us, but may not be natural to sixth-grade students.

One of the keys to being an effective teacher (and enjoying working with children) is to appreciate that their experiences and world views are quite different from our own. Providing students with new strategies that are interesting, understandable, and helpful to them can be a rewarding process.

Although it seems second nature to us, students need to be reminded that their efforts should have a direct relationship to their performance. By now students have learned through experiences in gymnastics, dance, soccer, baseball, and so forth, that practice is important. Students can be reminded that (1) practice is helpful, and (2) all of their learning experiences have provided them with knowledge that will help them succeed on tests, including the Proficiency Test. The limerick on the next page about "Chuck" is an example used to illustrate this point.

1. **Luck isn't enough.** Have you ever had a lucky number, lucky color, or even a rabbit's foot? (Hopefully fake!) Everyone believes in luck, some more than others. A famous NFL quarterback never wears new shoes if he has won a game when wearing one particular pair. It probably doesn't really make sense (new shoes might be better for gripping the turf and staying on his feet) but he thinks it helps. However, if he just believed in luck, he wouldn't be an NFL player. He also has to learn and practice a lot! Learning in your classroom and practicing what you learn is probably the best strategy you can have. Don't be like Chuck!

> There was a cool boy named Chuck
> Who thought taking tests was just luck.
> He never prepared.
> He said, "I'm not scared."
> When his test score appears, he should duck!

Middle school students may still equate mastery with speed, perhaps stemming from peer pressure. Although there will be some time constraints when the Proficiency Test is administered, plenty of time has been allowed for students to read the directions and carefully consider and respond to each question. Emphasize to your students that rushing will not be beneficial to their test performance, stressing that taking time to implement test-taking strategies will actually help them do better. The limerick below about "Liz" can be helpful in presenting this concept.

2. **Speeding through the test doesn't help.** In our world, speed seems important. We always hear about the "fastest computers," the "fastest running backs," and the "world's fastest bullet train." Speed gets peoples' attention and respect. But how fast you complete the Ohio Sixth Grade Proficiency Test does not affect your test score. The people who created the test did not want students to rush; they allowed plenty of time for most students to finish. They want you to show what you know, not how fast you can answer questions. Speeding will not help you use any of the strategies that are discussed in this section. Look what happened to Liz:

> There was a sixth grader named Liz
> Who sped through her tests like
> a WHIZ.
> She thought she should race
> At a very fast pace
> But it caused her to mess up her quiz.

If students learn nothing else about test-taking, they need to learn to read directions carefully. (Especially while the separate answer booklet to record answers requires a bit of searching for the right place to record the answer.) Remember that some students still do not (1) carefully read directions, or (2) recall directions due to anxiety. Helping students recognize and deal with anxiety goes hand in hand with mastering the skill of reading directions. The limerick below about "Fred" may help teach this concept.

3. **Read directions carefully.** Sometimes we make up our minds about things before we explore and study them. Sometimes we feel nervous or rushed and don't read or listen carefully. Sometimes students have problems with tests because they do not read and remember directions. They think that they know what will be asked. Or they rush through the directions. Both of these approaches get in the way of students' showing what they know!

Imagine you are a famous chef. You are really well known for your cakes; you make the best cakes in Ohio! One day a group of visiting kings and queens from foreign countries come for a very important visit to Ohio. You are asked to bake their favorite cake, one you never baked before. They give you a list of ingredients and directions. However, you barely look at the directions. "Who has time? And anyway, I know how to bake any cake without much direction." Unfortunately, you don't read that the cake needs to bake at 250 degrees, not the 350 degrees you are used to. You also don't read that it should only bake for 15 minutes, not the 30 minutes you are used to. What do you get? Crispy cake and upset royalty. Not a good combination!

Reading directions slowly, repeating them to yourself, asking yourself if they make sense, and calming yourself down, are powerful test-taking strategies. Think about Fred:

There was a nice boy named Fred
Who forgot almost all that he read
The directions were easy
But he said, "I don't need these!"
He should have read them instead.

Students (especially when anxious) tend to become stuck on one question, wasting time, increasing anxiety, and decreasing self-confidence. Teaching (1) the relative unimportance of any one question, and (2) the tendency for all persons to remember information once they relax and move on to other questions is helpful. The limerick on the next page about "Von" helps make this point.

4. Don't get stuck on one question. Everyone generally wants to do a good job. Few people want to give up when faced with a question that is difficult. Some people panic (get really nervous) when they come across a question it seems they can't answer. Letting yourself get stuck on a question that is hard is a poor strategy for two important reasons. One, on the Ohio Sixth Grade Proficiency Test, missing one question is not a big deal. The test has lots of questions, and gives you plenty of chances to show what you know. Two, scientists who have studied learning and remembering have found that when a student goes on to other questions, it helps remind them of other things they know – going on to other questions may actually help you remember what you thought you couldn't! Later, we will read about how to make good guesses on hard questions, but for now, just remember to circle the number of the question you couldn't answer, and go back to it later. Think about Von!

There was a sweet girl named Von
Who got stuck and just couldn't go on.
She'd sit there and stare,
But the answer wasn't there.
Before she knew it, all the time was gone.

Not only is there no penalty for guessing on the Ohio Sixth Grade Proficiency Test, but skills that teach "educated guessing" are helpful to students in other situations. Specifics about the "how-tos" of educated guessing will be provided throughout this chapter; however, most students are unfamiliar with this concept as a whole. They tend to see thinking and guessing as two separate ideas, one "good" and one "bad." Stressing that thinking can be used in guessing is an intriguing concept for most students. The limerick below about "Tess" describes this to the students.

5. Power guessing is a helpful strategy. Did you know that on the Ohio Sixth Grade Proficiency Test there is no penalty for guessing? Some of us have learned that guessing is "bad," and thinking is "good." Actually, guessing and thinking can go together with great results! It's okay to guess, and even better when you learn how to guess intelligently. Think about Tess!

There was a smart girl named Tess
Who thought it was useless to guess.
If a question was tough
She just gave up
Which only added to her stress.

Administering the Test : What Students Need to Know

Share this information with your students:

- Students will have a maximum of two and one-half hours to finish each test. Most students will be able to complete the work on a test within approximately 75 minutes.

- The tests will be given in the following sequence: Writing, Reading, Mathematics, Citizenship, and Science. Districts can choose to administer one test per day or multiple tests per day.

- The tests (as of the printing of this book) will consist of two test booklets, (one for Writing, Reading, and Mathematics and one for Citizenship and Science) and an answer booklet.

- All work must be done in the answer booklet. Students may work in the test booklet but the test booklet will not be scored. Any work that is part of answering the question must be written in the answer booklet.

- Each multiple-choice question has four response choices, only one of which is correct. There is no penalty for guessing. The expression "choose the best answer" may be used in the question, but response choices such as "None of the above" or "All of the above" are NOT used.

- Since frequently made mistakes are often used as response choices, students should be encouraged to check their answers.

- Students may use certain calculators and protractors for the mathematics test items. (No graphing calculators and calculators with certain word processing capabilities are allowed. Students should check with their teacher or test administrator to see if their calculator is allowed before the test begins.) Students will be given only a #2 pencil.

- Students will NOT be permitted to use reference materials.

- Charts, maps, and other materials in the classroom that could assist students with the test items will be covered or removed during testing.

- Short-answer and extended-response items must be legible to be scored and both print or cursive writing is permitted.

Specific Strategies for Specific Types of Questions

The tests of Mathematics, Reading, Citizenship, and Science present questions in three different formats: multiple-choice, short-answer, and extended-response. The Writing test requires the student to create an actual writing sample. A student can optimize chances for success and enhance a sense of competence and confidence by learning and practicing a variety of test-taking strategies specially geared for each format.

Test-Taking Strategies For Multiple-Choice Questions

All multiple-choice questions have four possible answers, only one of which is correct. There is no penalty for guessing. Choices such as "none of the above" or "all of the above" will not be used. Therefore, students have an even greater opportunity to use test-taking strategies that will result in positive results. Students will need to find the correct page in the answer booklet and fill in the bubble with a #2 pencil. The multiple-choice questions are graded by a scanning device that only reads #2 lead and neatly filled in bubbles. It would be a shame for a student to get a question wrong for these technical reasons.

Sharing the following six strategies and examples should be helpful to your students. Please note that these examples are also in the test-taking section of the student manual.

1. **Read the question and answers carefully.** Help your students recognize the importance of paying attention to the specifics of both the question and the answer choices. For example:

   What is true about the population of cities in Ohio?

   A. The population of Columbus is greater than the population of Cleveland.

   B. The population of Canton is greater than the population of Cleveland.

   C. The population of Cincinnati is less than the population of Canton.

   D. The population of Cambridge is more than the population of Cincinnati.

This question has lots of two things – cities whose names start with the letter "C," and the words "greater than" and "less than." Think how easy it is to mix up all of this if the question isn't read carefully! To find the answer read one at a time and cross out the answer choices you know are incorrect. Choose the best answer from what is left. If you did a very good job of eliminating the incorrect answer choices, you will only have one left, the correct answer, "A."

2. **Select your answer carefully.** Sometimes an answer will seem correct at first glance, but is not correct. For example:

Which branch of Ohio's state government makes laws?

A. Judicial
B. Executive
C. Legislative
D. Lawyers

At first glance the word "judicial" reminds a student of "laws;" judges enforce the law. However, they do not *make* laws, this is a responsibility reserved for the legislative branch of government. The correct answer is "C." You can cross out the answer choices you know are incorrect, like "D" and choose from what is left. It's okay to guess after you have considered each one if you guess intelligently.

Ohio is a leading producer of coal. Which people are needed to produce coal?

A. Semi-truck drivers
B. Factory workers
C. Miners
D. Chemists

At first, the answer "semi-truck drivers" seems like it could be right. After all, the coal has to be transported, a needed job. Factory workers may be needed somewhere, it's a possibility. Chemists may have a job testing and analyzing the mineral but they do not produce the coal. The question had to do with *producing* coal and the miners are directly involved in digging for and therefore producing the coal. "C" is the correct answer.

3. **Use partial knowledge.** Students can make reasonable choices with only partial knowledge of the subject. Helping students settle down and look for what they know in the answers, refocusing from what they do *not* know, is a useful strategy. Look at the following example.

Where would you find how many people lived in Cleveland in 1960?

A. An almanac
B. A thesaurus
C. A globe
D. A dictionary

Students can use their knowledge of what you find in each of these reference sources to find the correct answer. Students know that an almanac is the correct reference source to get this information. The correct answer is "A."

4. Use your pencil. Students can better organize their thinking and strategically "attack" the test by using their pencils. Physically crossing out answers that should be eliminated reduces distractions when deciding among the remaining choices. Circling the *important* information in the problem helps eliminate information that is not needed to answer the question. Since there is no penalty for guessing, students should be encouraged to circle the numbers of questions that they have either guessed on, or feel they could not answer at all. Let's use the same example from the previous strategy example:

(Where) would you find (how many people) lived in Cleveland in 1960?

    A. An almanac
    B. A thesaurus
    C. A globe
    D. A dictionary

The circles show what the question is asking: "*Where* to find, *how many people.*" Answer "C" can be scratched out because your students know globes do not show population. They know a thesaurus is a word book of some kind and does not give information on the number of people, and should put a line through answer "B." A dictionary gives definitions and meanings of words so "D" can be scratched out. Your students may not know exactly what information is in the almanac, but they have eliminated all other answer choices. "A" is the correct answer.

5. Use common sense. Instead of focusing on looking for "trick" questions, using common sense is a better use of student's test-taking time. Some answer choices simply do not make sense if one thinks about them at all. For example:

Ohio farmers grow corn and soybeans. What do farmers use to have good crops?

    A. Caves
    B. Fertilizer
    C. Honeycombs
    D. Bugs

Simple, common-sense thinking will indicate to the student that they probably have no recollection of anything that relates to caves and farming. Have they ever seen a picture of crops in a cave? Similar reasoning can be used for the "honeycombs" choice. The students may know that some bugs are good in a garden but should be able to reason that farmers do not "use them to have good crops." That leaves "fertilizer" as the only common sense answer choice, so "B" is the correct answer.

6. Do not always pick your first answer. This may seem the opposite of test-taking skills you've come to believe in, but these multiple-choice questions are constructed in a slightly different way than traditional multiple-choice questions. On the Sixth Grade Proficiency Test, frequently made mistakes are often used as an answer choice. Therefore, students must always check their answers. Their first choice may be a popular wrong answer that they selected by making a common mistake.

Solve the problem: 98 + 37 =

A. 125
B. 134
C. 135
D. 136

If the two numbers are added together and the student forgets to add the one that was carried, they could get answer "A." Answer "D" could also be chosen by making an addition error (8 + 7 =16). By checking their answers carefully, and writing out the problem in the margin of the test booklet, the student can solve the problem carefully and choose the correct answer, "C."

Test-Taking Strategies For Short-Answer Questions

Short-answer questions require a student to demonstrate an ability to explain or document knowledge beyond answering a multiple-choice question. Each specific content test, except for Writing contains different types of short-answer questions. A student's familiarity with each type of short-answer question will obviously assist in doing well on the test. However, just as important, learning how to respond to these questions develops thinking skills; helps students organize, analyze, and reason; and encourages them to use their knowledge to generate conclusions.

Short-Answer Strategies For Reading
Short-answer questions are open-ended items that require a short phrase or sentence,or may be a chart or graphic that needs to be filled in, allowing the student to respond to the content of the reading passage in an organized manner. Here are some tips on test-taking strategies for Reading:
 1. Read the question carefully.
 2. Underline important parts.
 3. Ask yourself if the question makes sense.
 4. Make notes in the margin with ideas that seem to answer the question.
 5. Review what you read to find more details.
 6. Organize the answer in your head, asking if the answer is logical and supported by details.
 7. Think about how the answer will fit in the space provided.
 8. Write your answer in the space provided.

Short-Answer Strategies for Citizenship

These short-answer questions ask students to explain a conclusion, provide examples, complete a chart, interpret information, or explain an answer. Some of these questions have multiple steps or components. In most questions, all information needed to answer the question will be provided. Students need to reassure themselves that they will not be asked anything impossible.

Teaching students how to scan and assess the entire question is important. Talking themselves through the "layout" of the question is an important skill. For example, if a map is provided, students may tell themselves, "The map will be used to answer questions." Scan the map. What are the cities, rivers, mountains, etc. that are noted? See where they are included in the questions. "Question #2 uses the word Columbus – so I'd better pay attention to the location of Columbus." Here are some important test-taking strategies for Citizenship:

1. Scan and assess the entire question.
2. Ask yourself what information the question is asking for.
3. Think through and look carefully at the information provided in the question (maps, etc.).
4. Ask yourself what given information can help you find the correct answer.

Short-Answer Strategies for Mathematics

Short-answer questions in mathematics require the student to demonstrate proficiency in hands-on problem solving. Students may be asked to carry out a calculation, examine a situation and describe why an answer is correct, measure or draw a figure, complete a table, or provide a numerical, verbal, or visual response to a solution. While it is obvious that students must master the mathematical skills to answer correctly, certain test-taking approaches can be valuable. Identifying the "real" question being asked is critical. Here are five specific test-taking strategies for Mathematics:

1. Carefully read the question and determine what kind of a response you are asked to give. Are you asked to show your work, explain how to solve a problem, or answer and explain?
2. Solve, figure, calculate, draw out diagrams, and plan what your response will be in the margins of the test booklet.
3. Look at the space you are given to answer the question. It may be a box, a line, a diagram to fill in, etc.
4. Reread the directions and the questions so that you are sure what the problem is asking you to do.
5. Write your answer neatly in the space provided, show your work in an organized way.

Short-Answer Strategies For Science

Short-answer items might ask students to provide an explanation for an answer they have chosen or a conclusion they have made; make and justify predictions; propose a procedure to resolve an investigation; interpret information from a chart, graph, paragraph, or drawing; explain simple cause-and-effect relationships; provide examples; or explain the cause of certain natural phenomena or observations. Here are some test-taking strategies for Science:

1. Read the question carefully to determine what the quesion is asking you to do.
2. Organize your thoughts by writing them in the margins of the test booklet.
3. Observe pictures and read charts or data carefully, noticing the labels and keys.
4. Neatly write your answer in the chart, on the line, or in the space provided.
5. Go back to the test booklet and check that you did all that was required and that you answered the question.

Test-Taking Strategies For Extended-Response Items

Extended-response items require a student not only to give an answer but to explain, summarize, or retell information in a slightly greater length than in a short-answer item. Extended-response items will be found in the Reading, Citizenship, Science, and Math sections of the test.

Extended-Response Strategies for Reading

Students will have open-ended items that require them to show their ability to organize ideas and respond to what they have read. Each reading passage will have at least one short-answer or extended-response item. Skills required are organizing ideas, analyzing and responding to text, and integrating text information with background knowledge. Here are some extended-response strategies for Reading:

1. Read the question carefully and determine what the "real" question is.
2. Reread the passage or skim quickly through it if needed.
3. Organize your response/answer by writing in the margins of the test booklet.
4. Look at the space you are given to write your response. Is it small or large?
5. Neatly write your answer in the space provided. (Print or cursive)
6. Your response should fit the space provided or be complete in answering the question. Try to use no more than the space provided. Being well organized will help you be as brief or as detailed as you need to be. The length is not as important as what you write. You are being asked to give a little bit more information than in a short-answer response item.

Extended-Response Strategies for Citizenship

Extended-response items ask students to interpret information from a three to eight line paragraph on a specific topic, reach a conclusion, and justify that conclusion or provide examples. The credit for answers are usually based on demonstration of the understanding of concepts, therefore students should always try to explain their answers. The more a student demonstrates an understanding, the more credit that may be applied. The following strategies for Citizenship can be helpful:

1. Read the question carefully to find out what the "real" question is.
2. Carefully study any chart, graph, map or information you are given. At times, you may be required to pull the answer out of the information given in the question.
3. Look at the space provided to you to answer the question.
4. Organize your answer by stating the answer and listing two or three reasons for your answer by writing in the margins of the test booklet.
5. Locate the space provided for your answer and, in a neat and organized method, write your answer.
6. Do not worry if your answer did not use the exact space provided.
7. Check your answer to see if you answered the question correctly and if you explained your answer to show a good understanding of the subject.

Extended-Response Strategies for Mathematics

Extended-response items require students to construct their own responses and to demonstrate problem solving, mathematical reasoning, and application of concepts and skills. Extended-response items require students to communicate their understanding of the problem situation, verify and interpret results with respect to problems, and justify their answers and solution processes. Each strand has at least one short-answer or extended-response item. Please note the following Mathematics strategies:

1. Read the entire question carefully and find out what you are asked to do.
2. Look at the space you are given to answer the question.
3. Make any calculations or plan your response in the margins.
4. Find the space your are to record your answer in, then neatly write your answer in the space provided and make sure you show your work, if asked, in an organized way.
5. Reread the question or directions to make sure you have done what you were asked to do and check your work for any mistakes.

Extended-Response Strategies for Science

Extended-response items might ask students to evaluate a procedure and point out its flaws and/or suggest improvements; make and justify predictions or conclusions; describe natural processes or interactions among the components of a biological or physical system; make and use inferences in resolving an investigation; and interpret information from a chart, graph, paragraph, or drawing. Credit for answers is based on demonstrating an understanding of concepts, therefore students should always explain their answers, when asked to do so. Here are some strategies for Science extended-response items:

1. Read the question carefully to find out what the "real" question is.

2. Carefully study any chart, graph, map or information you are given. At times, you may be required to pull the answer out of the information given in the question.
3. Look at the space provided to you to answer the question.
4. Organize your answer by stating the answer and listing two or three reasons for your answer by writing in the margins of the test booklet.
5. Locate the space provided for your answer and, in a neat and organized method, write your answer.
6. Do not worry if your answer did not use the exact space provided.
7. Check your answer to see if you answered the question correctly and if you explained your answer to show a good understanding of the subject.

Example Short-Answer and Extended-Response Items

The reading passage below is an example illustrated in the test-taking strategy section of the student manual. It can be used to demonstrate each of the written types of responses before the students go on to the practice items in their manuals. It would be helpful to review these with your students.

Sample Question:

Directions: Read the selection below and answer the questions that follow.

Most of us see pelicans when we go to the seashore. To us they seem like big happy birds, flying freely through the sky, swooping down to grab fish for a meal. Pelicans have been in existence for a long time, dating way before the fossils of humans were found on this earth. However, the life of pelicans is not as easy as it looks. Pelicans are exposed to many violent natural elements, such as storms, including hurricanes, and very windy conditions. They are also hunted not only by careless humans, but by animals when they are perched on the ground, such as alligators. Pelicans are fairly fast flyers when they are in the air, but they are clumsy on the ground. They are also very big and easy targets. So how do pelicans protect themselves?

Although pelicans will land on the ground and walk around, they have a real talent for balancing themselves in tight places. Pelicans can get a good night's sleep perched on the end of a pier, on a rock, or sometimes on the water itself. Pelicans also have a knack for drinking fresh water very quickly, keeping them away from predators and on the ground as little as possible. Pelicans are obviously not blue, like the water or sky, but they are light gray and white, and often times blend in with the caps on waves, making it difficult for them to be spotted. Over the years, many people have befriended pelicans. Pelicans have become the mascot of sports teams, and have had their pictures on T-shirts and other items. There are also clubs who want to help protect pelicans. Because of this, pelicans have many friends among humans, who want them to live long lives and be protected.

Sample short-answer question:

1. The reading passage above gave a lot of information about pelicans. What are two things that can be listed as dangers to pelicans?

> **1.**
>
> 1)_____
>
> 2)_____

Sample Answer:
Question #1 is an example of a short-answer question. The box represents the space that is given to write the answer. The answer should be short, meaning one to three words each. The answer must answer the question asked. In this case the student is ask to list two dangers. The answer space gives the student a total of two lines, one answer per line. A correct response might be 1) storms or bad weather, and 2) preditors like alligators.

Sample extended-response question:

2. Describe in detail what protections may help pelicans survive.

> **2.**
>
> _____
>
> _____
>
> _____
>
> _____
>
> _____
>
> _____
>
> _____

_____

_____

_____

_____

_____

_____

_____

_____

_____

Sample Extended-Response Answer:

Question #2 is an example of an extended-response question. Students should build their answer by writing ideas in the margins. Add to the ideas by skimming the passage again. Then begin writing in the space provided. Check the answer to see that the question has been answered and that the answer is complete. A sample student response might be:

> *Pelicans can find themselves in danger but have many ways of protection that will help them survive. They can stay safe while flying because they are fast flyers and can drink fresh water quickly so they aren't attacked while on the ground. They are light gray or white in color, making it difficult to spot them in the water. Some people see them as a mascot and try to protect them, too.*

Test Anxiety

Helping Your Students Overcome Test Anxiety

By the time you read this book, you, your staff, your students, and their parents have heard a great deal about the Ohio Proficiency Test. School personnel are anxious and concerned that their students do their best and that the test scores reflect the hard work that the faculty has put into educating their students. Parents are also concerned that the children do well. Many parents believe that a student's performance on the Sixth Grade Proficiency Test is going to directly affect the perceptions that others have of their child. They also want their child to do well, for a number of reasons, including their concern about the child's educational performance and their own anxieties about test-taking. Students are not oblivious to the fact that the Ohio Proficiency Tests have received so much press and attention in recent years. Although they can be reassured that their performance on the Sixth Grade Proficiency Test is not going to effect promotion or graduation, they know that high school students have had their shares of anxieties about failing. Your sixth graders are well aware that the Ohio Proficiency Tests are important milestones in their education. In addition, from a developmental perspective, sixth graders are very aware of their performance in relation to their peers, as well as the pressures that they feel regarding moving into the young adult world.

For these and other reasons, test anxiety can be a significant factor in how well your students perform on the Ohio Sixth Grade Proficiency Test. The purpose of this chapter is to provide you, as an educator, with a basic understanding of the origins of text anxiety and how this problem can be confronted in an educational setting to the betterment of your students. This discussion will also hopefully be of assistance to you in dealing with your students' test anxiety in other situations other than the Sixth Grade Proficiency Test.

Test anxiety is one of a number of fears and anxieties that are experienced by both children and adults. Those who work with, or parent children understand that some fears are typical for children of all ages. Developmental psychologists call these "age-related" fears. These fears are usually transitory, but at times they can become problematic when they are intense and/or interfere with a child's normal development and daily activities. All children experience anxiety when confronting new challenges, and the school setting in itself provides many unique challenges to the developing child. It would be rare to find a child who has not had a fearful or anxious response to something pertaining to their life at school, whether it be dealing with a new teacher, confronting a bully, learning a new concept, climbing to the very top of the climbing bars, or having to speak in front of the class. Children of different ages resolve these fears and anxieties in different ways. Younger children may go to an adult for support and guidance but older children are expected by others to be more independent and also feel themselves that they should resolve these problems on their own. Educators generally respond to children's fears and anxieties with support, direction, and reassurance, allowing children to overcome these difficulties and gain self-esteem from accomplishing this task.

A fear of taking tests is very similar to the fears noted above. As with other situations that cause your students to feel anxious or concerned, test anxiety should be treated the same way. Students need to be informed that test anxiety is not something they face alone, but children of all ages and even adults often times feel anxious and concerned when facing a test taking situation. Your students would also benefit by developing an understanding of how test anxiety develops, which will provide them with a mechanism for finding ways to remediate this difficulty. Relatedly, students will benefit from learning new, effective, and even pleasurable ways to reduce their anxiety and master test taking situations. The purpose of this chapter is to provide you with information that is necessary to be of assistance to your students in helping them overcome test anxiety. While many serious fears and anxieties are treated by mental health professionals, in this situation, the educator is the first line of defense. There are many relatively simple and effective procedures that the educator can employ to assist their students in feeling confident in taking not only the Ohio Sixth Grade Proficiency Test, but other tests as well.

Just What Are Sixth Graders All About Anyway?

As those of us who teach sixth graders know, this is anything but your "run of the mill" grade level. Sixth graders vary markedly in terms of their cognitive development, physical size, social interests, and judgment. Any of us who have looked at our own sixth grade class picture remembers the tall, womanly appearing girl standing next to the scrawny, youthful looking boy. We will also remember having part of our class still play with action figures while the other half of the class just wants to know where the action is! However, most sixth graders do share a number of commonalities which are helpful in designing interventions for test anxiety.

Sixth graders see themselves on the cusp between childhood and adulthood. They are just beginning to realize that the world is fraught with adult responsibilities and demands and are trying to get a sense of how they fit into the adult world. Sixth graders, for example, are just beginning to earn a living independently, perhaps delivering the small suburban newspaper, babysitting or dog-walking, or perhaps helping an older sibling mow lawns. In their style of dress they are also trying to bridge the gap between childhood and adulthood. How many of us have seen sixth graders wear the latest style worn by college students, although with perhaps cartoon characters, flowers, or teddy bears as designs or decorations? Sixth graders are beginning to realize how close they are to adulthood. They realize that they will be driving and exercising the right to vote relatively soon. As one sixth grader excitedly stated, "Soon I'll be driving down to that voting place and I'll be able to tell you what to do!" Sixth graders are also becoming increasingly aware of the impact that their actions have on their future. They are beginning to think about "getting good grades to go to college" and being concerned as to how their performance and abilities relate to that of their peers. While many sixth graders look at comparisons in terms of appearance or popularity, many of them are becoming aware that differences and comparisons also exist in terms of academics.

While younger children often times develop test anxiety for the simple reason that they want to perform well to please their parents or their teachers, the desire to do well and the anxiety that may accompany that concern is more complex for sixth graders. Test anxiety develops in students of this age when they view taking the Ohio Sixth Grade Proficiency Test, or other tests, as experiences that will have significant impact on their future. They want to see themselves as someone who can do well not only in the present but in the future. The intellectual and developmental changes that children experience in very late elementary school and early middle school give them the ability to consider how their present behavior impacts future behavior. Because of their ability to think abstractly and complexly, sixth graders are acutely aware that test performance may indeed be significant at some point in their life, if not right here in the present. As noted, sixth graders are also concerned as to how they appear to others. For many sixth graders, performing poorly or failing a proficiency test would be a sign to their peers that they are inadequate, certainly not something to which most students this age would like to admit. Sixth graders want to do well in the adult world and are aware that all sorts of test taking and other challenges are part of the adult experience. Sixth graders tend to equate failure in certain areas with the possibility of failure as an adult. While part of this problem is an offshoot of normal development, it is painfully apparent that some of this anxiety concerning the transition between childhood and adulthood is worsened by societal expectations. In a society where performance in middle school athletics directly relates to acceptance on high school teams and where middle school students are concerned about whether or not their mathematics curriculum will allow them to take Calculus II as a senior in high school, it is not surprising that sixth graders may be anxious about tests.

Sixth grade children who experience test anxiety, in addition to the developmental issues noted above, may simply have not learned adequate test taking strategies early in their academic career, and may also have not learned how to channel their anxieties and fears in constructive ways by mastering other fears during early childhood. Thus, while educators need to understand and appreciate certain developmental issues, some of the test anxiety experienced by sixth graders may be a result of inadequate previous learning, including previous experience with significant test anxiety.

A Framework for Understanding and Remediating Test Anxiety

Test anxiety can be lessened to a great degree by the application of simple psychological principals and techniques. Unfortunately, when many of us hear the word "psychological" we generally think of two or more inaccurate scenarios. In one situation, psychological interventions are viewed as a bad Woody Allen movie, with long-term intensive sessions, "laying on the couch" and discussing for years how early childhood trauma results in performance anxiety. The other scenario is taken right out of the old sci-fi movies where the unlucky abductee is strapped in a chair with a metal helmet attached to numerous electrodes, and is shocked when he thinks or says something that is not to the liking of whatever alien or mad scientist is in control. Fortunately, in terms of the treatment of test anxiety, both of these scenarios can be thrown out the window!

Extensive research has shown that children's fears can be greatly reduced with the implementation of cognitive/behavioral strategies. Cognitive/behavioral treatment is widely used for a variety of problems encountered by children and adults, including depression, anxiety, social interactional difficulties, long-term maladaptive behavior patterns, and so forth. These approaches work on a simple but very effective premise; that one's thoughts play an important role in maintaining the problems at hand. Cognitive/behavioral approaches assist the student or client to think differently about the world around them. The motto of cognitive/behavioral therapy is that changing one's thoughts leads directly to changes in behavior and attitudes.

All of us use cognitive/behavioral techniques, to one degree or another, in our daily lives. This is not a magical or novel concept, but there is extensive research that shows that these techniques, used in predictable and proven ways, are highly effective in behavior and attitude change. For example, it is probably safe to say that none of us enjoy going to the dentist. What stops us from turning the car around and going home, screaming in terror in the dentist chair, or crying in anticipation of dental work being performed?

What stops us, simply stated, is the types of thought processes that precede our visit to the dentist. Telling oneself, "It will be over in a little while," or "I've withstood this discomfort before" are all helpful ways of reducing anxiety and changing one's attitude toward the dentist as well as one's behavior in the dental chair. While procedures are being performed, many of us tell ourselves, "I'm not going to anticipate pain because he gave me enough novacaine," or "The noise is a lot worse than what is really happening." If the majority of the adult public did not employ these cognitive/behavioral procedures, going to the dentist would be a torturous and devastating experience.

Children respond very positively to interventions that allow them to master situations. Mental health professionals have found that children, both in therapy sessions as well as in school settings, enjoy learning about their thoughts and feelings and obtaining control over their lives. Cognitive/behavioral interventions work well in the sixth grade age group because children this age feel comfortable and respected when they are educated about ways to solve problems, and treated in a responsible and adult-like manner. Cognitive/behavioral interventions help children not only answer the "why?" of what is happening to them, but these interventions also produce fairly rapid and noticeable positive results. Most of the interventions described in this chapter are cognitive/behavioral in nature. These specific interventions, and the theory behind them, should also be useful to you in helping your students with a variety of other difficulties, both academic and social.

"Normalizing" Test Anxiety for Your Students

Fears are both normal and common in childhood, but as children become older they become more embarrassed and self-conscious about not being able to master their environment and control their feelings and behavior. Sixth graders are particularly sensitive to and embarrassed by feelings of anxiety. They are able to look back upon their childhood, and compare themselves with younger students and younger siblings. While in the young elementary school age group, it is typical for children to be afraid of, for example, horror movies, tarantulas, war, or storms. Sixth graders see themselves as moving into adulthood and feel that they should be invulnerable to anxieties. Sixth graders, because of their intellectual and social development, would be less likely to bring attention to themselves concerning fears and vulnerabilities. Thus, educators must be aware that test anxiety is not uncommon among all students, much less sixth graders, but that these students may be reluctant to admit that they are having difficulty.

Teaching your sixth graders that everyone experiences anxiety at times is often times helpful. Both children and adults who experience anxiety often times feel that there is something wrong with them. Teaching your students that there are logical, even scientific reasons for anxiety can make this difficulty more acceptable as well as more understandable.

Students often benefit by understanding that mild forms of anxiety are very useful in helping people accomplish their goals. Most people who have overcome great challenges have felt some degree of anxiety prior to attempting to accomplish that task. Mild anxiety serves as a way for the body and mind to mobilize it's resources, much like a gathering of soldiers before war. If indeed, for example, our military had no idea of an impending threat, troops and armaments would not be appropriately deployed in an effective manner. Being "on alert" allows one to get moving quickly and with purpose. Without feeling that there is a challenge that needs to be met, everything would drag along at a slow pace and in an unfocused manner. Professional athletes perform much better when they encounter a mild amount of anxiety before a game or a meet. A mild level of anxiety, where their attention is focused, their heart races a little bit, and they are in tune with what is going on around them, helps them focus their direction and pay attention to what they are going to do next. The autobiographies of successful scientists, actors, and adventurers all discuss, in one way or another, how a small amount of anxiety helps them perform at their peak, and has also led to all sorts of discoveries and achievements. The structure of DNA was discovered in a dream; this scientist was anxious and preoccupied with his frustration of not being able to find the answer he was looking for. The problem was so much on his mind that he dreamt the answer. He did not have a nightmare, nor did he "freak out;" instead, he had enough anxiety that he was able to focus on the problem and put thought and energy in to it. Sixth graders do not like to be perceived as different from their peers and certainly do not want to appear incompetent in the eyes of adults. Educating sixth graders that many successful people have used anxiety to their advantage is reassuring and informative.

Even extreme anxiety is not always an abnormal or useless response. Fear is an extreme version of an alarm reaction that your body naturally goes through in response to any type of threat. The painful feelings that people experience when they very anxious actually have a protective role. Years ago, psychologists and physiologists described this natural heightened arousal as the "fight or flight response." This is a built-in mechanism that allows all higher order animals to mobilize a great deal of energy quickly in order to cope with threats to their survival. This alarm reaction serves people well in situations that are realistically dangerous. Hearing a loud explosion and ducking for cover, or seeing a tornado in the distance and running the opposite direction is a normal "fight or flight" response. During these experiences, we feel what is labeled "anxiety." While, in contrast, persons getting ready for a scientific experiment or an athletic event may feel alert and focused, persons experiencing a "fight or flight" response may experience heart palpitations, a churning stomach, sweating, dizziness, and jumpiness. Obviously, if one is being attacked by a large and hairy animal, such a response can save one's life. However, if one is just faced with taking the Ohio Sixth Grade Proficiency Test, this level of anxiety is an overreaction. If a student is experiencing these types of painful, physiological and psychological symptoms, their first choice is going to be run from rather than confront the test.

As sixth grade students are in the midst of learning comparative quantitative skills, they may benefit from understanding how anxiety can be both helpful as well as damaging by looking at an "anxiety curve."

Illustration I

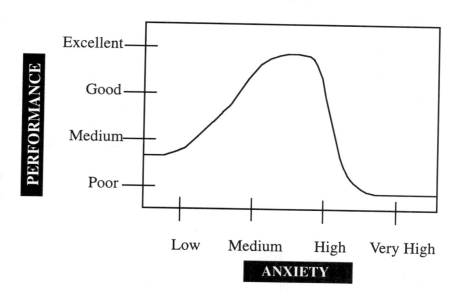

As this diagram depicts, low levels of anxiety are generally related to poor to medium performance. As anxiety builds, performance generally increases. However, there is a point where there is a sudden drop off; when anxiety becomes too high, performance becomes markedly impaired. This is what happens in test anxiety. Students need to feel comfortable with some degree of anxiety because this will facilitate their performance. Thus, they should not berate themselves for having some degree of anxiety; it actually has a positive effect. Focus should be made on differentiating between positive and healthy levels of anxiety versus more destructive feelings of being overwhelmed and terrified. These feelings are what is described as test anxiety, and negatively impact the student's ability to perform at a reasonable level.

The exercise described in the next illustration should help students understand how this anxiety curve relates to their own life. Students can find this example in their student workbooks. For example, have your students imagine what it would be like to ask someone of the opposite sex to a birthday party. How would their behavior differ if they experienced no anxiety, mild anxiety, or perhaps more extreme anxiety? In the situation where they felt no anxiety, they probably would present to their desired friend as less than desirable themselves. They would present with an "I don't care" attitude. Mild anxiety would make them focused on the task at hand, and present as interested and alert. Too much anxiety would cause psychological symptoms and avoidance.

Exercise #1: How much anxiety is helpful?

Using the "Anxiety Curve" as a guide, fill in the chart as to how you or a typical 6th grade student might feel in the following situations. The first one is done for you.

Type of Challenge	No Anxiety	Medium Anxiety	High Anxiety
1. Asking someone of the opposite sex to your birthday party.	You dress like a slob and say, "Hey, do you want to go? I don't really care."	You wait for the right moment, look him or her in the eye and ask shyly.	You get sick to your stomach, miss school, and ask your friend to do the asking.
2. Giving a speech at the 6th grade awards dinner.			
3. Taking an airplane ride alone, across country, to see your grandmother.			
4. Performing in front of your classmates at the school talent show.			

Anxiety can also be normalized by sharing with students that both children and adults fear a variety of objects and situations. Many fears have specific technical names, and although they are rarely used in day-to-day life, they are fun to read about and learn, especially for students who like to possess "rare" information to impress others. A list of some of these "fancy" names for a variety of fears are listed on the next page. Sharing this list with your class, and perhaps coming up with other "made up" names for fears, can inject some humor as well as learning in this situation.

Technical Name	Phobia
Acrophobia	height
Agoraphobia	open spaces
Aichmophobia	sharp and pointed objects
Ailurophobia	cats
Arachnophobia	spiders
Anthophobia	flowers
Anthropophobia	people
Aquaphobia	water
Astraphobia	lightning
Brontophobia	thunder
Claustrophobia	closed spaces
Cynophobia	dogs
Equinophobia	horses
Menophobia	being alone
Mikrophobia	germs
Murophobia	mice
Numerophobia	numbers
Nyctophobia	darkness
Ophidiophobia	snakes
Pyrophobia	fire
Thanatophobia	death
Trichophobia	hair
Xenophobia	strangers
Zoophobia	animals

How Do We Learn To Be Anxious Anyway?

There are three primary mechanisms contributing to the development of anxiety.

1. **Repetitive Learning.** Simple, accumulated, and repeated learning experiences, even those that seem relatively minor, all can "add up" to significant difficulties in the way that children conceptualize their problems and abilities. After years of these minor learning experiences, children's perceptions of themselves and their experiences are integrated into "who" they are; they do not know where these thoughts or feelings came from, and just accept them as part of themselves. For example, consider the child who has a great deal of comfort in working on a computer. Many of these children come from families in which learning new tasks is expected and rewarded. Over time, their parents have given them experiences in which they can feel successful in learning new activities, especially dealing with technology. When they enter school, teachers and peers complimented them on their ability to learn these types of activities quickly and competently. These children, if asked to describe themselves, would probably list "good with computers" as a primary descriptor as to who they are. Most likely, they would also note "I am a good problem solver," or "I am intelligent."

Test anxiety, like other aspects of a child's self-concept, skills, and coping mechanisms, develops over time. Students need to understand that while test anxiety can be overcome, improvement will take place over time. Using exercises such as the "positive self-talk" examples given later in this chapter, and recording a student's progress in handling their anxiety can give that student documentation as to how they are progressing over time. While younger elementary school age children generally enjoy visually seeing the fruits of their labor, sixth graders can also become excited over their ability to change their feelings and behavior. Having them record their experiences so they can be referred to at other times, and using interesting mediums, such as the computer, can make this exciting and rewarding for your sixth grade student.

The diagram below is just one example of a charting program that will allow a student to see the benefits of attempting change over time. Have students complete this exercise to prove to themselves that it's not always as bad as it seems.

Exercise #2: Was It As Bad As It Seemed?	
Situation That Made Me Anxious	
What Was I feeling? (Heart pounding, desire to leave, anger and irritation, etc.)	
What Was I Thinking? (For example, I'll never be able to do this; I hate this subject, etc.)	
What Did You Do About Your Feelings? (Never did the assignments; did part of it and quit, asked for help, etc.)	
What Did You Learn From Your Experience? (For example, if I think positive things, I am less nervous; getting in trouble for not doing a test is worse than not doing it at all, etc.)	

Sixth graders are getting to be masters at talking about their feelings. As they enter the early years of adolescence, they become quite introspective, concerned about how they feel about their own lives, the world around them, and also how others perceive them. Students at this age are always interested in literature which gives them insight into the behavior of themselves and others; basically, young middle school children are "budding psychologists." Students of this age are willing, in the appropriate setting, especially when the focus is not on them directly or they are in a private situation, to discuss how they feel about their lives and experiences. Giving students who are troubled by test anxiety an opportunity to record their feelings, try new strategies, and discuss the outcome with a significant adult, may help them. It is important to remind a child that learned behaviors take a while to unlearn so they do not feel set up for failure, but able to have reasonable expectations.

2. **Learning Through a Traumatic Experience.** Experiences that are traumatic in nature generally result in a very sudden and generally unpleasant learning experience. Phobias and other fears are most often learned through the type of scenario in which either a child or an adult is encountered with a situation which is surprising, overwhelming, dangerous, or in some way generates a very marked and extreme psychological reaction. The anxiety is an extreme version of an alarm reaction that one's body naturally experiences in response to any type of threat. From an evolutionary perspective, the painful feelings that humans experience when they are anxious actually have a protective role. Years ago, physiologists and psychologists described this heightened arousal as the "fight or flight" response. This is a built-in mechanism that enables all higher animals to mobilize a great deal of energy quickly in order to cope with threats to their survival. This alarm reaction serves people well in situations that are realistically dangerous. However, through learning experiences this "fight or flight" response can become non-adaptive, in the sense that a person becomes aroused in a situation which may not be dangerous in a realistic sense.

Your students certainly have experience with dangerous weather situations, especially in our home state of Ohio. Spring and early summer come not only with blossoming trees and flowers and the anticipation of the school year ending, but also with the possibility of torrential rains, violent thunderstorms, and tornadoes. Children and adults who have been caught in a dangerous weather condition, such as witnessing a tornado, having lightening strike nearby, or witnessing damage to property, may be particularly attuned to the possible dangerous nature of weather. The "fight or flight" reactions that occur when one is experiencing these frightening, and often times helpless, circumstances creates a state of arousal in the individual. Their heart races, they want to avoid the situation, and they think a number of negative thoughts such as, "I could actually die here." After such a traumatic experience, just a reminder of turbulent weather can evoke these feelings of anxiety. The hint of a thunderstorm, or a report on the weather channel, can cause panic in some of these individuals. Persons become anxious at even a hint of trouble.

Trauma does not have to be related to actual physical danger. Children and adults can experience an extreme physiological reaction to situations such as social embarrassment or failure. Many of us can look back on our lives and think about being mortified (even the words themselves equate to physical death) when perhaps we said the wrong thing on a date in middle school, or said something in front of the class which was incorrect or embarrassing. These types of situations can evoke a "fight or flight" response and result in anxiety whenever one finds themselves in a similar situation.

All test-taking is stressful. There is probably not one of your students that has not had a difficult time taking a test at one time or another in their academic lives, even the most competent of your students. For may students, however, test taking has been more than a worrisome experience; many students have failed a test only to be reprimanded by their parents, shamed by their peers, or perhaps just devastated by their own internal expectations. Some students have a "built in" physiological predisposition to be more anxious than others; test taking is even more problematic for them and they have a greater propensity to develop a "fight or flight" reaction.

It is helpful for students to learn that anxiety is a normal response to a difficult situation. However, when one experiences that response over and over again, even when they may have the abilities and capacities to handle the situation at hand, then this becomes a problem.

3. **Generalization.** Students with general doubts about their academic abilities often times generalize these doubts to a fear of failure on tests. Similarly, high achieving students who see school as a struggle or a battle will also look at tests in the same way. The concept of generalization is a useful teaching concept, not just in terms of test anxiety, but in terms of other learning situations.

Students who generalize about their own perceived limitations and their abilities often times experience test anxiety. This holds particularly true for sixth grade students, who may be newly exposed to changing classes and teachers throughout the day. Difficulties in one class, and feelings of frustration and failure, can easily generalize to other classes. In addition, a feeling of being overwhelmed with the entire middle school experience often generalizes to other aspects of a child's self-concept and behavior. Psychologists have found that it is often times common for young middle school students, especially sixth graders, to develop emotional and behavioral difficulties during this transition to a different social and learning environment. Research has shown that many of these difficulties have to do with problems in self-esteem, handling anxiety, and basically generalizing problems in one area to a lack of confidence and self-respect in other areas of the young adolescent's life.

The box on the next page lays out for your students the three ways in which we learn to be anxious. This information is also in the student workbook.

Three Ways You Learn Everything in Your Life!

1. **The first way we learn is by doing something over and over again.** By the time we are in the sixth grade, most of us can hit a softball or a tennis ball at least reasonably well. We may not be ready to be on the Sports Channel, but we also can get it across the net or at least down the field a little ways. But, have you ever thought how you learned this skill? Well, most of us kept whacking at the ball, missing it most of the time. Eventually, we would learn how to connect the bat or the racket with the ball, and feel pretty good about ourselves. Generally, our parents or our friends would tell us that we did a good job. Over time, we came to feel confident in our abilities to at least not make a total fool out of ourselves, and feel happy and comfortable when we played sports with our friends. We might not think that we're worth a million dollar sports contract, but we're not embarrassed about our abilities, and we are not afraid to play or try.

   However, imagine what it would be like to always feel like a failure. Let's say that we never were very good at hitting balls, and our friends and family didn't really care one way or another if we practiced. What do you think you would feel if by the time you got to the sixth grade you just weren't very good at those types of sports? Most likely, you would not see yourself as very athletic. If you were then forced to try out for the tennis team, the softball team, or probably any team, you would most likely feel very, very anxious, and very much like you wanted to get out of the situation as quickly as possible. Past learning experiences would cause us to feel anxious. Our heart would race faster, we would want to avoid the situation, and we would have all sorts of bad thoughts and feelings about ourselves. It is useful to think about ourselves as being made up of thousands of "little" day to day experiences. We need to have felt good about ourselves in the past to feel good today.

2. **People also learn when something REALLY BIG happens.** Some of us have had that experience when eating new foods. Think about going out to dinner with your family to a new Mexican restaurant. Before the meal is served, the waitress brings a big bowl of tortilla chips and salsa to your table. You are starving, having just spent the whole day shopping with your family and you can't wait to eat. You grab a tortilla chip and dip it right in the nice red salsa. About two seconds later, you've learned your lesson. Your mouth is burning and all the water in the world does not make it stop. You've learned once and for all to be very careful about eating anything that has to do with hot peppers.

   It probably makes a lot of sense not to eat a big mouthful of salsa in one bite, but sometimes we learn things that are not very helpful. Sometimes we have difficult experiences in school, especially when taking tests, and become so frightened and anxious that we decide that this is something we never want to do again. While staying away from big mouthfuls of hot salsa is probably a good idea, staying away from school work and tests for the rest of your life is not. Sometimes we learn things that help us but sometimes we learn things that get in our way of enjoying school and doing the best that we can. This is espeicially true when we have a bad experience.

3. **We also learn by generalization.** Generalization means that we take one thing that we have learned and extend the idea to other situations.

Let's look back at example number two, when we talked about eating that hot salsa. After that experience, you probably will think twice before eating anything that looks spicy, especially in a Mexican restaurant. You will probably be careful about green salsa too, and maybe about anything that looks like a hot pepper.

However, you can generalize too much. You might get worried about anything that looks red or green, or food that is served in a Mexican restaurant. Eventually, any type of new food might make you feel anxious and somewhat disgusted. This anxious reaction really gets in the way of enjoying new foods and new restaurants, and also enjoying sharing happy times with your friends and family.

Self-Talk; We Do It Anyway So Let's Do It Right
Early in this chapter, we talked about cognitive/behavioral interventions as a way of helping students reduce their anxiety and cope better in test-taking situations. One primary goal of cognitive/behavioral interventions is to reduce what is simply referred to as negative self-talk; thinking about situations in a way which promotes failure. Both children and adults with anxiety engage in a tremendous amount of negative self-talk. Psychologists have found that most anxious, as well as depressed, adults and also children, think in distorted, unrealistic, or illogical ways. Cognitive/behavioral therapists have described these distorted modes of thinking as cognitive distortions. These distortions are responsible for both creating and sustaining much of the anxiety experienced by children in a variety of situations, including situations related to tests and learning. When children learn to recognize and counter these unhealthful modes of thinking with more rational and positive self-talk, it goes a long way in helping them view themselves in a more balanced, objective, and realistic fashion. In time, this significantly reduces the amount of anxiety that they experience.

Most of us have seen in our own lives how external events (something that happens to us) leads to negative self-talk and ideas, and from there problematic feelings and difficult behaviors. For example, imagine hearing a rattly or whiny noise from our car's engine. That is called the external event. At that point, we can choose to internally talk to ourselves about this event in a number of ways. We might say to ourselves, "Well, this is going to be aggravating, but the worse thing that can happen is I have to put it on my charge card, but we will get the problem fixed." Negative self-talk would sound more like this, "I can never have a car that runs right and it's all the fault of that guy I married. If I put this on the charge card, we'll never get it paid off. And anyway, it's probably gonna be at least a few thousand dollars." What types of behaviors would result from differences in the way that one thinks about their situation? In the first situation, one would call one's spouse and figure out how to get the car to the shop in perhaps somewhat of an aggravated but generally controlled and reasonable fashion. In the second situation, one might throw the keys at one's spouse and say, "You take care of it!" and make a difficult situation even more difficult.

Psychologists have learned that children who have anxiety reactions engage in a great deal of negative self-talk. They are always telling themselves that situations are going to be much more worse than is realistic, that they are incompetent and incapable, and that all sorts of disasters will be forthcoming. For example, imagine one of your students in this situation; it is time for your third period class. You plan to give them a brief pop quiz on material they have been learning over the past week. One of your students finds a pile of handouts on your desk, and immediately assumes that a pop quiz is forthcoming. He either slinks to the back of the room, fiddling with his pencil and obviously wishing that he was anywhere else but in your class, or comes up to your desk and nervously asks you about whether such a quiz will take place and also the importance in terms of his grade. In more extreme situations, a student may cry, feign illness, and try to physically avoid the situation. Students such as these engage in immediate negative self-talk. Their first assumptions is that this pop test will be a miserable experience, one that they are sure to fail. Instead of focusing on how to cope with the situation, and focusing on their positive skills, they focus on the negative and tend to catastrophize, rather than cope.

Helping your students practice self-talk is important. Just as it takes time to learn negative self-talk, it takes time to learn better ways of thinking and coping. There are two major steps that your students can take to help them turn negative thoughts into positive ones. These are; 1) Questioning the validity of their negative thoughts (Is this thought realistic?); 2) Creating more positive ideas (How can I make my thoughts more positive and reasonable?).

There are some simple guidelines that will help your students change negative self-talk into positive self-talk. The exercises on the next page are in the student's workbook and should be helpful to all students, but especially those who immediately think in negative and unhelpful terms.

Exercise #3: Changing Negative Ideas Into Positive Ideas

You have to convince yourself that some of your ideas may not be correct or helpful, even though they seem very real. Ask yourself questions to "check out" if these ideas are true. Write down these questions and fill in the blanks about a negative thought you have about tests. (Or anything else!) Play detective!

- What evidence is there that my idea is true?

  _____

  _____

- What evidence is there that my idea isn't true?

  _____

  _____

- If I believe my negative ideas, what will happen?

  _____

  _____

- If I believe more positive ideas, what could happen?

  _____

  _____

Exercise #4: How to Create Positive Ideas

Positive ideas are strong ideas. No one ever did anything important by being "iffy." What would have happened if Christopher Columbus had said, "Well, I guess I can make it out there exploring the world, but it might not work out. Maybe I'll get sea-sick. I'll miss my mom. Gee, I wish I had studied more in Sailor School" and so on?

Making a positive statement has three parts.

1. Using the "I" word. "I am as smart as anyone else."

2. Not using the word "not!" "I will be calm during the test," instead of "I will not be nervous during the test."

3. Think of the opposite of your idea. If you feel dumb in math, state "I can think clearly about a lot of things, so I can give math a good shot."

Exercise #5: How To Face The Test Monster

There are other ways to overcome test anxiety, and some of them are even fun to do!

1. Draw a picture of how a person can succeed on the test. Drawing lets us imagine how we can tackle a problem. You might want to draw cartoon figures, or even animals instead of people. You might want to draw yourself!

2. Give yourself points for every thought or idea that helps you think positively about yourself and tests. Write them down. Ask your parents if they can post your list on the refrigerator when you reach 100 points. Ask if they will also give you a reward!

Thought	# of times I thought this	Total Points

3. Pay attention to all the good things about yourself. Feeling good about yourself will generalize into feeling good about taking tests — and doing other things in your life. Be your own best friend.

    Make a list of good things to say about yourself (your assets): _____

    _____

    _____

    _____

A Final Word

Sixth grade students desperately want to be accepted by their peers and by adults; simply stated, they want to be "normal." None of us likes being recognized for a problem, but this is especially true for young middle school students. Sharing with your students that test anxiety is normal for everyone, just to a greater or lesser degree, is an important theme that can be conveyed to your students no matter what the subject matter involved.

Students this age obviously have an interest in the adult world, although their time and energy is quite taken up with struggling with their own day-to-day difficulties. Sharing with students that test anxiety and related difficulties have been studied by psychologists, that this is an area of scientific concern, and that this is not just some type of personal abnormality, is important. Teaching them to deal with their problems in a scientific manner is equally important. Sixth grade students learn best when they can take a step back from their own self-absorbtion and anxieties and look at problems in a more objective manner.

Teachers of sixth grade students may find helpful to briefly review some basic articles or books on cognitive/behavioral interventions in an educational setting.

Writing

Sixth Grade Proficiency Test: Writing

Introduction: Strands and Learning Outcomes

The Sixth Grade Ohio Proficiency Test in Writing is based on Ohio's Model Competency-Based Language Arts Program. The test encourages the process as well as the outcome of writing: students may use a pre-writing exercise in addition to the main writing piece. Checklists are provided within the test to encourage revising and editing.

The Sixth Grade Ohio Proficiency Test in Writing is defined by four strands comprised of eight learning outcomes. The strands are outlined on the following page, and are explained more fully following this introduction.

Writing Learning Outcomes:

Strand I– Content

1. Focus on the topic with adequate supporting ideas or examples.

Strand II– Organization

2. Exhibit a logical organizational pattern that demonstrates a sense of flow and conveys a sense of completeness and wholeness.

Strand III– Use of Language

3. Exhibit word choice appropriate to the subject, the purpose, and the intended audience.
4. Communicate clarity of thought.
5. Include sentences of varied length and structure.

Strand IV– Writing Conventions

6. Use complete sentences except where purposeful phrases or clauses are desirable.
7. Write legibly using cursive or manuscript (print).
8. Demonstrate correct usage, correct spelling of frequently used words, and correct punctuation and capitalization.

Field Test Results

The Sixth Grade Ohio Proficiency Test in Writing was field tested in April 1995. Although the testing was limited, the results below were noticed as general trends.

- Students performed best on exercises designed to elicit narrative writing.
- Student performance was lowest on exercises designed to elicit summary writing.

Teachers should keep these trends in mind as you review for the test. You may wish to incorporate a little extra emphasis on summary writing within your current curriculum.

Test Format

The Sixth Grade Ohio Proficiency Test in Writing is divided into several sections. Students respond to the prewriting section (which is not scored) and complete two writing activities.

- The test administrator leads students through a script which reviews the writing process: prewriting, writing, revising, and editing.
- The test administrator reads or introduces the stimulus which will be the basis for the writing exercises. The stimulus might be an idea or scenario, a picture, or a piece of literature.
- Students complete the designated prewriting activity. This activity is not scored, and if a student chooses not to respond to the prewriting activity, he/she will not receive a lower score. The prewriting activity functions as the prewriting stage for both writing activities.
- Students respond to the first, and then the second, writing activity. Editing checklists are provided for students to check that their writing follows the requirements for a good writing piece.
- Each writing activity will ask for a different mode of writing. Modes include: summary, fictional narrative, personal experience narrative, persuasive, informational, and communication: letter, invitation, thank-you note, letter to the editor, directions, and journal.
- Four pages are provided in the answer book for each writing activity. Students do not have to use all of the available writing space.

Emphasis of the Test

The students are expected to show familiarity with the writing process, and use the skills necessary to write a good response. Responses should focus on the topic, use main ideas and supporting details, and have an organized and natural response that flows. Responses should clearly represent the purpose (mode) of writing through word usage, writing style, and structure.

Scoring of the Test

The rubric, or score-point description, adopted in the state of Ohio for evaluating sixth-grade student writing, is based on the eight learning outcomes listed previously and uses the numerical scale described below.

The rubric is a 4-point scale. This scale represents the different levels of writing proficiency demonstrated, based on the eight learning outcomes.

Scores are designed to be used in conjunction with illustrative rangefinder papers and are intended to describe characteristics of most papers at a particular score point. The aim is to determine the best fit; a paper at any given score point may not meet all characteristics.

Rubric

A 4-point response focuses on the topic, clearly addresses the purpose (mode), and has ample supporting details. It has a logical organizational pattern that demonstrates a sense of flow and conveys a sense of completeness and wholeness. It uses language effectively by exhibiting word choices which are appropriate to the subject, purpose, and intended audience. It includes sentences of varied length and structure and exhibits the use of complete sentences except where purposeful phrases or clauses are used for effect. It demonstrates correct usage, punctuation, capitalization, and correctly spells commonly used words. Its writing style varies according to purpose.

A 3-point response is related to the topic, generally addresses the purpose (mode), and has adequate supporting details. It has a logical order that demonstrates a sense of flow and a sense of wholeness and completeness, although some lapses may occur. It includes word choices which are appropriate to the subject, purpose, and intended audience. It includes sentences that are somewhat varied in length and type. For the most part, it exhibits the use of complete sentences except where purposeful phrases or clauses are used for effect. Some errors in sentence structure may occur, but they do not impede communication. It follows the conventions of usage, punctuation, and capitalization, and correctly spells commonly used words. Any errors that occur do not impede communication. Its writing style generally varies according to purpose.

A 2-point response demonstrates an awareness of the topic but may include extraneous or loosely related material. It demonstrates an attempt to address the purpose (mode) and includes some supporting details. It shows an attempt at an organizational pattern but exhibits little sense of flow or completeness. It has a limited and predictable vocabulary and makes word choices which may not show an awareness of audience, purpose, or subject. It contains errors in sentence structure and usage that limit its readability. It demonstrates some knowledge of capitalization, punctuation, and spelling of commonly used words. It contains an attempt to vary writing style according to purpose.

A 1-point response is only slightly related to the topic and offers few supporting details. It has little evidence of an organizational pattern. It has a limited or inappropriate vocabulary that obscures meaning and shows little or no awareness of audience, purpose, or subject. It demonstrates little knowledge of basic punctuation, capitalization, and the correct spelling of commonly used words. It contains errors in sentence structure and usage that impede its readability. It shows little or no attempt to vary writing style according to purpose.

An N/S (Not Scorable) is assigned if there is no response or if the response is unreadable, off topic, off task, illegible, or written in a language other than English.

Preparation for the Writing Proficiency Test

A healthy sixth-grade curriculum in Language Arts is excellent preparation for the Sixth Grade Ohio Proficiency Test in Writing. If your students are learning the conventions of the writing process – prewriting, writing, revising and editing – they are well on their way to conquering the Sixth Grade Ohio Proficiency Test in Writing.

However, as a standardized test, the Sixth Grade Ohio Proficiency Test in Writing will test your students' knowledge in a manner different from what you use in the classroom. In order to be best prepared for this test, your students need to become familiar with the format of the proficiency test.

Since the proficiency test is administered in March of each year, it is quite simple to incorporate specific learning outcomes into your daily curriculum. In addition to using activities and your normal classroom methods for teaching these outcomes, you can easily allow your students to become familiar with the format of the proficiency test by using practice items throughout the year.

The next section suggests specific activities that you might use to strengthen your students' command of specific learning outcomes. Many of these will be ones you use already, while others may be used as is, or as a springboard for more ideas of your own. Following the Strand Activities section is a section offering tips for approaching the test. Finally, the student manual contains many practice items which will make students comfortable with both the format of the test and the nature of the topics which will be presented to them.

The Writing Strands and Learning Outcomes

Strand I – Content

1. Focus on the topic with adequate supporting ideas or examples.

Students should respond to the topic and use appropriate details to support the topic. Readers look for responses that answer the topic without straying from the original intent. Content should be appropriate to the intended audience.

Teaching Tips and Activities for Strand I

- **Brainstorm!** Assign a topic and give students 2-3 minutes to write as many supporting details as possible. Topics might include a single noun (to elicit description), an argument (to elicit ideas for/against), or a fact (to elicit supporting "proof").

- **Speak Up!** Similar to the activity above, assign individuals a topic. Allow students to give a brief talk on their topic. Speeches should demonstrate a logical organization, include several supporting ideas or examples, and have a sense of completeness. Following each speech, the class can offer comments and suggestions for improvement.

- **Pick a Fight!** Create debating teams. Allow the class to brainstorm controversial topics of interest to them. Vote on the one to be used. Teams pick a side and organize their main point and supporting arguments. Caution them to be prepared to address arguments brought up by the opposing team.

- **Make Headlines!** Write a news article or radio bulletin. Keep it short and to the point. Practice delivering a clear and interesting message to your audience.

- **Order Now!** Write an advertisement. Can you sell an item in 25 words? In 10 words?

- **Two Thumbs Up?** Review a book, movie, TV show, or video game. Encourage students to use specific details showing their opinion of the material reviewed. Reviews can offer both positive and negative points.

- **Now Showing in Class 6B...** Draw a poster advertisement for a favorite book. Students should offer visual supporting details to encourage others to read the book.

- **Get a Job!** Write a persuasive letter to detail your qualifications and interest in the job of your dreams. Trade letters with classmates — would you hire each other?

- **S.O.S.! You're stranded** — on a deserted island, an unknown planet, locked in the school attic... Pick your location and write a "message in a bottle." Give detailed directions so your recipient can save you.

- **A Day in the Life...** Have students select one person from a busy poster or photo. Students should then create a fictional narrative about their subject. Include plenty of details and supporting facts about that person: family life, home, hobbies, friends...

Strand II – Organization

2. Exhibit a logical organizational pattern that demonstrates a sense of flow and conveys a sense of completeness and wholeness.

Students' papers should be clear and complete. Be sure to address the topic fully. Readers look for a naturally organized structure.

Teaching Tips and Activities For Strand II

• **Spider! Webs, clusters, lists, reading, research, note cards, outlines...** Practice various pre-writing activities to help students develop a feel for what belongs in a particular piece. Once the organization of the assignment begins to take place in their minds, allow them to develop the topic fully.

• **Act it out.** Use various props as inspiration for impromptu skits. Preliminary planning of skits should be very brief, focusing on how the story will begin, what will happen, and how it will end. If the skit "stalls," encourage the audience to provide suggestions to keep the plot moving.

• **It happened to me...** Write about a personal experience. Introduce the action, tell the plot, end the story. Use many details and lively language.

• **"I don't get it."** Explain a science or math concept to another person. Once they understand, ask which points made it especially clear to them. Can you put your explanation in writing? Keep it organized.

• **Lifestyles of the...** Pick a person or animal (famous, infamous, real or a character from a book) and imagine you are to conduct an interview with them. Brainstorm for ideas of questions you want answered. How can you organize your interview so that it flows? (This makes an excellent class activity on the blackboard.)

Strand III – Use of Language

3. **Exhibit word choice appropriate to the subject, the purpose, and the intended audience.**
4. **Communicate clarity of thought.**
5. **Include sentences of varied length and structure.**

Students should have a well-developed, varied vocabulary. They need the ability to construct sentences of various lengths and complexity as well as be familiar with word meanings, homonyms, and words in context. Students should be able to make their points clearly, and to make their writing interesting by using sentences of different lengths and structure.

Teaching Tips and Activities For Strand III

• **Rough Waters.** Choppy sentences make rough reading, sentences of the same length make reading monotonous. Create interesting sentences and paragraphs by using techniques such as sentence combining, varying beginnings and endings of sentences, and developing good transitions between thoughts. Have students practice these skills in the revision process of all of their writing.

• **Stroll, saunter, strut...** Remind students that the right word is often worth 5 words — use strong, lively vocabulary, but avoid embellishment for embellishment's sake.

• **Evaluate writing.** Develop a class checklist of characteristics that make an acceptable piece of writing. Students should practice using the checklist to evaluate all of their writing. This familiarity with the checklist will also help students feel comfortable with the checklists in the actual proficiency test.

• **Compliments!** This game can be used to help students choose interesting words and phrases to convey their ideas. Have each student tape a large piece of paper to his or her back. Every student must write a compliment on every other student's back. The game is an excellent way to reunite a group of students, or merely reinforce their self-confidence. Anonymity is fairly well assured, so some wonderful compliments can come from the most surprising sources. The results can remain private, or can be shared with the class (a "Sixth Grade is Great" bulletin board,

- **Fabulous Phrases File.** Begin a file or section of a bulletin board for great phrases students have written. Be sure to credit the authors!

- **To Whom am I Speaking?** Pick a topic and develop it for several audiences. Make sure the vocabulary suits the audience and the purpose of the piece. Topic example: A trip to the park. Possible modes/audiences: letter to grandmother; report for science teacher; driving directions for parents; invitation to friends for a party at the park.

Strand IV– Writing Conventions

6. Use complete sentences except where purposeful phrases or clauses are desirable.

7. Write legibly using cursive or manuscript.

8. Demonstrate correct usage, correct spelling of frequently used words, and correct punctuation and capitalization.

Students should be able to use and spell common words, and should be able to punctuate a sentence correctly. Students should write in complete sentences, and know when it is appropriate to use a phrase or clause. Students may print or use cursive for the proficiency test. Before the test, help each student decide which type of writing they will use. This decision should be based on what is most legible and most comfortable for the student.

Teaching Tips and Activities For Strand IV

- **Their, there, they're.** Students can keep a folder of frequently misspelled or misused words. As they proofread their work, this list will help them correct some of their personal weak spots. You might set up a system where they can place a check next to problem words for each time they spell or use it correctly in their writing. Removing a problem word from your list is an accomplishment!

- **once upon a time in the middle of the deep dark scary forest...** Let students write stories in all lower case, with no punctuation. Trade with a classmate and insert correct punctuation and capitalization.

More Teaching Tips and Activities to Reinforce Writing Skills

- **Write Daily.** Students might use any combination of journals, learning logs, responses to reading, informational pieces, correspondence, etc. Use journals to brainstorm story ideas; learning logs to work with graphic organizers; paper and markers to create a visual response to a story. Remind students to keep a log of story ideas for future use.

- **Use peer conferences** in both the brainstorming and the proofreading process. Conferences can boost egos with positive comments, and suggestions are fairly non-threatening when made in a peer group.

- **Offer a teacher conference** near the end of the revision process.

- **Publish good writing.** "Publication" methods include: posting work on the bulletin board, desktop publication and binding; and author readings.

- **Share your own writing!** Demonstrate how you use writing in your life. Read a letter you wrote to a friend, a short story, a series of math word problems, a letter you wrote to complain about an incorrect bill, directions for a substitute teacher. Allow the students to participate in a peer conference for you, and share your revised version with them as well.

- **Write with a reason.** Allow students to practice a variety of writing activities: to inform, persuade, report, entertain, and express emotion.

- **Write for a variety of purposes:** speech, brochure, newsletter, literary magazine, fable, math word problems, science experiments, reaction to a museum trip, etc.

- **Use writing effectively:** write to your mayor about a local issue; submit articles to the school newspaper; send letters of praise to a hard-working community member.

- **Vary the stimulus.** Topics can be self-chosen or assigned. Practice using visual prompts as well: posters, calendars, photos, unusual items (even ones they won't recognize), live events, walks outdoors (in nature and through city streets).

- **Create inspiration.** Students will keep their enthusiasm for writing if they are frequently allowed to select the topics and purposes.

- **Meet the press.** Suggest a review column to the school or local newspaper editor. Review books, movies, TV shows, music, video games, and the local attractions, all from a sixth grade perspective.

- **Meet an author.** Invite a local author to visit your school. Ask her to show the various drafts of a story she has written. Discuss how she writes: from the initial idea, to the final editing process.

Test-Taking Techniques for the Writing Test

The Writing Stimulus

Students should listen carefully and follow along in their books as the test administrator reads the writing stimulus. The stimulus might be a piece of literature, an idea or scenario, or a picture. The stimulus is used as the basis for new writing by the students.

Pre-Writing Exercise

The pre-writing exercises are not graded. Technically, students do not have to complete the pre-writing exercises. However, it is recommended that students complete this step, since it is designed to help them with the two written exercises. There may be one pre-writing exercise to help with both written exercises, or one for each exercise.

In the classroom, the pre-writing stage includes: selecting a topic; exploring the topic through brainstorming or clustering of ideas; determining the audience and purpose of the piece; gathering and organizing information and ideas for the topic, and focusing the topic so it best suits the audience and purpose.

Unlike some classroom writing situations, the general topics for the Sixth Grade Ohio Proficiency Test writing section have already been defined for the students. In addition, the audience and purpose of each written exercise will be pre-determined. The main focus of the pre-writing exercises for the test will be to explore the topic and to gather ideas. Students also will need to focus the topic so it suits the audience and purpose; this might occur actively during the pre-writing exercise, or students might do this more independently by using the checklists.

Students need to be familiar with pre-writing skills. Although students often brainstorm for ideas with groups in the classroom, they need to be able to conduct this activity on their own for the Sixth Grade Ohio Proficiency Test. Encourage students to practice brainstorming – the free flow of ideas – regularly. Editing should not occur during the pre-writing stage; any and all ideas should be written down.

For the Sixth Grade Ohio Proficiency Test, students will have room in the test booklet to list the ideas suggested in the pre-writing exercise. Students might be asked to list their ideas, or to cluster them in a cluster or web type diagram. It might be suggested that students mark their favorite ideas during the pre-writing stage. In some cases, the lists may be left unmarked and used as a general source for details to be included in the students' written exercises.

Using the Checklists Before Writing

Each written exercise will have a checklist of points which will need to be included in the written piece to constitute "best writing." Remind your students that these checklists can help them to focus their ideas before writing, as well as to check their work after writing.

During the Sixth Grade Ohio Proficiency Test, the students will hear the stimulus first. They will be told, in general terms, the nature of the writing exercises to follow. Next they will complete the pre-writing exercise.

Following the pre-writing exercise, students will hear the checklist and the directions for the written exercise. Remind your students to take a moment to collect their thoughts at this point. They might want to mark the checklist with comments ("audience," "purpose," "letter form"). They may wish to return to the pre-writing exercise to mark ideas they will include in their written exercise. Students may also make margin notes or margin outlines of their written piece before they begin to write.

The Writing Exercise

Once students know what they are writing (a letter, fictional narrative, non-fiction piece, etc.), the topic (as well as some details they want to include), the audience, and the purpose, they are ready to write.

The readers will be looking for evidence that students have sixth-grade level writing skills. Students should be familiar with the standards and formats for fiction, non-fiction, journals, directions, and letters. Readers want to see passages that focus on the topic, offer supporting ideas or examples, and exhibit good organization and a logical flow of ideas. Students should be aware of their sentence structure; they should vary sentence length and complexity. Students should show an understanding of appropriate word use, as well as an ability to spell commonly used words correctly. Punctuation should be used properly.

Remind students that the written exercises should stay on topic. Students should use details to support their main points. Caution the students that the readers are not mind-readers! If students want to show what they know, it needs to be written in the test booklet.

Using the Checklists After Writing

Once a student has completed a writing exercise, the work should be re-read and checked for errors in spelling, punctuation, capitalization, and completeness of sentences and ideas. A self-editing checklist might go as follows:

• Does the piece read clearly? Does it flow from beginning to middle to end?
• Are my ideas easily understood?
• Do I use enough supporting details with my ideas?
• Do I use proper grammar, spelling, and capitalization?

Next, students should review the checklist in the test booklet. Have all of the points been covered? Does the writing meet the requirements for "best writing?" Students are allowed to make editing changes in the test booklet. Encourage them to erase and rewrite neatly. A lower grade may be assigned if the work is illegible.

Remind students to read the directions at the end of the exercise after they have completed the written piece.

Taking the Test — Getting Familiar with the Test Format

The stimulus for the writing test can be a piece of literature, a picture, an idea, or a scenario. Using the stimulus, students may complete a pre-writing exercise which will apply to both of the writing exercises in the test. The pre-writing exercise is not scored.

On each administration of the Writing test, there are two writing activities, both based on the same stimulus. Students are given four pages for each writing activity. Students do not have to use all of the pages provided. The writing activities are scored according to the rubric cited earlier.

There are two complete Sample Writing Exercises or sample tests on the pages that follow. This provides two practice tests for the students. The same practice, simulated writing proficiency tests are in *Show What You Know on Ohio's Sixth Grade Proficiency Test* student workbook which is sold separately. The teachers edition and the answer key booklet have sample answers to each of the exercises.

Sample Writing Exercise #1

Writing

Directions: Read the following passage or follow along as the passage is read aloud to you.

> A Canadian organization created a program to teach children what to do if they get lost in the woods, on a mountain, or even in a large store. The program is called "Hug a Tree and Survive." Children learn to stay where they are, as soon as they realize they are lost. Parents or rescuers looking for a lost child will always begin the search where the child was last seen. So, if a child wanders off, it will be more difficult to find him or her. If a child "hugs a tree," it is much more likely that he or she will be found quickly.

Today you will use the ideas from this story to help you complete two writing activities. For the first activity, you will write a personal experience story. In your story, you will tell about a time when you were lost. You will describe where you were, how you became lost, and how you were found. Your story may be true or not true. For the second activity, you will write a set of directions to explain how to act if you are lost. You will describe how to improve your chances of being found, and how to stay safe while you wait for help.

Pre-writing

Directions: The headings below will help you with ideas for your personal story about being lost. Write your ideas on the lines provided.

Describe the background details of your story.

Who was involved? _____

_____

What was the occasion? _____

_____

When did this happen? _____

Where did the event occur? _____

_____

How did you become separated from the people you were with? _____

_____

List some of the feelings you had when you knew you were lost.

_____

_____

_____

_____

List your reactions to the situation. What did you do?

_____

_____

_____

_____

_____

_____

In the chart below, list some things you thought might happen in the left column. In the right column, tell what did happen. An example is provided.

I thought...	Actually...
My parents would be mad.	They were happy to find me.

Pre-writing

Directions: The web headings below will help you with ideas for your set of directions telling how to act if you become lost. Write your ideas in the spaces provided.

What to do if you are lost	What to do if you are afraid	Ideas for being found

Exercise A:
Personal Experience Narrative – Story

Directions: For Exercise A, you will write a personal story about a time when you were lost. In the story, you will describe the setting, the event, and who was with you that day. You will tell how you became separated from your group, what happened when you realized you were lost, and how you were found. You may use the information you wrote in the first pre-writing exercise. Your story may be true or not true. Be sure that your story is well organized and complete. You will write your story in the space provided.

The writing you do for Exercise A will be scored. Look at the box below. The checklist box shows what your writing must have to get your best score.

You will use your pencil to write your story. You may erase and cross out or make any other editing changes in your work. You may not use a dictionary or thesaurus in your writing. Spell the words the best way you know. Remember that writers often make changes as they work.

☑ Checklist A

I will earn my best score if:

- ☐ My story tells about a time that I was lost.
- ☐ My story gives details about the day, the location, and the people involved.
- ☐ My story describes how I felt when I was lost, and when I was found.
- ☐ My story tells how other people felt when I was lost, and when I was found.
- ☐ My story tells the process of getting lost and found.
- ☐ My story is well organized and complete.
- ☐ I use words that make my meaning clear. I do not use the same words over and over.
- ☐ I try to spell the words correctly.
- ☐ I try to use correct punctuation and capitalization.

Exercise A: Personal Experience Narrative – Story

Note to Teacher:
The student workbook provides
four full pages for the student to
respond to each writing exercise.

When you finish writing your story, use the checklist to revise and edit your work. When you have finished checking your story and you are satisfied with it, you may go ahead to the second activity, Exercise B.

Sample Response to Exercise A:

When I was four years old I went to Sea World with my family. I really like animals a lot, so I was very excited about seeing all the animals at Sea World.

During the day, we saw the killer whales put on a show. We watched the dolphins in a big tank where you could reach in and touch them. Then we watched a show with walruses and seals and some other animals. They were pretending that they were pirates.

On our way to leave, I saw a sign with a picture of a shark and an arrow pointing to a tank in the middle of the patio. I went to go look at the sharks. They were really neat, even though they were pretty small. You couldn't touch them, because they bite!

After I finished looking at the sharks, I turned around to ask my mother if I could get a drink for the ride home. She wasn't there! I couldn't see my mother, my sister, or my grammie anywhere. They hadn't followed me to the shark tank.

I was very scared. There were a lot of people around, and they were all tall, so I couldn't see very far. I called and called for my mother, but she didn't hear me. A woman asked me if I was lost and I said yes. She said to wait here and she would find someone who worked at the park. I was glad she said that, because I didn't want to go with a stranger.

Just as the woman returned, I saw my mother running to me. She was very happy to see me — so happy that she cried! I was glad to see her, and happy that she wasn't too mad at me for wandering off alone.

Now I make sure I tell my parents where I am going. I didn't like being lost!

Exercise B:
Set of Directions

Directions: For Exercise B, you will write a set of directions telling what to do if you get lost. You may use the information you wrote in the second pre-writing exercise. Be sure to provide several ideas for making sure you will be found, and what to do while waiting to be found. Use ideas you have learned, and others that make sense to you. Be sure to use words that make your meaning clear. Be sure that your story is well organized and complete. You will write your story in the space provided.

The writing you do for Exercise B will be scored. Look at the box on the next page. The checklist box shows what your writing must have to get your best score.

You will use your pencil to write your directions. You may erase and cross out or make any other editing changes in your work. You may not use a dictionary or thesaurus in your writing. Spell the words the best way you know. Remember that writers often make changes as they work.

✓ Checklist B

I will earn my best score if:

☐ My directions include steps to follow if you get lost.

☐ My directions offer several ideas for making sure you are found.

☐ My directions offer ideas for what to do while you wait.

☐ My directions tell how to keep safe and warm.

☐ My directions are well organized and complete.

☐ I use words that make my meaning clear. I do not use the same words over and over.

☐ I try to spell the words correctly.

☐ I try to use correct punctuation and capitalization.

Exercise B: Set of Directions

_____

_____

_____

_____

_____

_____

_____

_____

_____

_____

_____

_____

_____

_____

_____

_____

_____

_____

_____

_____

_____

_____

_____

> **Note to Teacher:**
> **The student workbook provides four full pages for the student to respond to each writing exercise.**

When you finish writing your set of directions, use the checklist to revise and edit your work. Take out your silent work to do at your desk when you have finished checking your work and you are satisfied with it. Or you may go back to your first writing, your story, and work on it some more.

Sample Response to Exercise B:

Imagine that you are camping with your family. On the first morning you wake up very early. Since you don't want to wake everyone up, you decide to play away from your tent. Soon you decide to explore the area. After a while you get hungry, and decide to return to camp. But you realize that you are lost! What should you do? Here are some simple directions to help you:

1. *Don't panic. It's OK to feel scared, but if you run around in a panic you will get more lost.*
2. *Call for help. Yell as loudly as you can, many times. Save your voice enough so that you can yell about every 5 minutes.*
3. *Don't move. Find a tree or bush and stay very close to it. You could even talk to it if you feel lonely or scared.*
4. *Make sure the area where you are is safe. You don't want to fall asleep on the edge of a cliff, for instance.*
5. *In between calling for help, play a game to keep your mind busy. You might look at the clouds and see what shapes they look like.*
6. *Don't eat any plants or drink any water unless you are sure it is safe. You can live quite a while without food.*
7. *If it begins to get dark, decide how you will keep warm during the night. You might make a pile of branches or leaves to cover and protect you from the weather. Be sure part of you still shows, though, in case rescuers come by.*
8. *If you get scared, talk to your tree. Give it a hug if you want. You can also think about things that make you happy, or times you have been scared and everything worked out alright. You are being smart and brave while you are lost, so be proud of yourself.*
9. *Keep calling for help!*
10. *If you hear voices calling your name, answer them. If you do not recognize the voices, it is probably rescuers who are helping to find you. No one will be mad at you for getting lost, they will be happy that you are fine.*

In the future, try not to go anywhere alone, and always tell your parents where you are going.

Sample Writing Exercise #2

Writing

Directions: Read the following Japanese saying.

"One kind word can warm three winter months." Japanese saying

Today you will use the ideas from this quotation to help you complete two writing exercises. For the first exercise, you will write a Thank-you Note. In your letter, you will write to a family member, friend, or teacher to thank them for the many things they have done for you. For the second exercise, you will write a Persuasive Piece. You will tell about a situation where someone has worked hard, but has received mostly criticism of failures rather than praise for their successes. You will try to convince your audience that this person is worthy of their admiration. In both writing activities, your story may be true or not true.

Pre-writing

Directions: The activites below will help you with ideas for writing your Thank-you Note. Write your ideas on the lines provided.

Think of some friends, family members, or teachers who have been important in your life. List them here, then circle the one you will write to in the writing activity.

_____   _____

_____   _____

_____   _____

_____   _____

What are some of the things this person has done for you? Why were they important? Use the chart below for your list. An example is done for you.

what they did for me...	why it was important...
cheered for me at my first soccer game	I was nervous, and not very good yet, so it helped me play my best

How has this person made you a better person?

_____

_____

_____

_____

_____

Pre-writing

Directions: The lists of ideas you create below will help you with ideas for your Persuasive Piece. Write your ideas in the spaces provided.

List some ideas of people or animals who often receive criticism rather than praise. Mark the one you will use in your writing activity.

_____   _____

_____   _____

_____   _____

_____   _____

Who is your audience for your Persuasive Piece? (Who needs to be convinced that this character is worthy of praise?)

_____

_____

_____

List the positive and negative points of your character's personality and achievements. Fill in the chart. An example is done for you.

Positive Points	Negative Points
good guard dog	always barks at other dogs
loves me	eats my father's socks

In the chart above, mark your strongest arguments in favor of this character.

Exercise A:
Thank-you Note

Directions: For Exercise A, you will write a Thank-you Note. In the letter, you will describe the events or situations for which you are thanking someone. You will give details that remind your reader of the event, and details which show your appreciation. You may use the information you wrote in the first pre-writing exercise. Your letter may be true or not true. Be sure that your letter is well organized and complete, and is written in the form of a letter. You will write your letter in the space provided.

The writing you do for Exercise A will be scored. Look below. The checklist box shows what your writing must have to get your best score.

You will use your pencil to write your story. You may erase and cross out or make any other editing changes in your work. You may not use a dictionary or thesaurus in your writing. Spell the words the best way you know. Remember that writers often make changes as they work.

✓ Checklist A

I will earn my best score if:

☐ My letter is written to someone who is important to me.

☐ My letter gives details about the times they have done something meaningful for me.

☐ My letter describes how I feel about this person.

☐ My letter tells how much I appreciate them.

☐ My letter is written in the form of a letter, with a greeting, body, and closing.

☐ My letter is well organized and complete.

☐ I use words that make my meaning clear. I do not use the same words over and over.

☐ I try to spell the words correctly.

☐ I try to use correct punctuation and capitalization.

Exercise A: Thank-you Note

_____

_____

_____

_____

_____

_____

_____

_____

_____

_____

_____

_____

_____

_____

_____

_____

_____

_____

_____

_____

_____

Note to Teacher:
The student workbook provides
four full pages for the student to
respond to each writing exercise.

When you finish writing your Thank-you Note, use the checklist to revise and edit your work. When you have finished checking your Thank-you Note and you are satisfied with it, you may go ahead to the second activity, Exercise B.

Sample Response to Exercise A:

March 5, 1997

Dear Katie,

   Thank you for being my friend. I know I don't say it very often, but your friendship is very important to me. Even though we haven't known each other very long, I know that you believe in me, and like me even when I mess up.

   Last week, you did something really special. When we were picking teams for soccer in P.E., you picked me first! I thought you picked me just because you liked me, since I can't play soccer well at all. When the other kids teased me, and you for picking me, it was great of you to just ignore them! When you told them I would be goalie, they laughed. But you just told me to watch the ball, and pretend it was my brother trying to get into my room — it worked! I made 6 saves, and only let in one goal. Even though we lost, your confidence in me made me know I can do well again.

   So, even though I sometimes tease you about stuff, I want you to know how important you are to me. Thanks for being a true friend.

Love,
   Rebecca

Exercise B:
Persuasive Piece

Directions: For Exercise B, you will write a Persuasive Piece. You may use the information you wrote in the second pre-writing exercise. You will tell about a situation where someone has worked hard, but has received mostly criticism of failures rather than praise for their successes. You will try to convince your audience that this person is worthy of their admiration. Be sure to provide several examples to support your argument. Be sure to use words that make your meaning clear. Be sure that your story is well organized and complete. You will write your story in the space provided.

The writing you do for Exercise B will be scored. Look at the box below. The checklist box shows what your writing must have to get your best score.

You will use your pencil to write your directions. You may erase and cross out or make any other editing changes in your work. You may not use a dictionary or thesaurus in your writing. Spell the words the best way you know. Remember that writers often make changes as they work.

✔ Checklist B

I will earn my best score if:

☐ My Persuasive Piece tells the characters involved in the situation.

☐ My piece gives details about how people often criticize the main character.

☐ My piece offers examples to show the main character deserves praise.

☐ My piece is written for my intended audience.

☐ My piece is well organized and complete.

☐ I use words that make my meaning clear. I do not use the same words over and over.

☐ I try to spell the words correctly.

☐ I try to use correct punctuation and capitalization.

Exercise B: Persuasive Piece

_____

_____

_____

_____

_____

_____

_____

_____

_____

_____

_____

_____

_____

_____

_____

_____

Note to Teacher:
The student workbook provides four full pages for the student to respond to each writing exercise.

When you finish writing your Persuasive Piece, use the checklist to revise and edit your work. Take out your silent work to do at your desk when you have finished checking your work and you are satisfied with it. Or you may go back to your first writing, your Thank-you Note, and work on it some more.

Sample Response to Exercise B:

My dog is always getting into trouble. Everyone complains about the bad things she does, and no one seems to notice the good things she does.

Last week was the "final straw," according to my mother. We got a letter from the neighborhood association that said our dog, Kerry, was barking too much. They said she barks as early as 5:30 in the morning and as late as 11:30 at night. My father complains that she keeps eating his socks. My mother is tired of vacuuming all the dog hair that she sheds. My brother is mad because she always steals his golf balls when he is practicing. Last night, my parents said maybe we should get rid of her.

NO!

I know that Kerry sometimes does bad things. But she does lots of good stuff, too. And I also have a plan to help keep her from doing bad things.

Kerry does many good things. She is an excellent guard dog. She barks when people come to the door, and if anyone even drives into the driveway she races to the door. Once when our doorbell was broken, my mother said we didn't even need to fix it with Kerry around.

She loves all of us. Every night she sleeps in one of our rooms, and then moves from room to room all night. She is nervous and sad when my brother or I sleep at someone's house. She likes to have her family safe in one place.

Kerry is very friendly, and would never bite anyone. She loves children. However, she looks big and scary, so my mom takes her with her when she goes for a walk at night. I think she would bite someone if they tried to hurt us.

Now for my plan to stop her bad habits:

- *She is never out as early or as late as the neighbors said, but she does bark whenever people or dogs go by on the sidewalk. My plan is to make sure we let her in the house if she starts to bark.*
- *My father should put his socks in the hamper!*
- *I will brush her at least twice a week, so she doesn't shed so much.*
- *We will keep her inside while my brother is practicing golf.*

I know Kerry has some bad habits, but she is a very nice, friendly, loving, smart dog. She is a member of our family, and we shouldn't talk about getting rid of her. Would you?

Reading

Sixth Grade Proficiency Test: Reading

Introduction: Strands and Learning Outcomes

The Sixth Grade Ohio Proficiency Test in Reading is defined by four strands, which encompass 18 learning outcomes. The strands and learning outcomes are outlined on the next page, and are explained more fully following this introduction.

The Reading chapter of this book features passages written by the author and other contributing writers. The example test items are numbered and correlate with the student workbook of "Show What You Know on Ohio's Sixth Grade Proficiency Test."

Reading

Strand I – Constructing/Examining Meaning with Fiction Selections
1. Analyze aspects of the text, examining, for example, characters, setting, plot, problem/solution, point of view, or theme.
2. Summarize the text.
3. Infer from the text.
4. Respond to the text.

Strand II – Extending Meaning with Fiction Selections
5. Compare and contrast aspects of the text, for example, characters or settings.
6. Critique and/or evaluate aspects of the text.
7. Select information for a variety of purposes, including enjoyment.
8. Express reasons for recommending or not recommending the text for a particular audience or purpose.
9. Explain how an author uses contents of a text to support his/her purpose for writing.

Strand III – Constructing/Examining Meaning with Nonfiction Selections
10. Analyze the text, examining, for example, author's use of comparison and contrast, cause and effect, or fact and opinion.
11. Summarize the text.
12. Infer from the text.
13. Respond to the text.

Strand IV – Extending Meaning with Nonfiction Selections
14. Compare and/or contrast aspects of the text.
15. Critique and evaluate the text for such elements as organizational structure and logical reasoning.
16. Select information from a variety of resources to support ideas, concepts, and interpretations.
17. Express reasons for recommending or not recommending the text for a particular audience or purpose.
18. Explain how an author uses contents of a text to support his/her purpose for writing.

Test Format

The reading test contains fiction, poetry and nonfiction reading selections. Students will answer multiple-choice, short-answer, and extended-response items. Each test contains 41 items, 36 of which are scored and five of which are embedded field-test items. The test items are distributed as follows:

Reading Item Distributions

Strands	Multiple-Choice	Short-Answer	Extended-Response	Totals
Fiction/Poetry Constructing/Examining Meaning (4) Extending Meaning (5)	4 - 12 3 - 8	1 - 3 1 - 4	0 – 1 0 – 2	5 - 16 4 - 14
Nonfiction Constructing/Examining Meaning (4) Extending Meaning (5)	4 - 12 3 - 8	1 - 3 1 - 4	0 – 1 0 – 2	5 - 16 4 - 14
Total number of items based on selection	24 - 28	7 - 9	2	36

( ) = Number of learning outcomes

Reading selections are from published sources and may include poems, short stories, essays, novel/book excerpts, plays, pamphlets, instruction booklets, and newspaper and magazine articles. Topics are varied, and selection length is up to 750 words. Tests contain two to four selections of fiction/poetry, and two to four selections of nonfiction. The selections together total about 1500 words, with a maximum of 2000 words. The number of questions for any given selection is, in part, determined by the length of the selection (longer selections have more questions).

Scoring of the Test

- Each multiple-choice question is worth one point.
- Each short-answer item is worth two points.
- Each extended-response item is worth four points.

Conventions of writing (sentence structure, word choice, usage, grammar, spelling, and mechanics) will **not** affect the scoring of short-answer or extended-response items unless there is interference with the clear communication of ideas.

The Scoring of Short-Answer Items

Short-answer items are scored on a 2-point scale based on these general scoring guidelines:

A 2-point response is complete and appropriate. It demonstrates a thorough understanding of the reading selection. It indicates logical reasoning and conclusions. It is accurate, relevant, comprehensive, and detailed.

A 1-point response is partially appropriate. It contains minor flaws in reasoning or neglects to address some aspect of the item or question. It is mostly accurate and relevant but lacks comprehensiveness. It demonstrates an incomplete understanding of the reading selection or inability to make coherent meaning from the text.

A 0 is assigned if the response indicates no understanding of the reading selection or item.

The Scoring of Extended-Response Items

Extended-response items will be scored on a 4-point scale based on these general scoring guidelines:

A 4-point response provides extensive evidence of the kind of interpretation called for in the item or question. The response is well-organized, elaborate, and thorough. It demonstrates a complete understanding of the whole work as well as how parts blend to form the whole. It is relevant, comprehensive, and detailed, demonstrating a thorough understanding of the reading selection. It thoroughly addresses the important elements of the question. It contains logical reasoning and communicates effectively and clearly.

A 3-point response provides evidence that an essential interpretation has been made. It is thoughtful and reasonably accurate. It indicates an understanding of the concept or item, communicates adequately, and generally reaches reasonable conclusions. It contains some combination of the following flaws: minor flaws in reasoning or interpretation, failure to address some aspect of the item, or the omission of some detail.

A 2-point response is mostly accurate and relevant. It contains some combination of the following flaws: incomplete evidence of interpretation, unsubstantiated statements made about the text, an incomplete understanding of the concept or item, lack of comprehensiveness, faulty reasoning, or unclear communication.

A 1-point response provides little evidence of interpretation. It is unorganized and incomplete. It exhibits decoding rather than reading. It demonstrates a partial understanding of the item but is sketchy and unclear. It indicates some effort beyond restating the item. It contains some combination of the following flaws: little understanding of the concept or item, failure to address most aspects of the item, or inability to make coherent meaning from text.

A 0 is assigned if the response shows no understanding of the reading selection or item.

Field Test Results

The Sixth Grade Ohio Proficiency Test in reading was field tested in April 1995. Although the testing was limited, the results below were noticed as general trends.

- Student performance was highest on multiple-choice items measuring outcomes 10, 16, and 17 identified in this chapter by the symbol "✔."
- Student performance was lowest on multiple-choice items measuring outcomes 1, 9, 14, and 18 indentified in this chapter by the symbol "✍."

Teachers should keep these trends in mind while reviewing for the test. You may wish to incorporate a little extra emphasis on the low-scoring areas within your current curriculum.

> **Key:**
>
> ✍ = Student performance was LOW during field testing.
>
> ✔ = Students performance was HIGH during field testing.

Preparation for the Reading Test

A healthy sixth-grade curriculum in Language Arts is excellent preparation for the Sixth Grade Ohio Proficiency Test in Reading. The reading skills tested in the proficiency test are skills you are already teaching. If your students enjoy reading and are becoming critical readers, they are well on their way to conquering the Sixth Grade Ohio Proficiency Test in Reading.

However, as a standardized test, the Reading Proficiency Test will test your students' knowledge in a manner different from those you use in the classroom. In order to be best prepared for this test, your students need to become familiar with the format of the proficiency test.

Finally, your students need to learn how to apply the reading skills they are acquiring in class to the specific format of a standardized test. The section which follows will offer specific tips for preparing for the Sixth Grade Ohio Proficiency Test in Reading.

Since the proficiency test is administered in March of each year, it is not difficult to incorporate specific learning outcomes into your daily curriculum. In addition to using activities and your normal classroom methods for teaching these outcomes, you can easily allow your students to become familiar with the format of the proficiency test by using the practice items in the student manual throughout the year.

The next section suggests specific activities that you might use to strengthen your students command of specific learning outcomes. Many of these will be ones you use already, while others might be a springboard for more ideas of your own. Following the Strand Activities is a section offering both teacher and student tips for approaching the test. Finally, the student manual contains practice items which will make students comfortable with both the format of the test and the nature of the reading selections which will be presented to them.

Taking the Test – Getting Familiar with the Test Format

The Sixth Grade Ohio Proficiency Test in Reading asks students to answer questions based on reading passages. The questions are in three different formats: multiple-choice, short-answer, and extended-response.

[The reading passage below is used to demonstrate the multiple-choice format, as well as the short-answer and extended-response formats.]

The Potato Chip Man
by William I. Lengeman III

For as long as he could remember Philip Rawletta loved potato chips. He loved 'em like a son...could have eaten 'em for a living. Even now, as he was approaching his fourth decade, Philip could think of nothing he loved more. Oh sure, there were his mother and sisters, his grandmother, and Emily, soon to be his wife. But there was no comparison there...it was like comparing apples and concrete.

It seemed absurd. It was only when he was eating chips that he was truly happy.

Philip attacked a bag of potato chips with such a frenzy that in no time he could reduce it to specks of dust in the bottom of the grease-coated bag. Then, of course, he drank down the crumbs, coughing and choking as he inhaled a few, and wincing with pleasure as the salt warmed his tongue.

Philip was not picky when to it came to potato chips. Anything would do: plain old garden variety chips, ruffled Cajun spice, grainy sour cream and onion. He loved the nice, uniform ones that came packed in a cylinder as well as the thick gourmet-styled waffle chips that he could buy at the health store.

It simply did not matter. If it was a chip, it was fair game. Philip gobbled them all down, to borrow his mother's words, "like they were going out of style."

His sisters, who were less polite, called him "piggish," and "disgusting." Philip munched away contentedly, ignoring them.

More than once, as she watched him tear into a bag, his grandmother remarked, "one of these days you're gonna turn into a potato chip." Philip always laughed or ignored her, and kept cramming handfuls of potato chips into his face.

Philip's obsession snowballed as he grew older. Alone in his apartment, he occasionally ate nothing but chips for a meal, substituting different types for the various courses.

This was a rare treat at first. But soon Philip's self restraint began to crumble. One chip feast a month gave way to two or three. Then it was once a week, and not long after that, twice. After six months in his new apartment, he was up to one meal a day of nothing but chips. He was downing as many as five large bags a day. The grocery store clerks often looked at his cart and asked, "Having a picnic?" Philip would smile and nod.

Philip worried about his health. But it seemed there was no turning back. He tried to take care of himself. He switched to fat-free chips at lunch and no-salt chips at dinner on Mondays, Wednesdays, Fridays and every other Sunday. He upped his intake of vitamins, minerals and amino acids, and drank more water. He exercised more regularly.

One cold, clear Saturday afternoon, in early November, Philip outdid himself. He devoured three giant bags of chips...BBQ, salt and vinegar, and ranch. He felt so bloated he was sure he would get sick. But he didn't. Instead he settled on the couch and slipped off into a deep sleep in front of a college football game.

When he woke, Philip could barely move. He tried to swing a leg over the edge of the couch. But the other leg came with it...uninvited. Philip realized that his legs were fused together.

He could see faint ridges running along his arm. Then he noticed that the creases were all over his body. They were neat and uniform, spaced about one inch apart, and ran from north to south on his legs, arms, stomach, chest, and, as nearly as he could tell, on his back. Philip's body was also thinner and wider. His arms and fingers had all but disappeared. After a half hour of struggle, he made his way to the bathroom, falling many times on the way. He was shocked when he looked in the mirror. He prayed to wake up.

His body was getting stiffer as he stood there. Philip could barely bend over enough to look at his body. It was thin and rounded and curved forward at both the top and bottom. It was hard for him to keep his balance. He fell forward, striking what was left of his head on the sink. He remembered what his grandmother had said. He'd have to give her a call and tell her all about it when he woke up. They'd have a good laugh.

About Multiple-Choice Questions

Most multiple-choice questions will have four possible answers. Students should be familiar with the following strategies:

- Read the question carefully.
- Read *all* of the answers; an answer which looks right on first glance may not be the best choice.
- Cross out answers you know are wrong. Try to eliminate at least two answers.
- There is no penalty for guessing. If you cannot determine the answer you should guess. In your test booklet, mark any questions you have guessed. If you have time at the end of the test, go back to these items and see if you still like your answer.
- Use common sense. If the meaning of the question is clear to you, the answer will make sense. Do not try to over-analyze a question.
- Be careful of answers containing words such as *always* or *never*. Unless directly stated in the reading passage, absolute answers are rarely correct.
- When asked which answer fits "best," realize that the correct answer might not summarize a passage entirely, or give all the reasons for something, but it will fit better than the other answers.
- Answers to "main idea" questions can be tricky, since all of the answers will contain ideas from the reading passage. Students might try to determine the main idea before reading the answers, and see if any of the answers fit with their interpretation.
- Be sure your answer choice answers the question. Some answers might use language from the reading passage, or from the question itself, and still be incorrect.
- Some questions are a variation of multiple-choice. For example, a compare and contrast question might ask students to fill in a Venn diagram with words from a word list. For this type of question, students should cross out the word that doesn't fit any of the blanks before beginning to place the remaining words.

Sample multiple-choice questions:

1. What concerns does Philip have about his potato chip eating habits?

   A. Companies will stop making his favorite chips

   B. Emily will not marry him

   C. His health will suffer

   D. His sisters will call him names

Analysis:
Answer "A" can be eliminated, since we know that Philip is "not picky" about the chips he eats — one brand is as good as another. Emily is mentioned in the first paragraph, but not referred to again. Therefore, it is safe to eliminate answer "B." Philip does have health concerns: he takes vitamins and exercises to remain healthy. Philip's sisters do call him names ("piggish," and "disgusting"). However, Philip is not bothered by the names, but he does worry about his health. Therefore, "C" is the correct answer.

2. How did living on his own affect Philip's eating habits?

    A. He ate more well-balanced meals

    B. He ate more potato chips, since no one was watching him

    C. His eating habits remained the same

    D. Philip bought more potato chips

Analysis:
*Answer "A" is clearly wrong. Philip ate few well-balanced meals. He did eat more chips when he was on his own, so "B" is a possibility. His eating habits did not remain the same: he experimented with multi-course potato chip meals, and varied types of chips. Answer "C" can be crossed out. Philip did buy more potato chips, but answer "D" does not refer directly to his eating habits. Answer "**B**" is correct.*

3. The best person to recommend this story to would be someone who

    A. likes fantasy stories

    B. is named Philip

    C. has a crabby grandmother

    D. loves a single type of food

Analysis:
Someone who enjoys fantasy stories might like a story about a man who turns into a potato chip, so answer "A" is a possibility. Answer "B" can be eliminated, since simply sharing the name of Philip does not mean the content of the story will be appealing to someone. Answer "C" can be eliminated, since the grandmother is not the main focus of this story. If a friend loves a single type of food, they might enjoy this story. It might be funny to think of eating so much of your favorite food that you become that food. Answer "D" is the best answer.

About Short-Answer Questions

Short-answer questions allow students to respond to the reading passage. Students must be able to demonstrate an understanding of the text, as well as the ability to organize their ideas, integrate text information with background knowledge, and form a complete answer. The following strategies should be helpful:

- Read the question carefully. Underline important parts. Be sure you are clear about the specific question.
- Make margin notes of your immediate reaction to the question. Skim the passage for additional details.

- Organize your answer in your head. Is it complete, accurate, logical, and supported with appropriate details?
- Write your answer in the space provided, referring to the margin notes you made.
- If you have time at the end of the test, reread the question and your answer. Does your answer make sense? Have you answered the question fully?

Sample short-answer questions:

4. What clues tell us what happened to Philip at the end of the story? Support your answer with references to the story.

4.

_____

_____

_____

_____

_____

_____

Sample Response:

At the end of The Potato Chip Man, Philip turns into a potato chip. During the story, we read a few clues that this might happen, and a few clues that it was happening. Philip's grandmother told him, "One of these days you're gonna turn into a potato chip." He always laughed at her and kept eating chips. Near the end of the story, Philip ate three bags of chips and was afraid he might explode. Even he was full, and maybe tired of chips. After his nap, the author gives several clues about Philip turning into a chip. He describes how his legs are stuck together, how his body is flatter, and how he has ridges all over his body. Then we know that his grandmother's warning has come true!

Some short-answer response questions will ask one question and others will ask several questions and only expect a single response. The student's response must answer both questions before the response is complete. See question #5 on the next page.

5. Did Philip really turn into a potato chip, or was it a dream?   How do you know?

```
5.

_____

_____

_____

_____

_____

_____
```

Sample Response:

I think Philip was dreaming that he turned into a potato chip. Near the end of the story, he falls asleep on the couch. When he "wakes up," he finds that he is turning into a potato chip. The rest of the story is told in sort of a dreamy description. We learn about how his body has changed, how he realizes what is happening, and that he remembers what his grandmother told him. I bet that when Philip wakes up he will stop eating so many potato chips! His dream was pretty scary.

About Extended-Response Questions

Extended-response questions ask for a complete understanding, and a valid interpretation, of a reading passage. Students should keep the following strategies in mind as they approach these questions:

• Read the question carefully. Underline important parts. Be sure you are clear about the specific question.

• What is your initial response to the question? Use the margin or blank space on the test page to make notes.

• Test readers want to see how well you can interpret a story. You may need to infer ("read between the lines") some ideas from the passage. Be sure to support all of your ideas with details or reasons.

• Skim or reread the passage and underline parts relevant to the question. Add these ideas to your margin notes.

• Number your notes in a logical order for answering the question.

• Answer the question in your own words, in a logical order, and with enough detail to show that you understand both the reading passage and the question.

Sample extended-response question:

6. What is the author's purpose for writing this story? What message is he trying to give the reader? How does the author use the action and characters of the story to deliver his message?

6.

_____

_____

_____

_____

_____

_____

_____

_____

_____

_____

_____

Sample Response:

In The Potato Chip Man, the author wants to tell readers that there is more to life than just one thing. Some people spend all their time playing one sport, or visiting with one person, or practicing one hobby. Although their interest may be a good one, concentrating on just one interest gets boring. Philip's main interest is potato chips. He spends all his time with them, he even feels that he loves them "like a son." Philip doesn't seem to spend any time with his family or friends, he just seems to plan his day around potato chips. Finally, just as his grandmother suggested, Philip dreams that he turns into a potato chip. Luckily, in his dream, Philip realizes that being a chip is not fun. We imagine that when he wakes up he will develop some different food interests. The author has used a very silly example to make a good point. Since he is interested in only one thing, Philip has no time for other activities, friends, or even foods. He has become bored, and boring. The same thing can happen to anyone; we need to make sure we develop different interests.

Putting It All Together:
Demonstrating Reading Skills
Within the Standardized Test Format

Note: The learning outcomes below are arranged out of order since the suggested activities for strands I and III, as well as those for strands II and IV, are similar.

Strands I and III: Teaching the Required Skills

Strand I - Constructing/Examining Meaning with Fiction Selections
Strand III - Constructing/Examining Meaning with Nonfiction Selections

"*Constructing Meaning*" tests the ability to understand the general meaning of a reading passage. "*Examining Meaning*" refers to the ability to analyze and interpret a selection.

Analyze
✍ 1. **Analyze aspects of the text, examining, for example, characters, setting, plot, problem/solution, point of view, or theme.**
✔ 10. **Analyze the text, examining, for example, author's use of comparison and contrast, cause and effect, or fact and opinion.**

In fiction, students should be able to quickly identify the characters and the setting of a reading passage. Students should be able to relate the plot, as well as the main problem and its solution. The point of view represents the vantage point from which the author tells a story, and the theme delivers the main idea or message of the passage.

For nonfiction, students need to be able to identify the various methods an author uses to make a story meaningful: comparison and contrast; cause and effect. Students should be able to distinguish between facts stated in a passage and opinions expressed by the author or others in the story.

Analysis can be practiced throughout the curriculum on a regular basis. Students might practice making analyses by:

• Summarizing a story or article: telling the main points along with their interpretation.
• Writing their own stories. Be sure each story includes specific characters, setting, plot, a problem and a solution, a point of view, and a theme.
• Examining the same topic as related from different sources: a newspaper article, a letter to the editor, and a television documentary, for example. How do the authors treat their subject? How do the facts and opinions expressed differ in each source?
• Discussing a scientific invention: What was the main problem? Who are the characters involved? Relate the plot and the setting, and discuss the solution.

Sample Reading Passage:

May 25, 1996

Dear Editor,

Since I began my subscription to your newspaper, I have noticed that your coverage of women's sports is much weaker than the coverage of men's sports. This is true at the high school, college, and professional levels.

We moved to this town in August of last year, and our children (a son in 9th grade, and a daughter in 11th grade) began playing sports on their local high school's teams.

We do our best to attend all of their games. I have noticed that the crowds seem to be fairly equal for both men's and women's soccer, basketball, and softball/baseball. However, I have noticed that your photographers appear six times as often at the men's events, and they seem to attend the women's games only if the team is doing exceptionally well. In addition, your paper tends to cover men's sports in article form, and limit women's sports to box scores. It is frustrating to find a story and photos about a men's soccer game, while the women's game, which was played *on the next field*, receives no coverage at all.

Must women athletes be tops in their league to receive press coverage? **Title 9**, which calls for equality in men's and women's sports, passed a *generation* ago. Will we need a legislative order to attain equality in press coverage as well?

I hope that you will prepare to provide better women's sports coverage for the upcoming summer Olympics, and continued coverage of all women's sports for many years.

Sincerely,
Amy Coes

Sample Questions:

7. Why is Amy Coes upset?

   A. Her daughter played poorly in an important soccer match

   B. Her copy of the newspaper is often missing the sports section

   C. No photos of her daughter appeared in the sports section

   D. The newspaper gives more coverage to men's sports than to women's

Analysis:
Answer "A" should be eliminated, since her daughter's athletic skills are not mentioned in the letter. Answer "B" should be read carefully: she complains that the sports section is missing enough coverage of women's sports, not that her paper is missing the sports section. Cross out answer "B." Answer "C" is too specific: she would like to see more photos of women's sports, though not necessarily of her daughter. Answer "D" is correct; the letter addresses the inequality of coverage between men's and women's sports.

8. Which of the following items is a fact, rather than an opinion?

    A. Title 9 calls for equality in men's and women's sports

    B. All newspapers give more coverage to men's sports than to women's sports

    C. A new law will demand equality in sports coverage in the media

    D. Newspaper photographers prefer to attend men's sporting events

Analysis:
Answer "A" states a fact about a law. The statement in answer "B" is too broad. Be careful of answers with "all" in them. Answer "C" reflects a comment the author made, but we do not know if there is a new law to this effect. Answer "D," like "B," is too general. Answer "A" is correct.

9. If you were the newspaper editor, how would you evaluate this letter? Has the author made her point? Does she present enough evidence to support her conclusions? Is her solution reasonable? Respond as if you were writing a return letter to Amy Coes.

9.

9. continued

_____
_____
_____
_____
_____
_____
_____
_____
_____
_____
_____

Sample Response:

Dear Ms. Coes:

Thank you for your letter about the coverage of women's sports. It is with great embarrassment that I must admit you are right. I have looked at recent sports sections for the past few months, and I found that we gave men's sports at least three times as much coverage as women's.

I am particularly upset about your comment, "It is frustrating to find a story and photos about a men's soccer game, while the women's game, which was played on the next field, receives no coverage at all." You are right, and we have no excuse.

I hope you will accept my apology, both to you and the rest of our female readers. We will follow your suggestion and improve our coverage in general, and we will make a special effort to cover more women's sports, and women athletes, during the Olympics this summer.

Thank you for calling this to our attention.

Sincerely,

The Editor

Summarize
2. Summarize the text. *[fiction]*
11. Summarize the text. *[nonfiction]*

A summry tells the main idea of a story or nonfiction selection and several of the most important supporting details. A summary uses inference and states the outcome or the story conveyed. A summary reduces a text to its essence, based on information in the passage as well as inferences, conclusions, and interpretations which can be made from the material.

Students can practice summarization by:

• reporting on a movie or play
• explaining the rules to a game
• telling why a decision was made (at home, school, in politics...)
• explain a news story for current events
• share a novel, story chapter, short story or poem

Share the following passage with your students.

Sample Reading Passage:

CONTRACT RAP
by
Gail Blasser Riley

Jack asked Jill to repair his board.
He **agreed** to ten dollars, what he could afford.
When Jack and Jill entered into this pact,
the two of them had made a **contract**.

Now Jack said he'd pay to get the job done
and that money's called **consideration**.
I listened to their rap; now say, can you guess?
Hey, you got it right; I was a **witness**.

Jill **promised** to return the board before three
and that's when the girl could collect her fee.
Jill returned the board at 2:09.
She fulfilled her **duty**; she arrived on time.

Jack, however, was out at the beach.
He refused to pay. He committed a **breach**.
When Jack wouldn't pay, what else could Jill do?
The girl called her **lawyer**. She decided to **sue**.

The case went to **court**, and what might you predict?
The **judge** ruled for Jill. This was the **verdict**.
Now Jack learned a lesson in court that day.
You promise? You breach? You skate? You pay!

Sample Question:

10. Which statement best summarizes this poem?

   A. Legal terms can be explained in Rap form

   B. A boy tries to cheat a girl by not paying her what he owes her

   C. Jack and Jill live near the beach and like to surf

   D. Jack learned not to make promises

Analysis:
Answers "A" and "C" are correct statements about this poem, but they do not summarize the content of the poem. Cross out answers "A" and "C." Jack did try to cheat Jill by not paying for the repairs she made. Since this statement tells the main content of the poem, answer "B" is correct. The idea in answer "D" is not made clear in the poem, so answer "D" is incorrect.

Infer
3. Infer from the text. *[fiction]*
12. Infer from the text. *[nonfiction]*

Students will use information in the text to understand ideas which are not directly stated.

Inferences can often be used to determine personal attributes of a character (emotions, biases, temperament), as well as a way to expand one's understanding of a selection. You might practice drawing inferences by:

- Reading a play. Emotions and feelings are often described as stage direc tions ("she stomped her way across the room"). Act out the play in your classroom and discuss how the audience must infer from the actions (or the words) of the characters. If possible, see a play you haven't read. Have students keep a log of inferences they are able to make.
- Reviewing a Congressional Bill. Notice what is included and what is omit ted to determine the intentions of the bill's authors.
- Reading poetry. Poets are very economical with words. Examine how moods and scenes are created without expressing them directly.

Discuss the passage and the questions below with your students.

Sample Reading Passage:

Curtistown, OH, October 10: Drive through Curtistown in May, and you will see a lovely small city with traditional homes and gardens. As election day approaches however, the town's front porches and flower gardens are overshadowed by a multitude of campaign signs. "Re-elect Cavenaugh for School Board," "Marumoto for Mayor," "Jacobson for State Congress."

It is the school board race which has this town eagerly awaiting election day. The school board has 3 seats available this November, and it is a very close race among 5 contenders.

Evelyn Cavenaugh has represented the town on the school board for the past three years. She is a vice-president at State Bank, and has two grown children. Cavenaugh was appointed to the board following the death of board member Jacob Reiss in 1993. Since the upcoming election will be Cavenaugh's first, she is making a great effort in her campaign. Cavenaugh's positions include: FOR lengthening the school day by 30 minutes, so that the school year can be shortened by 13 days; AGAINST increasing taxes to update elementary school science textbooks; FOR raising taxes to develop a daycare for children ages 2 to 4.

Thomas Karaguesian has lived in Curtistown for all of his 55 years. Karaguesian was a member of the school board from 1973-79. Even though his children are grown, Karaguesian feels strongly about the local school system. "We need to support our schools in word and in deed. We can't shortchange our children's futures by cutting funds, or by dropping school volunteer programs." Karaguesian feels that a fair balance can be found to support the school without making taxes too high. His positions include: FOR allowing sports Boosters to raise funds for specific teams; AGAINST lengthening the school day; FOR developing a program to use school facilities during the summer months.

Karl Kroeger will seek one of the vacant school board seats. Kroeger owns a local landscaping firm, and has three children in the local school system. According to Kroeger's campaign manager, his positions include: AGAINST lengthening the school day; FOR raising taxes to update science textbooks; FOR a tax levy to develop a daycare center.

Mika Takeda has three children in the local elementary school. She is a partner in the law firm Marumoto, Takeda & Richardson. Takeda is running for school board with a bias towards elementary education. "If we neglect the younger children, we will fail to develop a strong base for their later education. Let's focus on building a strong education in the early grades, and work our way through the system. Our current method of fixing problems in "spots" is merely a bandage approach — we need to completely re-evaluate our educational values." Takeda has taken no stand on most current issues, since she feels the school system needs a total reevaluation.

Local builder Stan Winston is also seeking re-election. Winston has served on the school board since 1990. During his tenure on the board, he has helped the school system to grow from a single building to three buildings. Winston has one grown child, and one in high school. Winston's positions include: FOR allowing sports Boosters to raise funds for specific teams; FOR raising taxes to develop a daycare center; AGAINST lengthening the school day.

Recent polls (see chart) show Takeda and Cavenaugh in the lead, with the other three candidates fighting for the third post.

Which candidate would you vote for if the election were today?			
Candidate	August 1	September 1	October 1
Cavenaugh	28%	26%	22%
Karaguesian	16%	18%	20%
Kroeger	18%	20%	18%
Takeda	18%	22%	25%
Winston	20%	14%	15%

Sample Questions:

11. Candidate Takeda has become more popular since the polls began, yet she has not declared her position on any of the issues. Why might her popularity be increasing? Use examples from the article to support your answer.

11.
_____

_____

_____

_____

11. continued

_____

_____

_____

_____

_____

Sample Response:
Mika Takeda believes that the whole educational system in Curtistown needs to be reevaluated. She also believes that the school board should stop putting bandages on smaller problems and should work to fix the main problems. Although she has not declared her position on any current issues, she clearly believes in children and in helping the school system. As her campaign has had more time, these ideas must have become more popular with the voters.

12. If the current trend continues, what percentage of voters would vote for Thomas Karaguesian on November 1?

   A. 16%

   B. 18%

   C. 22%

   D. 20%

Analysis:
Since Karaguesian's support has grown by 2% with each monthly poll, we would assume his support would be at 22% on November 1. Answer "C" is correct.

Respond
4. Respond to the text. [fiction]
13. Respond to the text. [nonfiction]

When students respond to a passage, they will relate it to personal experiences or feelings.

Students respond to situations every day! For specific practice, you might:
- Invite a discussion of school food! How does it compare to food at home?
- After finishing a poem or story, ask if anyone has a similar story to relate.
- Choose a character from a story. How would students feel if they were in the same situation?
- Discuss an important community issue. How will it affect students? How do they feel about the decisions made by local officials?

Response practice can be done across the curriculum:
- math word problems (How would you design your garden in the space shown?)
- science experiments (Do you think animals should be used for experiments?)
- history texts (Would you have liked to have lived during the Revolutionary War?)
- newspaper articles (How might we help a family whose home burned down?)
- fiction (Have you ever had to "survive" a new situation on your own?)

Share the passage below and the questions that follow with your students.

THE NEW LEADER
by LaRita Marie Heet

Ten year old Alex leaned into the car, tossing his backpack into the back seat, then jumped in to sit beside his mom.

"Hi, honey. How was school today?" she asked, leaning over to kiss his cheek.

"Fine. Ernie got detention again, nothing new there."

His mom laughed. "Poor Ernie, can't he stay out of trouble for a single day?"

"Yeah, right! You know Ernie better than that. Hey, guess what? I have great news!" He reached around and pulled an envelope from his backpack. "Here," he said, holding it out to his mom.

She kept her hands on the steering wheel. "Alex! You know I can't read that while I'm driving. Why don't you read it to me?"

He nodded, and began reading her the letter from his Webeloe Den Leader. He looked over at her when he finished it. "Isn't that great news?"

"Wait, did I miss something here? Mr. Goggin is moving, and isn't going to be your Den Leader anymore, and you're happy about it? I always thought you liked Mr. Goggin."

Alex nodded excitedly. "I do; I like him a lot. But didn't you hear the part about needing a new den leader? Ernie nominated you!" He grinned at the look of surprise on her face. "We all agreed. You already go on campouts with us, and you help out with our badges and special projects, so you practically know everything about it. Even Mr. Goggin says you'd be perfect for the job. So will you do it, Mom?"

Her blue eyes were serious as she looked at him. "I don't know, Alex. I mean, helping out with campouts and projects is awfully different than being in charge of the entire den. I'll have to think about it, okay?"

Alex nodded, the disappointment evident in his expression. He'd thought for sure that his mom would love to be Den Mother. She'd always been different than the other moms — cooler, he thought — but since his dad had died suddenly three years before, she and Alex had grown even closer.

"It's not that I don't want to, Alex," she told him. "It's just that becoming a leader is hard work — you have to go through this whole leadership training class. And then I'd have to study and memorize lots of things. It would be so time-consuming... Besides, I might have to miss work for a day for the class, and you know how mad that makes my boss."

Alex nodded, trying to understand, but her excuses didn't seem that convincing to him. It was true that studying and reading didn't seem to be her favorite things — he never really saw her with a book or newspaper. She seemed to prefer outdoor activities instead — like camping and fishing and baseball. Still, it didn't seem like it'd take that much time.

But Alex didn't want to pester her, so he tried to wait until she brought it up again.

At the next den meeting, Mr. Goggin announced that he hadn't been able to find a new den leader. The boys would need to be split up and put in different dens.

During the ride home, Alex's mom noticed his unhappy mood. He told her what had happened, but kept his eyes fixed on the passing scenery, not looking at her once.

His mom glanced over at him. "And you think this is all my fault, huh?"

Alex shrugged, examining his fingernails intently. He couldn't help but be angry with her — she knew how much the Scouts meant to him.

She tried to apologize, but he just shrugged again, and as soon as they got home, he went straight to his room. His mom knocked on his door a short time later.

"Alex, I have something I need to tell you. I'd hoped you'd never have to find out, because I would hate for you to think any less of me. But now, I have no choice but to be honest with you." She looked nervous, as Alex stared at her. What could she possibly have to tell him? For a moment, he wondered if he'd end up on one of those talk shows — "My Mom's Secret Life" — then he turned his attention back to what she was saying.

"This is very embarrassing for me, honey, but the truth is... I mean, the reason I can't be your Den Mother is because... well, I don't know how to read," she said quietly, looking down at his comforter...

Sample Questions:

13. If one of your parents told you that they couldn't read, how would you react? Give specific examples of your emotions and any actions you might take.

13.
_____
_____
_____
_____
_____
_____
_____
_____
_____
_____
_____
_____
_____

Sample Response:

If my mother told me she couldn't read, at first I would be very surprised. Like Alex's mom (in the story), I'm sure she would have been able to "fake it" for many years. I guess that at first I might be sad that she kept a secret from me, but then I would want to help her learn to read.

Since she might be embarrassed to have me teach her, I could help her sign up for a tutor or a reading class. I would try to be patient with her progress, just as she is patient when I am learning something new. Once she could read pretty well, I would have all her friends write her a letter, put the letters in a scrapbook, and give it to her for a surprise. Then she would know how proud I was of her bravery in admitting she couldn't read and what she accomplished when she did learn to read.

General Activities to Reinforce Skills for Strands I & III

- **Break it down.** List the major components of a story. How are the pieces related? Would a change in one piece change the story? What if it were told from a different point of view? Try the same activity with a newspaper or magazine article.

- **Act it out.** Let groups of classmates select a short story to dramatize as simply or elaborately as you wish. The class might want to enact their plays with puppets, costumed students, or with a simple extemporaneous skit.

- **The silver screen.** Practice drawing inferences with silent "movies." Students can act out a scene with no words. Classmates should list everything they learn: actions, moods, characters' wishes, etc.

- **What do you mean by that?** Draw inferences by reading letters to the editor in your local paper. What is said in each letter? What else do you know? How do you know this? Use stated information to support your inferences.

- **Begin Book Groups.** When the class is reading a book together, divide the class into small groups for discussion purposes. No teachers allowed! Groups should discuss feelings and reactions to the reading, ask questions about parts they don't understand, and offer interpretations of passages or character actions in the story. Pressing questions and inspired revelations can be shared with the entire class. For groups who have trouble getting started, a few "starter questions" might be posted on the chalk board.

- **Keep reading folders.** Students should keep track of books they read. Folders can include the title, author, type of book and a brief summary. Folders should include both written and pictorial responses to books.

Strands II and IV:
Teaching the Required Skills

5. Compare and contrast aspects of the text, for example, characters or settings. [fiction]
✍ 14. Compare and/or contrast aspects of the text. [nonfiction]

Students need to be able to identify similarities and differences within a passage. They should be able to notice these similarities and differences even if the author has not compared/contrasted them directly within the text.
Students should be able to compare and contrast any given elements from their reading.

Source materials for practice of this skill include:
- fiction passages
- two articles on the same issue by writers with opposing opinions
- a novel and the movie version of the novel
- a photograph of your town many years ago and the same spot today

With compare and contrast, students are looking for similarities and differences. The simplest way both to teach this skill and to keep track of these similarities and differences is to construct charts and diagrams. Venn diagrams might be used to compare two characters in a novel, or to compare a novel to the movie interpretation. A two-column chart can be used to list only the similarities or only the differences between two characters.

Encourage students to go beyond the obvious when seeking similarities and differences. Students who are able to make inferences from the reading which will fit on the compare/contrast diagram are demonstrating a greater knowledge and understanding of the material. Try the exercises below with your class.

PITCHER MOUNTAIN
by Karinne Heise

Once we passed the funny-looking cows, we knew we were almost there. The long-haired cows, Scottish Highlanders, grazed in a meadow fenced in by old stone walls made of New Hampshire granite. In the back seat, my two brothers and I bounced as my dad steered our old red Scout off the blacktop and onto the dirt road that took us to the top of Pitcher Mountain. A white-haired man at the entrance to the road waved to us and my dad rolled down his window.

"How're the beh-ries this ye-ah?" Dad asked, using his fake New Hampshire accent.

"It's a good ye-ah for pickin'," answered the man, wiping his hands on the apron he used to collect money. "Head on up to numbah 10. That's whe-yah you'll find the best beh-ries."

We all waved, Mom and Dad in the black bucket seats in front and us kids in the back; the Scout spurted a bit of gravel from its tires and up we bumped on our yearly August trek to pick blueberries.

A weathered wooden flagpole marked the parking area on the top of the mountain. We clambered out of the car onto a grassy knoll surrounded by the high-bush blueberries covering the entire mountain top. Strapping coffee can containers around our waists with rope so we'd have both hands free for picking, we set off toward a path that meandered through the bushes, each in search of the best bush.

For my dad, the best bush was one near other pickers so he could eavesdrop on their conversations and then entertain us with impersonations on our drive home. My mom, efficient and eager, scouted out bushes with the largest clumps of berries while my younger brothers tended to find bushes near the large granite boulders jutting up along the ridge line so that they could take breaks from picking for games of King of the Hill. I liked to find the bush which would set me up with the best northwestern view. The blues and greens nearby were always distinct; green leaves offset the blueberries in front of me and dark green forests surrounded the deep blue lakes in the valley below the mountain. Each layer of green hills in the distance, though, grew more faint until my eye could barely distinguish the Green Mountains in Vermont from the blue horizon of the sky.

The first berries I picked plunked loudly and unsatisfyingly in my can. Each berry seemed like an effort and too small to make a difference. But once I had covered the bottom of my can, the berries dropped silently and I didn't think about what I was doing. I sneaked peeks at the mountains and listened to the buzz of the insects and the white-throated sparrows singing, "O sweet Canada Canada Canada" overhead. And every so often, I indulged in eating a handful of the sweet, juicy berries.

At the designated time, we met by the car to see who had picked the most berries and who had the bluest tongue and teeth. Mom somehow won both competitions. It was tough to step from the cool fresh breezes of the mountain top into the hot stale air of the car, until Mom announced, "Blueberry pie for dessert tonight!" I could smell the pie the whole way home.

Sample Questions:

14. How did the noises the berries made in her can affect the author's mood about picking blueberries?

14.

_____

_____

_____

_____

_____

_____

Sample Response:
At first, the berries made noise, and she felt like she wasn't making progress. Once the bottom of the can was covered, the berries made no noise and she just kept picking without thinking about it.

15. In *Pitcher Mountain*, the mother is eager to collect berries for pie, while the father is eager to collect experiences. How does the author demonstrate the goals of each parent? How do their different styles make the day more fun? Use examples from the story to support your ideas.

15.

_____

_____

_____

_____

_____

_____

_____

_____

_____

_____

15. continued

_____

_____

_____

_____

_____

_____

_____

Sample Response:

The author of Pitcher Mountain shows that her father collects experiences by describing how he tries to talk with a New Hampshire accent, and how he likes to pick berries near other people so he can listen to their stories and tell them to the kids in the car.

The mother wants to make pie, so she picks berries from the full bushes. She must pick quickly, though, because she also eats enough berries to have the bluest tongue! She keeps the kids excited by talking about making pies.

If both parents were too serious about picking berries, the kids would probably quit. If both parents just played, there wouldn't be enough berries for pies. In Pitcher Mountain, everyone seems to enjoy the outing; they like driving there, picking out their spots, having contests, hearing stories on the ride home, and making pies for dessert.

6. Critique and/or evaluate aspects of the text. [fiction]
15. Critique and evaluate the text for such elements as organizational structure and logical reasoning. [nonfiction]

To critique and/or evaluate aspects of a reading passage, students will usually consider the choices an author makes as he or she is writing the piece. What choices were made (point of view, organization, etc.)? Did these choices make the passage more effective?

For critique and evaluation, students need to develop a critical eye. Just as they might evaluate the function of each part of a plant in science, they should discuss the choices involved in writing. Does each piece make the whole the best it can be?

For practice:

- Discuss the goals of the author. What point is he or she trying to make?
- List the choices which the author made: number and importance of characters, organization of an article or story, point of view, etc.
- How did these choices affect the power of the story? If different choices were made, how would the story be changed? Discuss how different choices might make an equally good piece, but might not fit with the author's original goals.

Try the poem below and the questions that follow for more practice.

Whose Will Be Done?
by Babs Bell Hajdusiewicz

Each poem I write has a mind of its own,
Its willful unfolding remains to be shown.
I get an idea
                        t
            and   o s
                        s   it around
often unsure of where I am bound.
I write the first line...
                            ...Hmmm...like it a lot!
And these words? They seem to develop my plot.
Another few lines...yes, that could go there...
Wh   s
      oo p
                        maybe these lines don't fit a-n-ywhere.
Let's see...
            how's it read from back at the start?
No...those lines don't fit at all with this part..
        But this is much better...it seems to convey
                exactly the message I wanted to say.
Hmmm...strike the first line
                and delete the third;
Substitute here
                and insert a word
Read it again beginning...
                                    ...to end
the message is altered...But...
                    look what I've penned!

Each poem I write has a mind of its own,
Its willful unfolding remains to be shown.

16. This poem describes the process of writing a poem. The poet uses some unusual typesetting within the poem (see the words "toss," "whoops," etc.). Does this format help the meaning of the poem, or hurt your ability to read it clearly? Is this format a successful way to tell her story? Support your answer with references from the story.

16.

_____

_____

_____

_____

_____

_____

_____

_____

_____

_____

_____

_____

_____

_____

_____

_____

Sample Response:
When you first read this poem, you wonder if the poet hit the wrong letters on the keyboard. But once you realize what she is doing, "tossing" words around for her poetry, it makes the poem more fun to read. Her format makes it clear that she has fun writing, and that it is still fun even if things come out different from what she thought might happen.

17. Who are the main "characters" in this poem?

```
┌─────────────────────────────────────────────────────┐
│  17.                                                  │
│  _____ │
│  _____ │
│  _____ │
│  _____ │
└─────────────────────────────────────────────────────┘
```

Sample Response:
The words of the poem seem to be the main character, and the poet is more of a support-ing character. The poet is like a director of her poem — she tries to keep the words in place, but she is willing to move them around to make the poem work. The words try to find their own places in the poem, and can even change the meaning of the poem if they want to.

7. Select information for a variety of purposes, including enjoyment. [fiction]
✔ 16. Select information from a variety of resources to support ideas, concepts, and interpretations. [nonfiction]

Students will need to be able to choose resources (print, media, community resources, etc.) to support or amplify a reading passage.

For this skill, students should be familiar with basic resource materials:
- library card catalogs
- dictionaries
- encyclopedias
- tables of contents and indexes for books, magazines and newspapers.
- community resources of varying types

Next, students must be clear about what information they are seeking.

With some "find information" questions in hand, try the following exercises:
- allow students to brainstorm for where information might be found
- analyze each response to determine the probability of finding answers there
- have each student vote for one resource which he or she thinks will hold the answer
- test your answers! How many of your resources worked? Which ones were best, and why? Which ones didn't work, and why?

The Christmas Diary
by Amy Ruth

And so, the diary remained in the trunk, a secret not yet discovered. Many years went by. The girl's son passed on in the spring of 1943.

The girl's youngest grandson returned to the house and cleaned out his father's things. He brought his daughter, Martha Rose, with him.

When they climbed the stairs to the attic, they found the old trunk. Together, Martha Rose and her father lifted the lid. Dust flew about. The hinges whined and complained.

Inside, sitting on a blue calico dress, was the red leather diary. Martha Rose lifted the diary carefully. From the inside front cover she read:

Martha Rose MacTaggert, age 12
MacTaggert Farmstead, Nebraska

The girl gasped and cried out, "Why, that's my name."

The father smiled, surprised and delighted by the find. "She was your great-grandmother," he said. "I did not know she kept a diary."

They took the diary home and read past midnight, straining to read the great-grandmother's childhood words. The walnut ink, once a deep brown, was now faded. But the girl had written a neat cursive hand; her letters were slanted and perfectly shaped.

"Looks like art," said Martha Rose.

"It was," her father agreed.

January 1, 1870
Dear Diary,
I don't know how they succeeded, but Mama and Papa brought Christmas through the ice and snow after all. If I never receive another present again, I shall not mind. Today I make the promise to write a thought in this diary every day. It will be the story of my life. Surely it will bore others, but I do not care. The words I write here are my own gift to myself.

October 11, 1872

Dear Diary,

Am not fond of the dress Mama had me wear today. The blue calico does not flatter me so. I should wear red silk and feathers in my bonnet if I had my way.

Next to the entry she drew a flowing silk dress with bows and pearl buttons down the front.

August 1, 1873

Dear Diary,

Papa says I shall go to school year-round if I like. I do, I do! I shall board in town during the week with Aunt Millie and return to the farm on the week-end. Happy, happy day! Mother says she is sad to see me go, but presented me with two composition books to begin my lessons.

December 12, 1874

Dear Diary,

Argued with the chickens over their eggs. They are stubborn creatures with mean spirits. They take joy in pecking at my ankles with their sharp beaks. I should not judge the poor creatures, though, for they do not like to mind anymore than I!

And so she continued, day after day, every day, for five years. She recorded sicknesses, deaths, birthdays, and family reunions. She described trips to town to buy cloth, buttons, a new tea kettle, or sacks of flour, sugar, and coffee. Sometimes, the girl pressed wildflowers, newspaper clippings, and other keepsakes into her diary. She saved report cards, a reward of merit she earned in eighth grade, and her high school commencement program.

December 31, 1875

Dear Diary,

I must say good-bye now. I write here one final time. Soon I start anew. Wish me luck, dear diary, dear friend.

The following week, the girl was married to a lawyer. Then she moved with her husband to Colorado. Together, they made a new life.

When they had finished reading, the girl wondered, "What do we do with it now?"

"It is yours to do with as you wish," the father replied

"Would other people want to read it, too?" she asked.

Her father nodded. "Why, at my museum, people are always coming in asking to see so and so's diary. Then they sit and inspect it oh so carefully, often taking pages of notes."

"So they can understand how life used to be?" she suggested.

Her father nodded.

"Could we take it to Nebraska?" she asked. "Is there a place for it there?"

Her father nodded again, and smiled inwardly at his daughter's fine wisdom.

At the Nebraska State Historical Society, Martha Rose slipped the diary out of its box and unwrapped it from its covering. She handed it to the librarian.

"I'd like to give this here," she said, her voice a little sad, a little shaky. "It was my great-grandmother's when she was young, like me."

"A generous gift," the woman said. "We have no children's diaries from this time period."

Sample Questions:

18. Which of the following books would be most likely to include parts of Martha Rose's diary?

    A. "Children of Nebraska: 1850-1900"

    B. "Settlers of Colorado"

    C. "The Founding of the Nebraska State Historical Society"

    D. "Christmas in Colorado"

Analysis:

Although Martha Rose did move to Colorado, her diary was written before this time. Answers "B" and "D" should be eliminated. The diary was given to the Nebraska State Historical Society, but well after its founding, so answer "C" is incorrect. Answer "A" is correct, since young Martha Rose lived and wrote her diary in Nebraska between 1850 and 1900.

19. If Martha Rose, the great-granddaughter, wanted to learn more about experiences her great-grandmother might have had after the time of the diary, where might she look?

    A. "19th Century Law and Lawyers"

    B. "Fifty Years in Nebraska: 1875-1925"

    C. "Colorado: from Settlement until 1900"

    D. "The United States from 1800-1950"

Analysis:

Answer "A" is too narrow — although Martha Rose married a lawyer, we couldn't expect any information about their life to be in this book. Answer "D" is too broad, since it covers 150 years in the entire country. Answer "B" seems likely, until we remember that Martha Rose moved to Colorado after she married. Answer "C" is correct. This book covers the state she lived in, for a fairly narrow time period. We could expect to learn about life in Colorado during Martha Rose's adulthood from this book.

20. A group of Nebraska school children want to make a presentation about Martha Rose's childhood. In addition to the diary, what resources might they use in their presentation? How should these resources be used? Give reasons for your selections.

20.

Sample Response:

The students might visit the library and the Historical Society to find more information. They should look for newspapers from the years of Martha Rose's childhood. It would be interesting to learn about what her town was like, what was important to the people, how people earned a living, what they did in bad weather, and so on. The students should try to find any other diaries from that time. An adult diary might show different ideas about some of the same things Martha Rose discussed. The library or the Historical Society might also have some early pictures or drawings of the town, of people, or of local buildings. It might be interesting to compare these pictures with pictures of the area today. The students could make their presentation as a slide show, a reading, or even as a play.

8. Express reasons for recommending or not recommending the text for a particular audience or purpose. [fiction]

✔ **17. Express reasons for recommending or not recommending the text for a particular audience or purpose. [non-fiction]**

Students should be able to judge whether a certain text is appropriate for a given audience or purpose.

As you read anything in class — from math word problems to science articles to short stories — discuss for whom the work is intended. What reasons do you have for making this decision? Why would a dinosaur picture book be appropriate for a four-year-old, but not for a paleontologist? Or would it be appropriate for both? Under what circumstances?

Sample Passage:

"Spring has sprung, the grass is riz, I wonder where the flowers is." My mother sings this little rhyme every spring, when she is tired of winter, and eager to see her crocuses and daffodils. For some people, spotting the first robin means spring has arrived. For my mother, nothing is official until the daffodils are in full bloom.

I come from a long line of gardeners. I remember playing in my grandfather's garden, disagreeing with him over the pronunciation of "tomato." I spent many hours pulling weeds and harvesting vegetables, flowers, and blueberries in my mother's garden. As an adult, I have lived all over the country — with a garden in every spot. Vacations often include trips to visit, and learn from, other people's gardens. Many friends have been made in rather unlikely spots: hardware stores, garden shops, peeking through fences to get a better glimpse of a garden. Only another gardener can understand this desire to peer into a mysterious back yard.

Recently, we moved to Ohio. As I unpacked boxes, I planned gardens in my head. A dear friend — knowing that a gardener's house is not a home until the gardens begin — sent lily bulbs for our new yard.

Our children watched with some confusion as I carted many wheelbarrows of dirt to the new gardens. Soon the confusion turned to curiosity, and I had two helpers. Within an hour, the helpers wanted a garden of their own. Today their garden holds tiny seedlings: flowers (sunflowers, moon flowers, poppies), herbs (chives, sorrel, parsley), and vegetables (onions, beets, spinach). Some of their harvest will be vegetables which are new to them, but they will savor their flavors, warm from the earth. With a new generation of gardeners, spring will always have a special meaning in my family.

Sample Questions:

21. The best person to recommend this essay to would be someone

A. with young children

B. who has lived all over the country

C. who would plant an indoor garden, if they didn't have a yard

D. who enjoys the birds of spring

Analysis:
All of the answers refer to passages from the essay. However, since the main focus of the essay is the joy that spring awakens in gardeners, answer "C" is correct.

✍ **9. Explain how an author uses contents of a text to support his/her purpose for writing. [fiction]**

✍ **18. Explain how an author uses contents of a text to support his/her purpose for writing. [nonfiction]**

Students should be able first to determine an author's purpose for writing a piece. Next, students need to be able to explain how the contents of that piece support the purpose.

For practice with these learning outcomes, critique a story or an article, examining how the different elements contribute to the author's purpose.

For example:

Hatchet
by Gary Paulsen

Author's purpose: To show that a troubled boy can set aside his own problems to face major challenges in a life-threatening situation.

contents	how it supports author's purpose
divorce of parents	demonstrates how a major item in Brian's life can seem minor when compared with his later troubles
pilot's heart attack	Brian's reaction to this shows that he is not quite ready to take on adult responsibilities and challenges
lost in the wilderness	Brian realizes that his actions will determine whether he survives. He takes responsibility for himself and gains confidence in his skills

Try the passage on the next page with your students.

THE RESCUE OF THE NINE-BANDED RABBIT-TURTLE
by Gail Blasser Riley

Many thousands of years ago, the Nine-Banded One surveyed the mountainous countryside as he skittered across the land on legs so short they appeared barely able to propel his strange body. The giant ground sloth and mastodons paid little attention to him as he traveled across the kingdom. While the dire wolves and the saber tooth cats hissed and fought against one another, the Nine-Banded One traveled by, unnoticed in the background.

The Nine-Banded One knew he should feel thankful and relieved, as he had no natural predators. Instead, relief had long ago given way to a quiet anger. Sorrow and emptiness mixed to form a terrible ache in his heart. He was lonely. Though he had been told a long time before that others of his kind existed, he had yet to discover them, and he grew frustrated in his search.

One day, the Nine-Banded One ventured toward the land of the human, a land said to hold great wonders, but also torture and misery for all those who dared enter.

The Nine-Banded One traveled rough terrain for days. Finally, he arrived at the land of the human. As he crossed into this forbidden territory, the Nine-Banded One stopped in his tracks, raised his head and flared his nostrils. The strange new scents filled him with fear and excitement all at once.

As he approached, the humans who saw the Nine-Banded One cried out shrill sounds that pierced the creature's tender ears. The humans raced away and cowered. They crouched behind rocks and trees as they viewed this strange armored being. For a short while, the humans watched and talked amongst themselves.

Soon, however, as the setting sun's blaze illuminated the clearing, the humans crept slowly forward to investigate this new life form that had entered their kingdom. One by one, they reached out to brush a finger across the creature's back. Each time, the Nine-Banded One tingled warmly to the touch and inched forward, seeking more of this strange, delightful feeling.

Though the humans at first pulled back in fear of this unknown skin, their curiosity gradually overtook their cowardice and they came to investigate again and again. "Rough," boomed one human. He touched the unusual hide, looked at his hand and looked back to the hide once more.

"Bumpy," another of these upright creatures declared.

These speech sounds pleased the Armored One. He began to feel comfortable and welcome.

In time, the humans came often to stroke the creature and share their love and earthly belongings. They seemed to enjoy his playful antics and his generous return of affection. Seeking a name for their new companion, the humans explored many possibilities.

"He bears nine bands," observed one human.

"He resembles the rabbits and turtles of our land," offered another.

"We shall call him 'Nine-Banded Rabbit Turtle,'" decreed a wise one.

But, as humans tend to do, another of their kind challenged the decree. "He is an armored one. We shall call him 'The Armored One.'"

Though the new creature would always be "The Nine-Banded Rabbit-Turtle" to many, "The Armored One" became his official calling.

The Armored One lived for a joyful period in the presence of the humans, honored and held dear by all who came to know him.

This joy was short-lived, however. The Armored One soon fell prey to a human virus, a sickness it had never encountered in its own kingdom. The remedies offered by the humans proved worthless and the Armored One soon grew increasingly ill.

As the days passed, the Armored One could scarcely move about. The humans offered wise remarks, advising the Armored One to return to his homeland, believing that the creature might in some way shed this illness in his natural habitat.

But the Armored One had grown to cherish these humans who had made him a center of their world, who had stroked him and loved him and tended to him in a way that those who inhabited his native land never had.

In time, as he fought his sickness, the Armored One came to be known as the Armored Ill one. He lived out his last days in the land of those who had loved and cared for him.

... And today, the small heartier armadillos who roam the human kingdom remember their ancestor and follow his legacy by living in peace and harmony with the human creatures.

Sample Questions:

22. What is the author's purpose in writing this story?

   A. To tell the biological history of the armadillo

   B. To create a folk tale about how the armadillo got its name

   C. To show a scene of the early-American southwest region

   D. To tell how humans have been bad luck for animals

Analysis:
*Answer "A" is incorrect, since we have few scientific facts in this story. Answer "B" seems right, since we learn about how the animal got two names, and then became the Armored Ill one (armadillo). Answer **B** is correct. Answer "C" describes an aspect of the story, but not the main purpose of the tale. Answer "D" is too broad, and draws conclusions which are not demonstrated in the story.*

23. Explain how the "Nine-Banded One's" loneliness is important to the author's purpose in this tale. Refer to the story to support your answer.

23.

Sample Response:
When the armadillo lived in the animal world, all of the other animals ignored him. He had heard that there were others of his kind, but he could never find them. He was so lonely, that he decided to go to the human world, even though he heard it was dangerous. When he traveled to the human world, he received a lot of attention from the humans. He enjoyed being petted and loved by someone. The humans were kind to him, and gave him a name. The author is telling this tale to explain the armadillo's name. She uses the animal's loneliness to explain why he went to the human world, and then got his name.

General Activities to Reinforce Skills for Strands II & IV

• **Post it!** Create a bulletin board with stories and articles about one subject. Compare and contrast the different approaches to the subject, the different decisions each author made, and the intentions the authors had in writing their pieces.

• **Stop the presses!** Rewrite a story or article. Try telling it from a different point of view, organizing the information in a different way, or having different characters express the key points. Is your story able to meet the author's goals effectively? Why did the author make the choices he/she did?

• **Decisions, Decisions...** Examine how authors get an important point across to the reader. In fiction, an emotional moment might be expressed in words, actions by the character involved, or reactions by other characters. In nonfiction, a controversial issue might be discussed within the text by the author, in a quotation from one source, or in quotations from several contradictory sources. Which methods work best? Why might an author choose different methods for different situations?

• **First things first.** Discuss the power of a story or article's organizational structure. Why do some stories use flashbacks? Why might a magazine article begin with an anecdote, before the "issue" is stated? How do different techniques affect the impact of the piece?

• **Compile an anthology.** Allow the class to select the criteria for their anthology. It might be a collection of stories, advertisements, jokes, poems, or they might choose a theme (nature, sports, politics, etc.). Discuss why items have been chosen. Compare and contrast the merits/faults of items during the final selection phase. Debate how to organize and display the collection.

• **A day in the life of...** If the class has enjoyed a particular book or article, make an effort to learn more about the author or the subject. Allow students to brainstorm for resources which will answer their questions. In addition to biographies, encyclopedias, and past magazine articles, don't forget to include the author (if living) as a possible source of information.

• **Out of the book experiences.** Authors use the contents of their work to support their purpose for writing, but so does everyone! Examine decisions made by the school board, decisions made on the playground, and those made in the world. For example, the contents of the refrigerator support the purpose of dinner and general nutrition. Look for examples all around you.

**Suggested Activities to Reinforce General Reading Skills
(as well as a love of reading)**

• **Write book reviews.** Create a class newsletter, binder, or bulletin board for book reviews. Reviews should include the title, author, a brief description, why recommended, and the reader's name. Students looking for reading suggestions can browse the recommendations.

• **Read every day.** Pleasure reading materials should be self-selected. Encourage students to read for pleasure for 30 to 40 minutes every day.

• **Vary the selections.** Personal and classroom reading should cover a variety of topics and types of reading materials. Reading selections can be in various fields (science, historical fiction, folk tales) and of various styles (short stories, news articles, posters, labels, directions).

Mathematics

Sixth Grade Proficiency Test: Math

This book is about success. Everyone likes to succeed, especially on tests. Tests are given to see what you know. It feels great, when asked, to be able to show what you know. A good many people succeed on tests, not because they know all of the facts or answers, but because they are able to use what they know to figure out what they don't know. They make use of their H.O.T.S. (Higher Order Thinking Skills).

Hopefully, this information will help students develop a knowledge base, and higher order thinking skills, so that they can be successful not only on the proficiency test, but in all of life's testing situations.

It is important to note that only 20% of the items on the proficiency test will deal with Knowledge and Skill items. The bulk of the test and the consequent scoring will be based on the Conceptual Understanding (40%) and the Application and Problem Solving (40%) abilities of students.

Mathematics Learning Outcomes

Strand One: Patterns, Relations, and Functions
1. Apply the relation between doubling the side of a regular figure and the corresponding increase in area.
2. Determine the rule, identify missing numbers, and/or find the nth term in a sequence of numbers or a table of numbers involving one operation or power.

Strand Two: Problem Solving Strategies
3. Apply appropriate notations and methods for symbolizing the problem statement and solution process.
4. Identify needed and given information in a problem situation as well as irrelevant information.
5. Validate or generalize solutions and problem solving strategies.

Strand Three: Numbers and Number Relations
6. Compute with whole numbers, fractions and decimals.
7. Find equivalent fractions.
8. Change freely between fractions and decimals.
9. Order combinations of whole numbers, fractions, and decimals and ordering fractions and decimals by using symbols $<, \leq, >, \geq$, and $=$ and/or by placing them on a number line.
10. Use ratio and proportions in a wide variety of applications.

Strand Four: Geometry
11. Visualize and show the results of rotation, translation, reflection, or stretching of geometric figures.
12. Recognize, classify, and/or use characteristics of lines and simple two-dimensional figures including circles: and apply models and properties to characterize and/or contrast different classes of figures including three-dimensional figures.

Strand Five: Algebra
13. Use the distributive property in arithmetic computations.
14. Explain and reflect differences between calculators with arithmetic logic and calculators with algebraic logic when symbolizing a keying sequence and in the display as each key is pressed.
15. Use variables to describe arithmetic process, to generalize arithmetic statements, and to generalize a problem situation.

Strand Six: Measurement
16. Determine perimeters, areas, and volumes of common polygons, circles, and solids using counting techniques or formulas.
17. Convert, compare and compute with common units of measure within the same measurement system.
18. Measure angles with a protractor. Goniometers and compasses are not allowed for the test.

Strand Seven: Estimation and Mental Computation

19. Apply appropriate stategies to find estimate of sums, differences, products, and quotients of whole numbers and determine whether the estimate is greater than or less than the exact result.

20. Estimate the sum, difference, product, or quotient of decimal numbers by rounding, and the sum, difference, or product of fractions and/or mixed numbers by rounding the fractions to 0,1/2, or 1.

Strand Eight: Data Analysis and Probability

21. Collect data, create a table, picture graph, bar graph, circle graph, or line graph and use them to solve application problems.

22. Read, interpret, and use tables, charts, maps, and graphs to identify patterns, note trends,and draw conclusions.

23. Apply the concept of average and calculate the arithmetic mean and mode of a given set of numbers.

24. Make predictions of outcomes of experiments based upon theoretical probabilities and explain actual outcomes.

Test - Taking Tips for the Mathematices Proficiency Test

1. Answer the question exactly. If test question asks for an estimate, exact numbers will be marked incorrect even if the exact answer that is given may be correct. If an estimate average is requested for a column of numbers, and students know that they may use a calculator, a common error may result if students just find an average using the calculator. The test will be looking for students to use an estimating technique to find an estimated total and then find the average of that total. Students may feel that an exact answer is more correct, but in this testing situation this would be a misconception.

2. Read every part of the problem carefully. One example in the test booklet shows a visual or diagram of a sale advertisement. An estimate of a total sale or purchase is requested. If students do not read all the words in small print, they may not see "for a set of three", words that would radically alter their estimate. An estimate is an answer that tells <u>about</u> how much money would be needed to buy the items. It would not be an exact answer.

3. Read to know what is really being asked, and answer all parts to the question. Often the test item does not require an answer to a problem, but rather asks for "related facts," or " formula for the solution," or "similar equations." If students are not prepared for this, they may correctly solve for "n" only to find that they were not asked to do so. Be sure to do all steps of the problem requested in the test item, for many of the items on the practice test have two and three parts to the solution.

4. Be careful writing in your Answer Booklet!!! When you are ready to write your answer, be certain that it is carefully transferred to the correct space provided for that response. At the time of the writing of this book, the format of the sixth grade answer book has all multiple choice answers grouped in one part of the book, and all the short-answer and extended responses grouped in another section. This was done to correct the over-writing that caused scoring problems on the fourth grade document (when students wrote longer responses than expected and their writing over-lapped the mulitple choice answers). Unfortunately, the test items are mixed in the booklets, requiring students to locate the proper place in the answer booklet for their response. This will require that students turn pages to different sections of the answer booklet as they work. Students can best be prepared for this by offering them similar situations within the regular classroom assessment activites. This style of answer booklet may be eliminated in the future.

5. Responses need to be as exact as possible. Student should be encouraged to use their best expository style when writing the answers to the short and extended responses. They should be encouraged to plan an answer using a chart or web, write it carefully, then re-read to see if they have written exactly what they have intended to say. The correct understanding and use of vocabulary will be important. Know that the math test is also very much a test of how well a student can read the item and comprehend what is being asked. It is also a test of how well the student can express their thought process in diagrams and in writing using exact mathematical labels and terminology. In this sense, vocabulary is being tested, even though definitions are not an item on the test.

6. Use a #2 pencil. Fill in multiple choice bubble spaces completely.

7. Skip if you don't know the answer. If you do not understand a question, or have no idea what the response might be, skip that question and go on. Be certain that if students skip an answer that they are careful to also skip that space in the answer booklet. Students also need to be encouraged to go back to these items if they have time and make educated guesses about the possible answer. Students can be taught to go from what they know to what they don't know if this strategy is demonstrated as new concepts are presented in class. This concept can also be used in co-operative problem solving.

8. Go back and check your answers! If student finishes the test early, encourage rereading the written responses and rechecking the computation. Look to see if the response given really answers the question that was asked. Try to solve the problem another way and see if the answer is still the same. Check by using the inverse operation.

9. Write neatly in the test booklet, but don't be afraid to use it. Cross out answers that you know are wrong so that you won't have to reread them. Underline the key words that tell what the test item is really asking. Draw pictures, make lists and charts that will lead to a solution. Then write your response carefully.

10. Calculators may be used on this test. Students need to know that different kinds of calculators will compute operations in different orders. Be certain that students know how to operate the calculator they will be using as well as possible. Warn students that using the calculator on this test will not insure a higher score if they do not also read carefully and reason accurately as well. Test items will require that students know the difference between calculators with arithmetic logic and those with algebraic logic. This is best shown when students can have both kinds of calculators in front of them while the order of operations is being taught. On only 8 of the 23 items on the practice test could a calculator be used, and of those items one is looking for irrelevant facts in the problem and three others are looking for estimates. In only four items would the use of a calculator facillitate a solution, and NO item could be completely answered by using the calculator. Students need to be advised of this fact.

How the Test is Scored

Each multiple-choice item on the test is worth one point; each short-answer item is worth two points; and each extended-response item is worth for points. Altogether, the thirty-four multiple-choice items are worth 34 points; the ten short-answer items are worth 20 points; and the two extended-response items are worth 8 points. The total test score is 62 points.

Mathematics Test Distributions

Type	Number of Items	Total Points	Total Percent
Multiple Choice	34	34	55
Short Answer	10	20	32
Extended Response	2	8	13
TOTAL	46	62	100

Conventions of writing (sentence structure, word choice, usage, grammar, spelling, and mechanics) will not affect the scoring of short-answer or extended-response items, unless there is interference with the clear communication of ideas.

Short-answer items will be scored on a *2-point scale* based on these general guidelines:

A *2-point* response shows a complete understanding of the concept or task, logical reasoning and conclusions, and correct set up and/or computations.

A *1-point* response contains minor flaws in reasoning, neglects to address some aspect of the task, or contains a computational error.

A *0* is assigned if the response indicates no mathematical understanding of the concept or task.

Extended-response items will be scored on a *4-point* scale based on these general guidelines:

A *4-point* response contains an effective solution. It shows complete understanding of the concept or task and thoroughly addresses the points relevant to the solution. It contains logical reasoning and valid conclusions, communicates effectively and clearly through writing and/or diagrams, and includes adequate and correct computations and/or set up when required. It may go beyond the requirements of the item.

A *3-point* response contains minor flaws. Although it indicates an understanding of the concept or item, communicates adequately through writing and/or diagrams, and generally reaches reasonable conclusions, it contains minor flaws in reasoning and/or computation, or neglects to address some aspect of the item.

A *2-point* indicates gaps in understanding and/or execution. It contains some combination of the following flaws: an incomplete understanding of the concept or item, failure to address some points relevant to the solution, faulty reasoning, weak conclusions, unclear communication in writing and/or diagrams, or a poor understanding or relevant mathematical procedures or concepts.

A *1-point* response indicates some effort beyond restating the item or copying given data. It contains some combination of the following flaws; little understanding of the concept or item, failure to address most aspects of the item or solution, major flaws in reasoning that led to invalid conclusions, a definite lack of understanding of relevant mathematical procedures or concepts, or it omits significant parts of the item and solution or response.

A *0* is assigned if the response indicates no mathematical understanding of the concept or item.

About the Mathematics Learning Outcomes

This section will cover each learning outcome in all Mathematical strands. The chapter is filled with practice items, lesson ideas, and teaching hints for each learning outcome to be tested on the Ohio sixth grade mathematics proficiency test. During the Sixth-grade Proficiency Field Test, student performance was assessed on multiple choice items. Student performance was highest on multiple-choice items measuring outcomes 6, 11, 22, and 23. We have placed the symbol "✔" next to these learning outcomes. Students performance was lowest on multiple-choice items measuring outcomes 1, 9, 13, and 17. We have placed the symbol "✍" next to these learning outcomes. Only the ones that have been identified as high or low are marked.

> **Key:** ✍ = Students performance was LOW during field testing.
> ✔ = Students performance was HIGH during field testing.

In order to successfully lead a majority of students to master these learning outcomes the use of certain manipulatives and supplies are recommended. Although these may not be used in taking the test, they are excellent tools for the students to learn the concepts needed in order to be successful. Pattern tiles (including a transparent set for the overhead), graph paper, paper printed in blocks of 100 (used when visualizing decimal / fractional equivalents), meter sticks, rulers with inch and centimeter / millimeter markings, calculators that have algebraic logic and fraction capabilities, and a small journal book (for vocabulary and for writing explanations and thoughts in math) can all be very beneficial. Useful, but not as essential are reflecting mirras (tinted plastic forms for examining lines of symmetry and drawing reflections), counting disks (for probability), geoboards, tape measures, and various art supplies. In a learning environment that includes these kinds of supplies, a students will realize that mathematics is more than just numbers without ever being told this directly. These tools also employ most of the multiple intelligences, and thereby reach most students at a level where conceptual learning may take place.

Strand One: Patterns, Relations, and Functions

1. Apply the relationship between doubling the side of a regular figure and the corresponding increase in area.

Test items will involve 3, 4, and 6 sided, regular polygons. Students will need to *look up* understand the vocabulary used, that is, regular, polygon and congruent. (A regular polygon is a many-sided figure with all sides and all angles congruent or equal.) Pattern tiles are very useful during the instruction of this concept.

Exercises:

1. Each side of the square tile shown equals one unit. To make a square where each side is two times as large, how many tiles would be needed? Sketch your solution in the space provided.

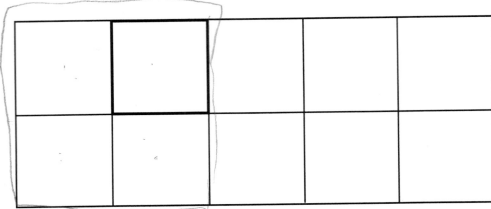

Analysis:

*This would be considered a short response item. The sketch should show a square with sides that are each two units in length, for a total perimeter of eight, and an area that is four times as large. **Four tiles would be needed.** Students must be careful to answer the question and not just do the sketching.*

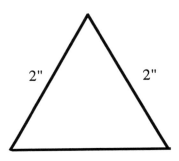

2"   2"

2. The equilateral triangle shown has sides that are 2" in length. Determine how many equilateral triangles with sides that are 1" in length will fit inside this figure. Sketch your solution on this figure.

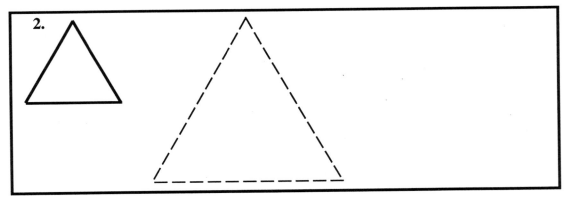

Analysis:

*The relationship is that the area becomes **four times** as large whenever the sides are doubled.*
See the diagram right.

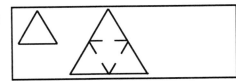

2. Determine the rule, identify missing numbers, and/or find the *n*th term in a sequence of numbers or a table of numbers involving one operation or power.

Students need to be able to recognize, describe and extend a variety of patterns, and to be able to use patterns to make generalizations and predictions. Test items require the student to continue a pattern by identifying or supplying the missing element(s) and/or describing the rule. Students will observe the number patterns in either a sequence of numbers or a table of number pairs.

A number pattern of a test item can include whole numbers, fractions, and decimal numbers, or numbers with exponents. The number pattern used in a sequence of numbers, or in a table, may be a combination of addition, subtraction, multiplication, or division. Patterns involving exponential numbers will involve only one operation.

Students should be familiar with the terms equation and variable, and be able to express most problems in the equation format.

Exercises:

3. Dante works in his father's store after school running errands. He makes $3.00 an hour. What two numbers are needed to complete Dante's chart?
    Use the equation: $e = 3 \times n$

# of hours	$ earned
1	$3
2	$6
3	$9
4	$12
5	
6	

A. $30, $36

B. $15, $18

C. $10, $12

D. $8, $9

Analysis:
*You solve this by using an equation like; $e = 3 \times n$, where e equals earnings and n equals the number of hours. The correct answer is answer choice "**B**," or $15, $18.*

s	0	3	6	9	12
r	6				

4. Solve this equation to correctly complete the table above: $r = 6 + s$

    A. 6, 9, 15, 18

    B. 9, 12, 15, 18

    C. 3, 9, 12, 15

    D. 12, 15, 18, 24

Analysis:
The sequence will be increasing by 6 since $r = 6$ when $s = 0$. As an equation the problem looks like this: $6 + s = r$. The first number in the table will be $6 + 3 = 9$. The correct sequence is found in answer choice "B."

Strand Two: Problem-Solving Strategies

3. Apply appropriate notations and methods for symbolizing the problem statement and solution process.

Students will need to be able to communicate mathematically and apply mathematics productively. They will be asked to represent problem solving situations using appropriate drawings, graphs, tables, number phrases or sentences, mathematical symbols and/or words. The problem situations are usually presented in worded format and may be accompanied by a chart or illustration. They will not involve the use of inequalities.

Exercises:

    5. A recipe for brown beans calls for 8 tablespoons of molasses. One tablespoon contains 55 calories. Which equation could you use to solve for how many calories molasses adds to the recipe?

        A. $55 \times n = 8$

        B. $n = 55 \times 8$

        C. $8 \times n = 55$

        D. $55 \div 8 = n$

Analysis:
*Because the recipe calls for 8 tablespoons of molasses each having 55 calories, **"B"** is the correct equation. An estimated answer would be the best way to show the error of the other three equations. Think: How much would 10 x 50 be? (500). That is close to what is needed in this problem. "A", "C," and "D" have answers that are less than 100, and could not possibly be correct in this case. This is an example of identifying the rule. **These examples do not require a solution.** The ask only that a student be able to select the expression that would correctly solve the problem.*

6. Four girls were competing for places on the track team. What equation shows how to find the time difference between the slowest and the fastest runner?

Runner	Jane	Ruth	Lan	Keisha
Time in seconds	50.8	50.1	51.2	51.9

Choose the equation which could be used to correctly solve this problem.

A. $51.9 + 50.1 = n$

B. $51.9 - 50.1 = n$

C. $(50.8 + 50.1 + 51.2 + 51.9) - 4 = n$

D. $50.8 + 50.1 + 51.2 + 51.9 = n$

Analysis:
This example uses a table or chart as well as words to state the problem. Answer choice "B" is the correct answer or $51.9 - 50.1 = n$. There is no need for the students to solve for "n."

7. There are six contestants in the Spelling Bee. Sandi finished second, and Carrie finished next to last. Tomika finished just before Carrie, and Jon finished right behind Sandi. Karthik did not finish last. In what place did Darlene finish? Use a drawing to solve this problem.

A. Second

B. Third

C. Fifth

D. Sixth

Analysis:
Using the information given in the problem, the student will determine the place held by each of the six remaining students. Logical reasoning must be used to solve this problem. Students can draw a picture to figure it out. The correct order that each placed in the Spelling Bee is: 1st-Karthik, 2nd-Sandi, 3rd-Jon, 4th-Tomika, 5th-Carrie, 6th-Darlene. The correct answer is that Darlene finished in sixth place, or answer "D."

4. Identify needed and given information in a problem situation as well as irrelevant information.

Students will examine problems and determine whether sufficient information has been given to solve the problem. They may be asked to state what information is still needed, or tell what given information is unnecessary.

Exercises:

8. 270 customers came into Claire's Shoppe on Thursday. They spent a total of $5,072.00 dollars. On Friday, the customers spent $275.00 dollars more. How many customers shopped at Claire's on Friday?

   Are you given enough information to solve the problem? What information is needed and what information is unnecessary? Explain.

8.

Analysis:
Students need to be prepared to ask themselves, "HOW can I get a REASONABLE ANSWER?" and then be able to tell if they have the information needed to get that answer. An average of what each customer spent each day could be a clue that would lead to a solution, but there is no way to answer the problem with only the information that has been given. Therefore, a correct response would point out that there is not enough information given to know how many customers shopped at Claire's on Friday. The information that is needed would be the number of people on Friday in relationship to or compared with the number of people that is given for Thursday. As long as students can show that they understand which information is needed and which is not, they will be able to answer a similar item correctly.

5. Validate or generalize solutions and problem solving strategies.

Problems that assess this learning outcome may have students demonstrate their understanding of different problem solving strategies that require critical thinking and the ability to generalize. Students can only internalize this depth of understanding (to the point of being able to generalize and relate similarities between problems) through repetitious use of all problem solving strategies.

Students may be asked to:
a) find and extend a pattern, applying the rule to a problem situation
b) draw conclusions about a large set of data by using a small sample of that data
c) solve a simpler problem (with smaller numbers) and then apply that solution to a more complicated problem
d) use logical thinking to choose appropriate operations
e) make a model, table, chart, list, or diagram of a problem
f) identify likenesses and differences
g) work backwards
h) guess and check
i) add missing information, when it is common knowledge

Problems that assess this learning outcome may use any of the problem solving strategies stated above. Students may prepare by solving one problem several different ways.

> **It is important for the students to know that the focus of these test items is not on finding the answer to a specific problem, but on re-examining the problem, the solution, or the answer.**

Exercises:

9. A cake is decorated with four rows of flowers. The first row has six flowers. The next row has seven flowers. The pattern is repeated one time. How many flowers will there be on the cake? Draw a picture of the cake.

> **9.**
>
>
>
>
>
>
>
>
> **How many flowers?** _____

Analysis:

This is an example of a problem that may be solved by making a drawing or by finding a pattern. The pattern will show that 6 + 7 must be mulitplied by 2 because the problem says the design is repeated. The equation that states this would be: $2(6 + 7) = n$.
A drawing may look like this:

*The correct answer is **26 flowers**.*

10. The sixth grade at Smith Middle School has an enrollment of 316 students. There are 30 more girls than boys. How many girls are there in this sixth grade? Show your solution and give your answer.

> **10.**
>
>
>
>
>
>
>
> **How many girls?** _____

Analysis:
*This problem can be solved using the "guess and check" method, or by working backwards. Students should first subtract the 30 form 316 to find the number that will represent an equal number of boys and girls. (286) They will then divide this number in half. (286 ÷ 2 = 143) There are 143 boys and 143 + 30 girls or **173 girls**.*

11. About 60 students were called to the office. There were 5 hallways that they could use to get there from various classrooms. About how many students used each hallway?

   A. 30

   B. 24

   C. 12

   D. 60

Analysis:
This item is an example of a problem that focuses on choosing the correct operation. Students are being asked to find an average or estimate. They would divide 60 by 5 to get an average of 12 for an estimate. 60 divided by 5=12, about 12 students used each hallway. The correct answer choice is "C."

12. Keisha, Tara, Josh, and Shawn were the finalists in a poetry contest. Shawn won 3rd place. Tara did not win 2nd. If Josh won 1st place, what place did Keisha win? Explain how you got your answer.

12.

Analysis:
This problem is one that requires the use of logical reasoning to find a solution. Students could best solve this item by using a chart to organize the information given. The correct response would need to indicate that **Keisha came in 2nd place**.

Strand Three: Numbers and Number Relations

✔ **6. Compute with whole numbers, fractions and decimals.**

Test items will focus on understanding and applying operations in problem situations. Students will need to determine what computations are needed to solve problems given in worded format and compute the answers. The following parameters are used for computations involving whole numbers, fractions and decimals.

a) Addition and subtraction of whole numbers including four-digit numbers.
b) Multiplication of whole numbers including four-digit factors.
c) Division of whole numbers including two digit divisors.
d) Addition and subtraction of fractions including fractions with the same and those with different denominators.
e) Fraction items include mixed numbers.
f) Decimals up to thousandths place will be used.

It is also expected that the concepts of improper fractions, mixed numbers, least common denominator, and comparison and simplification of fractions be prerequisites for computation with fractions. Since the use of calculators is permitted with this test, the real focus again is on determining which operation to use to solve the problem. It is also important for the students to know how to use their calculators with maximun efficiency. Any math book currently used in the classroom will provide practice in these basic computations and skills.

Exercises:

13. Mrs. Clark buys dresses worth $6,850 and coats worth $10,460 for her shop. She makes a down payment of $7,500 with the order. How much will she still owe at the time of delivery?

   A. $6,850 + $10,460 = $17,310

   B. $10,460 – $7,500 = $2,960

   C. $7,500 + $6,850 = $14,350

   D. ($10,460 + $6,850) – $7500 = $9,810

Analysis:
*This is an example of a word problem involving addition and subtraction of four-digit whole numbers. To solve the student would add the amounts spent on the products and then subtract the down payment from that total. The correct answer is "**D.**"*

14. The district manager traveled 1457 miles and used 47 gallons of gas. How many miles did he average on a gallon of gas?

   A. 322.58 mpg

   B. 31 mpg

   C. 32.9 mpg

   D. 32.258 mpg

Analysis:
*This item uses division of whole numbers in an everyday situation. Students need to solve by dividing 1457 mi. by the 47 gal. to get an average of 31 miles per gallon. The correct answer is "**B.**"*

15. A go cart dealer sold 158 carts for $8,500 each. What are his total sales going to be?

   A. $53,790

   B. $13,430

   C. $1,343,000

   D. $134,300

Analysis:
*Students must know how to work with whole numbers and multiplication. Multiply to find this answer. $8500 x 158 = $1,343,000. The correct answer is "**C.**"*

16. When Josh got home from school 1/3 of the cake was left. If he ate 1/4 of what was left as his snack, how much of the cake did he eat?

   A. 1/12

   B. 1/6

   C. 1/8

   D. 1/4

Analysis:
Multiplication of fractions would solve this item. 1/3 x 1/4 = 1/12. The students could also draw a picture of the cake as described in the question and try to visually solve the problem, like the picture of Josh's piece of cake here. The correct answer is "A."

Josh's Piece of Cake

Another way to give a visual of this concept is to use folded paper. Have students fold a paper into thirds one way. Have them shade one third of the three thirds. Then they are to open the paper and fold it into fourths in the other direction. When they shade one fourth of this the result will be to have one twelfth shaded two ways or in two colors.

$$\frac{1}{3}$$  $$\frac{1}{4}$$  $$\frac{1}{12}$$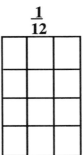

17. Lonnie was told to use a 40 pound bag of jelly beans to fill two and a half pound bags for a special sale. How many bags will he be able to fill?

    A. 100

    B. 16

    C. 24

    D. 8

Analysis:
This problem is an example of the use of a mixed number which will need to be changed to an improper fraction and then inverted because of the division rule. It is a complex item that will require that students be familiar with several basic skills and be able to use them in a logical order to solve. 40 divided by 2 1/2 = 40 divided by 5/2 or 40 x 2/5 = 16. The correct answer is "B."

18. Susan bought these items at the school bookstore: a pen for $0.19, a notebook for $0.35 and 5 bookcovers for $0.28 each. How much did she spend?

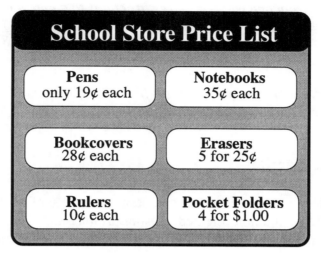

School Store Price List

Pens only 19¢ each	**Notebooks** 35¢ each
Bookcovers 28¢ each	**Erasers** 5 for 25¢
Rulers 10¢ each	**Pocket Folders** 4 for $1.00

A. $0.82

B. $ 1.94

C. $1.66

D. $2.17

Analysis:
*This problem involves multiplication and addition of decimal numbers. Since Susan bought 5 bookcovers, the student will multiply 5 x $0.28 and get $1.40, for the total price of the bookcovers. This will then be added to the other single items purchased by adding, $0.19 + $0.35 + $1.40 = $1.94. The correct answer choice is "**B**."*

19. Basketball is the favorite sport of 1/2 of the class. One fourth of the class likes football best. Only 1/8 chose soccer as a favorite sport. What part of the class did not have a favorite sport?

A. 1/4

B. 1/2

C. 1/16

D. 1/8

Analysis:
In order to solve this problem, students must add and subtract fractions with
unlike denominators. They must first find a common denominator, then add the fractions,
then subtract that total from one whole. Convert fractions to a common denominator, as
follows: $\frac{1}{2} = \frac{4}{8}$, $\frac{1}{4} = \frac{2}{8}$ *Then add all three fractions together.* $\frac{4}{8} + \frac{2}{8} + \frac{1}{8} = \frac{7}{8}$
One whole is represented by $1 = \frac{8}{8}$, *then the part that did not pick a sport must be found*
by subtracting the part that picked a sport (7/8) from the whole class (8/8) as follows:
$\frac{8}{8} - \frac{7}{8} = \frac{1}{8}$ *The correct answer is "D," 1/8 of the class did not state a favorite sport.*

7. Find equivalent fraction.

Items that address this outcome will reflect and permit a variety of models and strategies, and will not be solely computation oriented. Test items may include fraction models, and other pictorial representations of fractions to assess the student's understanding of equivalent fractions.

Exercises:

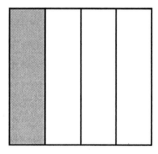 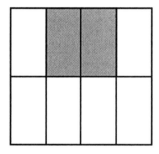

20.   Label each of the drawings above by their equivalent fraction.

20.

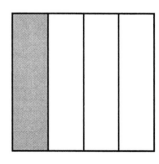 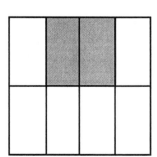

_____   _____

21. Three out of every four chickens on Pleasant Valley Farm lay extra large eggs. There are 120 chickens on the farm. How many lay large eggs?

$$\frac{3}{4} = \frac{?}{120}$$

A. 20

B. 30

C. 90

D. 100

Analysis:

This problem can be solved by completing the equivalent fraction that is also a ratio. Since 4 is contained in 120 a total of 30 times, then by multiplying 3 x 30 you get the equivalent numerator. The correct answer would be 3 x 30 = 90 chickens lay large eggs, "C."

Teaching Tips for Learning Outcome #7

The use of pattern tiles can be extremely effective in teaching this concept. Because the hexagon is exactly covered by 2 red trapezoids, 3 blue rhombuses or by 6 green triangles, students are able to see quickly how these different parts can be equivalent. If your school does not have pattern tiles, a set of black line masters called *Show What You Know – Grade 6 Math Masters* are sold separately. The masters can be copied onto different colored construction paper and laminated so they hold up.

The following is a game that teaches students to quickly calculate and exchange equivalent fractional values using the pattern tiles.

TRADING TILES

Number of players: 3 - 5

Materials needed: Pattern tiles (blocks), One die or a spinner with six numbers

Rules:
• Put a bank of pattern tiles in the center of the playing area.
• Roll a die to determine which player takes the first turn.
• Then, in turn, each players rolls a die and takes the number of triangles indicated from the bank.
• After taking the triangles from the bank, the player must trade for any larger tiles that are equivalent to the number of tiles he has.
• Each player should have the fewest number of tiles possible at all times.
   Example: If a player rolls a five on the die, they receive five green triangles from the bank. They must quickly trade for one red trapezoid and one blue rhombus. If the same player has a red trapezoid from a previous turn, they must trade the two trapezoids in for a yellow hexagon at this time. (Continued on next page)

Teaching Tips for Learning Outcome #7 (Continued)
• It is the responsibility of all of the players to make sure that correct trades are made each time. In the event that a player trades incorrectly, that player will forfeit one green triangle to the bank. This will occur when the next player has taken their turn. Sample trades: 4 triangles = 1 red trapezoid and 1 triangle. If a player already has a blue rhombus, the four triangles may be traded with that blue rhombus for a yellow hexagon.
• The winner is the first player to accumulate five regular hexagon tiles.

8. Change freely between fractions and decimals.

Fractions and/or decimals are presented in real-life situations or contexts. The problem situations require students to change freely between fractional and decimal notation. Illustrations of fractional models and other pictorial representations may be provided for some items. Students may find it helpful to associate these ideas with their established knowledge of money values that are expressed in hundredths of dollars all the time.

Exercises:

22. Show the space represented by the fraction 1/4, by shading the unit squares. Then express that fraction as a decimal and as a percent.

22.

Decimal ___ • ___ ___

Percent ___ ___ %

Analysis
The shading should show one fourth of the square shaded in like the square at right. The fraction 1/4 converted to a decimal is 0.25 and as a percentage it is 25%. Students need to be able to easily take fractions back and forth between percentages, decimals, and fractions.

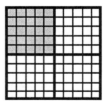

✍ **9. Order combinations of whole numbers, fractions, and decimals by using the symbols <, ≤, >, ≥, and = and/or by placing them on a number line.**

Developing an awareness of the relative sizes of fractions and decimals and ordering fractions and decimals are essential to the understanding and application of concepts and operations involving fractions and decimals. Test items may require the use of a number line or symbols for comparing and ordering combinations of whole numbers, fractions and decimals. Illustrations may accompany test items, when appropriate. Students will do well to know if a fractional part is nearer to 0, 1/2, or 1 whole. This distinction will really help them in ordering fractions.

Exercises:

23. Which decimal would be correctly rounded to 2.648 in thousandths place?

   A. 2.64735

   B. 2.64718

   C. 2.64753

   D. 2.64488

Analysis:
The correct answer is "C," or 2.64753. The number seven is in the thousandths place. Since the number to the right of the seven is a five or larger, the seven is rounded up to 8.

$$\frac{5}{8} \qquad \frac{2}{3} \qquad \frac{1}{2}$$

24. Write the fractions listed above in order from the one of least value to the one of greatest value. Use the space provided to show your work. Find common denominators or draw pictures.

24.

   Order from least to greatest: _____ _____ _____

Analysis:
In order to compare values, the fractions must be compared with a common denominator or converted to like forms. (ie. percentages or decimals) The correct order from least to greatest is 1/2 , 5/8 , 2/3. The fractions can be compared by converting to a common denominator of 24 as follows: 1/2 = 12/24, 5/8 = 15/24, and 2/3 = 16/24. Converted to decimals, the fractions can be compared as follows: 1/2 = 0.50, 5/8 = 0.625, and 2/3 = 0.666. And as percentages, 1/2 = 50%, 5/8 = 62.5%, and 2/3 = 66.6%.

TeachingTips for Learning Outcome #9
Students may need to be told that larger fractions do not automatically mean greater value, but rather more parts in the whole. They may also need practice in recognizing that fractional numbers can be sorted into those close to 0, 1/2 , or 1 whole. Knowing these concepts are important in this testing situation.

---

10. Use ratios and proportions in a wide variety of applications.

Test items may have students apply ratios and proportions to real-life situations and sets of numbers such as sports statistics and scale drawings. Given a problem situation or setting, students may be asked to determine whether two ratios form a proportion and explain why or why not. Test items will include pictorial percentage models and illustrations when appropriate. Ratios will be expressed in one of three ways.
(2 to 4, 2:4, or 2/4)

Exercises:

    25. Complete the proportion by solving for n. There are 6 golf balls in one package. How many golf balls will be in 9 packages?

$$\frac{1}{6} = \frac{9}{n} \qquad n = \underline{\hspace{2cm}}$$

        A. 24

        B. 32

        C. 54

        D. 36

Analysis:
The answer is n = 54 or answer choice "C." To solve this, students can cross multiply and get 54 = 54.

26. One croquet set has 4 mallets and 2 balls. How many mallets and balls will a dozen similar sets contain?

   A. 36 mallets and 18 balls

   B. 48 mallets and 18 balls

   C. 12 mallets and 2 balls

   D. 48 mallets and 24 balls

Analysis:
Two answers are required for this. The number of mallets can be set up as a proportion of 1 set to 4 mallets or, 1/4 and twelve sets to 48 mallets, or 12/48. The number of balls can be figured in the same way: 1/2 = 12/24. The correct answer is "D," there would be a total of 48 mallets and 24 balls in 12 similar sets.

27. LaTia is making frames for her artwork. Side AB of the larger frame is 50cm. Side BD is 35cm. If the smaller frame is of similar proportions, and side RS is 30cm, what will be the length of side SU?

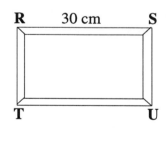 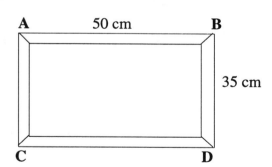

   A. 40 cm

   B. 15 cm

   C. 21 cm

   D. 55 cm

Analysis:
The ratio or proportion of the larger frame ACDB is 50/35. The ratio or proportion of the smaller frame would have to be 30/21. This proportion can be obtained through cross multiplication. Solving the proportion problem below gives you the correct answer, where x = 21. $\frac{50}{35} = \frac{30}{x}$ *The correct answer choice is "C."*

Strand Four: Geometry

✔ **11. Visualize and show the results of rotation, translation, reflection, or stretching of geometric figures.**

Rotation, translation, reflection, and stretching are four ways geometric figures can be changed or transformed. The following list describes each kind of transformation.

a. rotation: the image of a figure moved through an angle about a point in a plane.
b. reflection: the mirror image of a figure about a line of symmetry or a point on a plane.
c. translation: a slide image of the original figure.
d. stretching: (also called expansion or contraction) the image of a figure having a size change of a particular magnitude.

Test items may have students identify a transformation or draw a particular transformation of a given figure on a grid or graph. Students will not be asked to define the terms, but a working knowledge of the vocabulary is necessary to complete what will be asked. Students may be asked to use ordered pairs to identify or label the vertices of the figure drawn.

After the concept is presented and practiced, try the exercises on the next page.

Exercises:

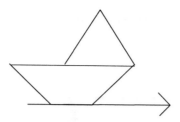

28. Translate the figure above in the direction of these arrow as indicated.

28.

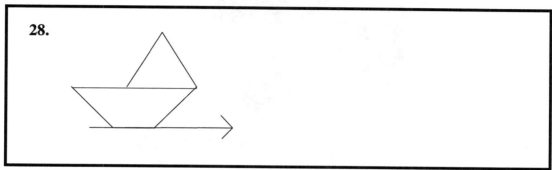

Analysis:
The drawing should be similar to the drawing at right.

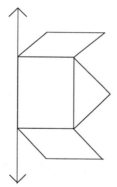

29. Draw a reflection of the design on the opposite side of the arrow.

29.

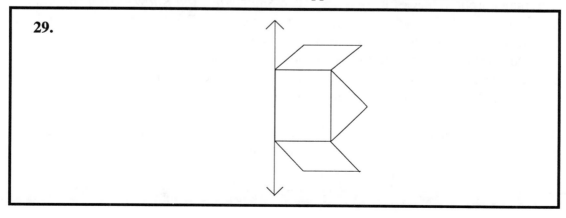

Analysis:
A reflection is the mirror image of a shape. The reflections should be like the design shown at right.

30. Name the transformation used to create the quilt pattern above.

    A. Traction

    B. Reflection

    C. Rotation

    D. Translation

Analysis:
The correct answer is rotation, the student should be able to see the rotating pattern in the sample quilt. Answer choice "C" is correct.

Teaching Tips for Learning Outcome #11
You may purchase black line masters called *Show What You Know - Grade 6 Math Masters* that include a set of designs made from pattern tiles. There is, for example, a transformation that is a reflection as it appears. It may be reproduced to a transparency, cut into fourths, and used on the overhead to show students how a translation, reflection, and rotation are achieved. The students can then create an asymetrical pattern of their own, and try each transformation on paper.

The demonstration at the overhead is an extremely effective and efficient way to present this concept. The individual practice follow-up reinforces a concept that students may find difficult to perceive at first.

More Teaching Tips for Learning Outcome #11

The last part of this learning objective, that involves the understanding of stretching, was also covered by example question number 28 on page 24 of this book. The example problem, that is about the similar picture frames, asks students to name or recognize the congruent sides of similar geometric figures. The larger picture frame is a good example of a stretched figure.

12. Recognize, classify, and/or use characteristics of lines and simple two-dimensional figures including circles: and apply models and properties to characterize and/or contrast different classes of figures including three-dimensional figures.

Students should be able to identify, describe, compare, and classify lines that are parallel, intersecting, or perpendicular. Test items may have students recognize, classify, compare, and apply the characteristics or properties of simple plane and solid figures, including prisms, pyramids, cones, cylinders, and spheres.

Students will not be required to define terms, however, recognition and use of terminology, models, characteristics, and properties is expected. These may include terms associated with, and visual representation of lines, (e.g. parallel, perpendicular, intersecting); two-dimensional figures (e.g. diagonals, sides, quadrilaterals such as squares, rectangles, rhombuses, parallellograms); three-dimentional figures and their parts (e.g. base, face, edge, vertex, rectangular and triangular prism, cone, cylinder and pyramid).

Please try the exercises on the next page.

Exercises:

Glass	*Cereal Box*	*Beach Ball*	*Toy Box*
Sugar Cone	*Can of Soup*	*Megaphone*	*Basketball*

31. Name the items above that represent a three dimensional figure of a cylinder.

    A. Glass, Can of Soup

    B. Megaphone, Sugar Cone

    C. Basketball, Beach Ball

    D. Cereal Box, Toy Box

Analysis:
The correct answer is "A," the glass and can of soup are cylindrical objects. Students should be familar with cone, sphere, prism, pyramid, and cylinder shapes.

Teaching Tips for Learning Outcome #12
For students to be successful in answering these test items they must have a working knowledge of the vocabulary mentioned above. One of the best ways to reach all students with this knowledge is through the hands-on activity of building models of these polyhedra. The *Show What You Know - Grade 6 Math Masters* provides black line masters of patterns (webs) for making models of several polyhedra. After the student makes the models, the identifying labels can be cut out, shuffled and students can then match the labels to the correct polyhedra. This makes a great hands-on learning activity.

Strand Five: Algebra

✍ **13. Use the distributive property in arithmetic computations.**

Test items may assess the students' ability to use the distributive property in arithmetic computations, or may involve a problem situation in which students apply the distributive property to the solution of the problem.

At this grade level, the distributive property will apply to whole numbers, decimals, fractions, and mixed numbers, but not to postive and negative integers. Also, at this level, this property is usually applied to the operation of multiplication.

$$6 \text{ x } 21 = (6 \text{ x } 20) + (6 \text{ x } 1) = 120 + 6 = 126$$

Exercise:

32. Solve the equation below with the correct use of the distributive property of multiplication.

$$8 \text{ x } (10 + 5) = \text{ ?}$$

- A. 75
- B. 65
- C. 85
- D. 120

Analysis:
The answer is found by solving inside the parentheses first and then multiplying. The correct answer is "**D**," or 120. To solve: 8 x (10 + 5) = 8 x 15 = 120

33. Which equation is NOT a correct use of the distributive property?

- A. 8 x 10 = 4 + (4 x 10) + 1 = 80
- B. 8 x 12 = (8 x 10) + (8 x 2) = 96
- C. 8 x 7 = (8 x 5) + (8 x 2) = 56
- D. 8 x 9 = 8 x (6 + 3) = 72

Analysis:
The correct answer is "A," because the rule applies that you solve the inside of parentheses first. This problem gives you the answer 45 not 80.

Teaching Tips for Learning Outcome #13
Students can remember the order of operations in solving equations by remembering the phrase: "Please Excuse My Dear Aunt Sally." The letters in bold stand for the different mathematical operations in the exact order of how you should use them.

Please = **P**arentheses
Excuse = **E**xponents
My = **M**ultiplication and
Dear = **D**ivision
Aunt = **A**ddition and
Sally = **S**ubtration

14. Explain and reflect the differences between calculators with arithmetic logic and calculators with algebraic logic when symbolizing a keying sequence and in the display as each key is pressed.

Assessing the students' understanding of the difference between calculators with arithmetic logic and calculators with algebraic logic is the focus of items developed for this objective. Each item will include an illustration of a keying sequence and what is displayed on the calculator as a result of that sequence.

Calculators that are programmed with only arithmetic logic will compute each operation as it is entered into the calculator by the sequence of the keys that are pressed. Calculators programmed with algebraic logic will hold the operations in memory and compute these operations using the rules of order of operations. (P.E.M.D.A.S. or paranthesis, exponents, multiplication, division, addition, and subtraction.) It is essential that students are familiar with this concept in order to understand what is being asked on these items.

It is also important that the students be aware of the kind of functions that are possible using the calculators they are given for the test and in class. Students should be very familiar with how the calculator they are using on the test works the operations.

The exercises for this learning outcome begin on the next page.

Exercises:

34. When this series of keys is pressed on each calculator, the answer on the display of Calculator A would be different from the display of Calculator B. Which calculator is programmed to use the order of operations? Explain your answer.

Calculator A [10] [+] [8] [x] [4] [=] (72.)

Calculator B [10] [+] [8] [x] [4] [=] (42.)

34.

Which calculator? _____

Explain your answer. _____

_____

_____

_____

_____

_____

_____

_____

_____

_____

_____

_____

Analysis:
*The answer would be "**Calculator B.**" The student should explain that the algebraic logic of calculator B solves by the order of operation. Since multiplication is calculated before the addition in the algebraic logic and calculator B solved the problem by taking the 8 x 4 first, and then added ten to get an answer or 42. Answers may vary.*

15. Use variables to describe arithmetic processes, to generalize arithmetic statements, and to generalize a problem situation.

This objective emphasizes recognizing and/or using variables in problem solving situations and mathematical phrases and equations as statements. Students may be given a mathematical sentence and asked to write an equation that would express that statement.

Exercises:

35. You can buy two calculators for $24.00. What is the cost of each? First write an equation. Then solve and show your work.

35.

_____

Analysis:
Students should write an equation first. The equation should read 2n = $24.00 *or*
n x 2 = $24.00. *The student's work should show how they got their answer. They need to demonstrate that they understand the arithmetic process of setting up the equation and finding the solution. The correct answer is* n = $12.00.

36. You had $40.00 in your wallet when you began to shop. You know that you spent $36.00, because you still have $4.00 left. You also know that the shirt you bought was $7.00. What did you spend on the running shoes? Which equation solves the problem?

    A. $40.00 – $36.00 = n

    B. $36.00 – $4.00 – $7.00 = n

    C. $7.00 + n = $36.00

    D. $4.00 + n = $40.00

Analysis:
There is unnecessary information given in this problem. If students can eliminate the unnecessary information they can work with only the important information to set up the equation. It isn't necessary to know what you started with ($40.00) and it isn't necessary to know that you have $4.00 left. The most important information that you know is that you spent $36.00 and that the shirt cost $7.00. Answer choice "C" is correct.

37. The owner of a sporting goods store knows that he will have to sell a sleeping bag for $73.00 in order to make $11.00 on the sale. What did the sleeping bag cost the store? Write the equation and solve.

37.

_____

_____

Solve and show your work here.

Analysis:
The correct equation is: $n + \$11 = \$73$. The solution is $n = \$62$

Strand Six: Measurement

16. Determine perimeters, areas, and volumes of common polygons, circles, and solids using counting techniques or formulas.

Items may require students to find the perimeter, area, and volume of 2 and 3 dimensional figures. Students should have a working knowledge of how to compute these answers for many geometric figures, including triangles, squares, rectangles, parallelograms, rhombuses. trapezoids, circles, cubes, prisms, and pyramids. Some items may require students to know how to calculate the surface area of all the faces of cubes, prisms, and pyramids.

Formulas will be provided for volumes and areas of solids, circles, and polygons that are not squares or rectangles. Students will need to be able to find the perimeter or area of a square or rectangle without a formula being provided in the item.

Exercises:

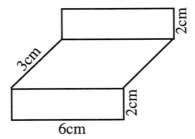

38. How much cardboard is needed to make the shape above for an art project?

    A. 6 x (2 + 3 + 2) = 42 cm. sq.

    B. 2 + 3 (2 x 6) = 17 cm. sq.

    C. (6 + 2 + 3 + 2) = 13 cm. sq.

    D. (3 X 6) + (2 + 2) = 22 cm. sq.

Analysis:
Students should set up an equation like this: 6 x (2 + 3 + 2) = n, and then solve for n. Where n = 42cm.sq. The cardboard needs to be 6cm wide by 7cm long or 42 square centimeters. The correct answer is "A."

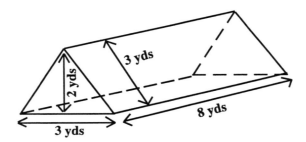

39. The four top sides of a tent need to be waterproofed. The bottom does not need to be waterproofed. What is the surface area that will have to be treated? Explain how you got your answer and show your work.

39.

_____

_____

_____

_____

_____

_____

_____

Show your work here.

Analysis:

Students should know how to find the areas of the side panels easily, that is by multiplying the length x width. The area of a triangle is computed by taking 1/2 of the altitude x base. They need to remember to double the answers that they get for the two sides. Their work should look like this:

$$\left(\frac{1}{2} \ (2 \times 3) \times 2 = 6 \ sq. \ yd. \right) + \left((3 \times 8) \times 2 = 48 \right) = 54 \ sq. \ yds.$$

Teaching Tip for Learning Outcome #16

Students benefit by using pattern tiles to become really familiar with the names, shapes and properties of various polygons. The polyhedra webs mentioned in the Teaching Tips for Learning Outcome #12 are valuable tools for this learning outcome as well. Once students have constructed the 3-D rectangular prism, the triangular pyramid, and the cube, the student can measure those figures to determine their surface area and volume. It is also helpful for students to see the web as a flat surface first. This gives them a concept of how the surface area differs from the volume of a 3-D figure. The black line master for making your own pattern tiles and polyhedra webs can be purchased separately in *Show What You Know - Grade 6 Math Masters.*

✍ **17. Convert, compare, and compute with common units of measure within the same measurement system.**

Students will need an understanding of the relative size of common units of measure for length, capacity, weight, and time. Items may require conversion and/or computations involving units of measure within the same measurement system. Conversion factors may be given for some items; for example, an item requiring conversions between feet and miles.

Units may be those used within the U.S. standard system (inch, foot, yard, mile, fluid ounce, cup, pint, quart, gallon, ounce, pound, ton, second, minute, hour, day, week, year) and those of the metric system (millimeter, centimeter, decimeter, meter, kilometer, milliliter, liter, kiloliter, milligram,gram,and kilogram).

Exercises:

40. Which metric measure closely matches the size of this gallon jug?

    A. 4L

    B. 4mL

    C. 4kL

    D. 4 milliliters

Analysis:
The correct answer choice is "A," or 4mL. Students need to know what metric measure is appropriate for different items.

41. If 1,000 mL = 1 L, then complete the table by writing the correct exchanges for the measures in the table.

mL	L
385 mL	
1,000 mL	1 L
	12L
5,000 mL	
	43L

41.   **Show your work here.**

mL	L
385 mL	
1,000 mL	1 L
	12L
5,000 mL	
	43L

Analysis:
This test item deals with exchanges within the same units of measure and the exchange is given. Students can find the answers by mulitplying or dividing by 1,000 to convert the exchanges. The correct answers are: **385 mL = 0.385 L, 12,000 mL = 12 L, 5000 mL = 5 L, and 43,000 mL = 43 L.**

18. Measure angles with a protractor.

Students need to be able to use a protractor to measure angles. Students may be asked to draw a figure and then measure its angles. Measurements must be made to the nearest whole degree.

Recognition and the use of standard labeling methods and terminology related to angles is expected. Terms may include right angle, acute angle, and obtuse angle. Students may use protractors on the Sixth Grade Proficiency Test in Mathematics. Goniometers may not be used.

Exercises:

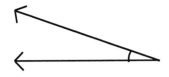

42. Measure and choose the correct label for this angle by the number of degrees and name of the angle.

    A. 30° acute

    B. 35° obtuse

    C. 25° acute

    D. 20° obtuse

Analysis:
The angle measure 30 degrees and is an acute angle. "A" is the correct answer.

43. Use a protractor to draw a 115 degree angle.

43.

Analysis:
A 115 degree angle looks like this:

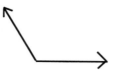

44. What kind of angle is a 115 degree angle?

    A. acute

    B. oblong

    C. reflex

    D. obtuse

Analysis:
A 115 degree angle is an obtuse angle. The correct answer is "D."

Strand Seven: Estimation and Mental Computation

19. Apply appropriate strategies to find estimates of sums, differences, products, and quotients of whole numbers and determine whether the estimate is greater than or less than the exact result.

Items for this objective may be completed using any of a number of effective estimation strategies. The most commonly used strategies are:

a. front-end estimation - Use the front-end numbers to obtain an initial estimate and all other numbers to adjust or refine that first estimate.

b. rounding - Used to obtain mentally manageable numbers for computation. Flexibility is needed in order to adjust the degree of rounding necessary for a particular situation operation or the numbers involved.

c. compatible numbers - Looks at all numbers involved to see if any can be paired or combined to make computation easier. (6.1,4), (7,2.5) are numbers about equal to 10. (63,44) close to 100, etc. This strategy involves flexible rounding of numbers that can be fit together for ease in mental computation.

d. clustering - This can be used when all the numbers in the set "cluster" around the same value, then a reasonable group average could be computed by multiplying that number by the total number of items in the set.

e. special number - This would be like finding powers of ten, or common decimals or fractions that are easy to compute and using them to mentally compute an approximate answer.

Students may be asked to describe their estimate in relation to the exact result, telling how much more or less the exact answer would be.

Exercises:

45. The best estimate for 42 x 59 would be:

    A. 90

    B. 2400

    C. 2000

    D. 20,000

Analysis:
To find the best estimate the student should try rounding to tens, the best answer would be 40 x 60 = 2400. Answer choice "B" is correct.

46. Three students were weighed before wrestling practice. Tom weighed 93 pounds. Shawn weighed 87 pounds. Drew weighed 113. Use front end estimation to find the approximate combined weight.

    A. 90 + 80 + 100 = 270

    B. 90 + 90 + 100 = 280

    C. 90 + 90 + 110 = 290

    D. 100 + 100 +100 = 300

Analysis:
The best answer is "A." Front end estimation requires students to round the numbers to the first number at the front. (ie. 93 = 90, 87 = 80, and 113 = 100)

20. Estimate the sum, difference, product, or quotient of decimal numbers by rounding, and the sum, difference or product of fractions and/or mixed numbers by rounding the fractions to 0, 1/2, or 1.

Items testing this objective require students to round decimal numbers, to estimate sums, differences, products, or quotients. Other test items may require the student to round fractions to 0, 1/2, or 1 to estimate the sum, difference, or product of fractions and/or mixed numbers.

Items focus on extending estimation strategies to situations involving decimals and fractions. Students will be expected to apply strategies using rounding and/or special numbers to make estimates.

Students will be expected to give an estimate when asked and not give the actual computed answer. Giving the exact answer and not the estimate as directed will be considered incorrect.

Exercises:

47. Gina bought souvenirs while she was on vacation. She got 3 T-shirts for $14.95 each, 2 framed prints for $9.95 each and 10 postcards for $0.50 each. Estimate how much she spent to the nearest dollar.

   A. $10 + $15 + $0.50 = $25.50

   B. $10 + $45 + $10 = $65.00

   C. $20 + $45 + $5 = $70.00

   D. $20 + $15 + $5 = $40.00

Analysis:
Calculate the correct amount paid per item and then round the amount paid for each of the three items to the nearest dollar. The correct answer choice shows the next step which is to add the three estimates together. "C" is the correct answer.

48. Choose the best estimate for: $1\frac{3}{4} + 5\frac{7}{8}$

   A. $1 + 5$

   B. $2 + 6$

   C. $0 + 6$

   D. $2 + 5$

Analysis:
Both mixed numbers are rounded up to the next whole number because the fraction is equal to or greater than 1/2. The correct answer is "B."

Strand Eight: Data Analysis and Probability

21. Collect data, create a table, picture graph, bar graph, circle graph, or line graph, and use them to solve application problems.

Items testing this objective emphasize the construction and/or use of a chart, table or graph to record and sort information. Students need to know how to construct a table or graph, determine an appropriate scale for an axis of a specific graph and know all the parts needed to make a graph or table complete so that they can determine the completeness or the accuracy of the data presented. Some items require students to use tables and graphs in the solution of a problem. Items may also require students to judge the accuracy of the representation of the data. (Does the chart give a false impression?)

Exercise:

49. Construct a bar graph to show the favorite colors of the 27 students in Room 302 using the tally chart of your survey. Remember to include all the parts of a correct graph.

Color	# of Votes
red	☰☰☰ ||||
blue	☰☰☰ ☰☰☰ ||
green	||||
yellow	||

49.

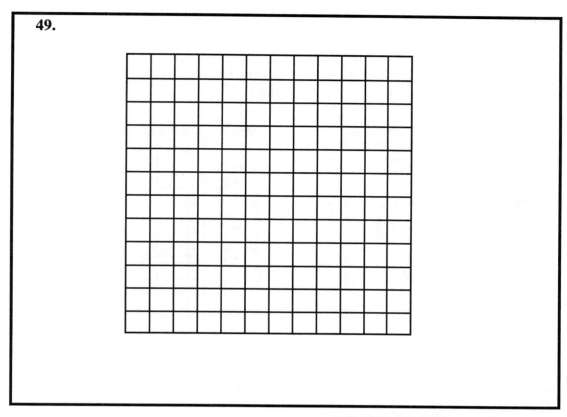

STUDENT FAVORITE COLORS

Analysis:

The graph should include a title, a scale with the label 'number of students' on the vertical axis, and the names of the colors on the horzontal axis. Bars should correspond to the information given and should look like the one pictured at right.

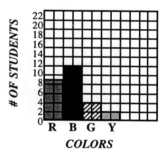

✔ **22. Read, interpret, and use tables, charts, maps, and graphs to identify patterns, note trends, and draw conclusions.**

This objective tests a student's ability to read and interpret tables, charts, maps, and graphs. Students should also be able to note patterns, predict trends, and draw conclusions from the graphs. Test items may include tables, charts, picture graphs, bar graphs, circle graphs, and line graphs.

Exercise:

50. Examine graphs A and B. Both graphs are showing the same data but look very different. Explain the differences and the similarities between the two graphs and what they are illustrating.

Student Attendance Over 4 Months

Student Attendance Over 4 Months

Graph A

Graph B

50.

Analysis:
The student attendance in Graph A appear to be missing more school because of the way the numbers on the vertical axis were chosen. Actually, the information on both graphs is the same. The only difference is the intervals between numbers on the vertical axis. This makes the graph lines look very different from the other.

✔ **23. Apply the concept of average and calculate the arithmetic mean and mode of a given set of numbers.**

Test items will have students find the arithmetic mean or mode in a problem situation. In the test items the word average refers to the arithmetic mean, which is the sum of a group of numbers that is divided by the number of addends. (Some people use the word average as a generic term to refer to all measures of central tendency, like mode, mean, and median, much the same ways as people tend to say Kleenex rather than tissue and Scotch tape rather than cellophane tape.

The modes are the number(s) that occur most often in a set of data. It is possible to have more than one mode. (An example would be: 5 and 7 are the modes in this set;   1, 2, 2, 4, 5, 5, 5, 6, 7, 7, 7, 8, 8, 10.)

The median is the middle number whenever a set of data is arranged in sequential order, or the point between the two middle numbers if there are an even amount of items in a set. In the sample set above there are 14 items. The median would fall between 5 and 6 and it would be 5.5 or 5 1/2.

Exercise:

51. Mr. Day's math students received the following scores on a recent quiz.

100, 100, 95, 90, 90, 85, 85, 80, 80, 80, 80, 75, 70, 70, 70, 65, 60, 60, 55, 40

What is the mode of this set?

A. 90

B. 80

C. 70

D. 100

Analysis:
The mode is 80, because there are four scores of 80. Answer "B" is correct.

52. What is the median of the same set on the previous page?

    A. 80

    B. 75

    C. 85

    D. 90

Analysis:
The median is 80, because the 10th and 11th numbers are 80. Answer "A" is correct.

53. What is the correct calculation of the mean?

    A. 75

    B. 76.5

    C. 77

    D. 78.5

Analysis:
The mean is the total of items divided by the number of items. $1530 \div 20 = 76.5$
The correct answer is "B."

24. Make predictions of outcomes of experiments based upon theoretical probabilities and explain actual outcomes.

Students should be able to apply their knowledge and understanding of probability to determine simple experimental probabilities and explain actual outcomes. They should be able to express the probability as a fraction (1 chance in 4 is 1/4) or describe which event is more likely or less likely to happen in a problem situation. Students should also be able to interpret probabilities in terms of percents. (Example: Explain the weather report that there is a 70% chance of rain.)

Test items may include pictorial representations when appropriate.

Exercise:

54. Use the drawing of a spinner to find the probability (P) of spinning a flower.

    A. P = 4/4

    B. P = 3/4

    C. P = 2/4

    D. P = 1/4

Analysis:

The correct answer is 2/4 or 1/2. Answer choice "C" is correct. The student needs to understand that of the four probable outcomes, there are two chances that the spinner will stop on a flower.

55. Using the same spinner, how many stars is it probable to spin in 20 spins? Show how you found your answer.

55.

_____

_____

_____

Show your work here.

Analysis:

The probability that the spinner would stop on a star can be expressed as 1 out of four or in the ratio 1/4 or the percentage 25%. The probability of how many stars in 20 spins is 25% of the 20 spins or 0. 25 x 20 = 5, so the probability equation will look like this:

$P = \dfrac{5}{20}$ *The correct answer would be 5 out of 20, 5/20, or 25% of the time.*

Citizenship

Sixth Grade Proficiency Test: Citizenship

Introduction: Strands and Learning Outcomes

The outcomes for the Citizenship Proficiency Test were developed by a committee of Ohio educators and business people using a consensus-building process.

The Citizenship test covers six strands comprised of twenty-two learning outcomes, based on the draft of Social Studies: Ohio's Model Competency-Based Program. Each form of the test includes some embedded field test items. There are 5 field test items embedded in the citizenship test, making a total of 51 items, only 46 of which are counted to obtain the students' citizenship scores. These field test items give the Ohio Department of Education the potential to continue adding to the item bank for future test forms.

Each form of the test contains 34 multiple choice items, 10 short-answer items and 2 extended-response items. Altogether the 34 multiple choice items are worth 34 points, the 10 short-answer items are worth 20 points and the 2 extended-response items are worth 8 points, making a total of 62 points. In all, the multiple-choice items account for about 55% of the total score, short-answer items, 32%, and extended-response items, 13%.

The Citizenship Learning Outcomes
Strand I - American Heritage
1. Demonstrate knowledge of and ability to think about the relationship among events:
   a. Group significant individuals by broadly defined historical eras.
   b. Utilize multiple-tier time lines.
2. Utilize a variety of resources to consider information from different perspectives about North America:
   a. Identify the central idea an historical narrative attempts to address.
   b. Inquire into the relative credibility of sources
3. Identify significant individuals from the past in North America and explain their contributions to the cultural heritage of the United States.
4. Identify a significant individual from a region of the world other than North America and discuss cause-and-effect relationships surrounding a major event in the individual's life.

Strand II - People in Societies
5. Compare the gender roles, religious ideas or class structures in two societies.
6. Draw inferences about the experiences, problems, and opportunities that cultural groups have encountered in the past.
7. Describe how the customs and traditions of immigrant and other groups have shaped American life.

Strand III - World Interactions
8. Utilize map skills:
   a. Apply latitude and longitude to locate points on maps and globes.
   b. Distinguish between relevant and irrelevant information on a map for a specific task.
9. Interpret and analyze maps, charts, or graphs to formulate geographic ideas:
   a. Utilize time zones to compute differences in time and to describe their impact on human activities.
   b. Determine and explain relationships among resources, economic activities, and population distribution.
10. Use maps of North America or the world to identify physical and cultural regions and to show relationships among regions.
11. Examine instances of contact between people of different regions of the world and determine the reasons for these contacts.

Strand IV - Decision Making and Resources

12. Describe the role of each factor of production in producing a specific good or service and suggest alternative uses for the resources involved.
13. Identify the factors that influence:
    a. Consumer decisions to demand goods or services.
    b. Producer decisions to supply goods or services.
14. Identify the factors that determine the degree of competition in a market and describe the impact of competition on a market:
    a. Identify advantages and disadvantages of competition in the marketplace.
    b. Explain the general relationship between supply, demand, and price in a competitive market.
15. Use information about global resource distribution to make generalizations about why nations engage in international trade.

Strand V - Democratic Processes

16. Identify the main functions of the executive, legislative, and judicial branches of the United States national government and cite activities related to these functions.
17. Interpret how examples of political activity illustrate characteristics of American democracy.
18. Classify characteristics of government that are typical of a monarchal, democratic, or dictatorial type of government.

Strand VI - Citizenship Rights and Responsibilities

19. Analyze information on civic issues by organizing key ideas with their supporting facts.
20. Identify and analyze alternatives through which civic goals can be achieved and select an appropriate alternative based upon a set of criteria.
21. Identify ways to resolve private and public conflicts based on principles of fairness and justice.
22. Identify examples of citizen participation in political systems around the world.

Scoring of the Citizenship Proficiency Test

Multiple-choice items ask students to choose the correct answer out of a list of possible responses. Short answer items ask students to explain a conclusion, complete a chart, interpret information, or provide a rationale for an answer they have chosen. Extended-response items ask students to interpret information from a three-to-eight line paragraph on a specific topic, reach and justify a conclusion, or provide examples. Since credit for answers is usually based on demonstrated understanding of concepts, students should be encouraged always to explain their answers when asked to do so. The more understanding that a student demonstrates, the more credit may be assigned. Each strand has at least one short-answer or one extended-response.

Item Type and Point Distribution

Type	Number of Items	Total Points	Total Percent
Multiple Choice	34	34	44
Short Answer	10	20	32
Extended Response	2	8	13
TOTAL	46	62	100

The following table shows the distribution of the test items on the Citizenship Proficiency Test. Each strand has at least one short-answer or one extended-response item. The number of learning outcomes is denoted in the table by a number place in parentheses.

Item Distribution by Strand

Strands	Multiple Choice	Short Answer	Extended Response	Totals
I. American Heritage(4)	5–9	1–3	0–1	7–10
II. People in Societies (3)	4–8	1–3	0–1	5–8
III World Interactions (4)	4–7	1–3	0–1	5–7
IV. Decision Making and Resources(4)	5–8	1–3	0–1	6–9
V. Democratic Processes (3)	4–8	1–3	0–1	5–8
VI. Citizenship Rights and Responsibilities (4)	4–7	1–3	0–1	5–7
Total Number of Items	34	10	2	46
Total Number of Points	34	20	8	62

How Short-Answer Items are Scored

Each short-answer item could receive any of the following scores: 2 points, 1 point, or 0 points

2 Points - The response must be complete and appropriate. The response must also demonstrate a thorough understanding of the concept or item. It indicates logical reasoning and conclusions. It is accurate, relevant, comprehensive, and detailed.

1 Point - The response is partially appropriate. It is mostly accurate and relevant but lacks comprehensiveness and demonstrates an incomplete understanding of the concept or item. It contains minor flaws in reasoning or neglects to address some aspect of the concept or item.

0 Points - A zero is assigned if there is no response or if the response indicates no understanding of the concept or item.

How Extended-Response Items are Scored

The extended-response items can receive any score from 0 to 4 points or N/S.

4 Points - The response provides evidence of extensive interpretation and thoroughly addresses the points relevant to the item. It is well-organized, elaborate, and thorough. It is relevant, comprehensive, detailed, and demonstrates a thorough understanding of the concept or item. It contains logical reasoning and communicates effectively and clearly. It thoroughly addresses the important elements of the item.

3 Points - The response provides evidence that an essential interpretation has been made. It is thoughtful and reasonably accurate. It indicates an understanding of the concept or item, communicates adequately, and generally reaches reasonable conclusions. It contains some combination of the following flaws: minor flaws in reasoning, neglecting to address some aspect of the concept or item, missing details.

2 Points - The response is mostly accurate and relevant. It contains some combination of the following flaws: incomplete evidence of interpretation, unsubstantiated statements made about the text, incomplete understanding of the concept or item, a lack of comprehensiveness, faulty reasoning, or unclear communication.

1 Point - The response is a partial understanding of the concept or item but is sketchy and unclear. It indicates some effort beyond restating the item. It contains some combination of the following flaws: little evidence of interpretation, unorganized and incomplete response, failure to address most aspects of the concept or item, major flaws in reasoning that led to invalid conclusions, a definite lack of understanding of the concept or item, or demonstrates no coherent meaning from text.

0 Points - The response indicates no understanding of the concept or item.

Facts from the Field Test

Test items based on the citizenship learning outcomes were field tested in April 1995. While a number of students responding to each test was limited, some general observations regarding student achievement can be made. The summary below is based upon review of student performance on multiple-choice items only. Scored examples of short-answer and extended-response items found on the practice test will be available in the winter of 1996.

The symbol "✔" will be used to indicate the learning outcome where student performance was highest on multiple choice items. The students had high performance on items measuring outcomes 3, 7, 11, and 13. The symbol "✍" next to a learning outcome indentifies the learning outcomes where student performance was lowest on multiple choice items. The students had the lowest performance on items measuring outcomes 12, 16, and 18. You may refer to the Key on the next page.

> **Key:**
> ✍ = Students performance was LOW during field testing.
> ✔ = Students performance was HIGH during field testing.

About the Citizenship Learning Outcomes

The following pages will cover all of the Strands and Learning Outcomes in detail. Following each learning outcome will be several simulated Proficiency Test problems and some teaching tips that can be used to review the content of the learning outcome with students. The student manual includes all of the sample problems.

Strand I - American Heritage

Items in the American Heritage strand ask questions related to the student's understanding of chronology and historical relationships. Specific chronological events are provided as part of the test items. Items in this strand also examine various sources of information about historical topics. Some prior, but not extensive, knowledge of events and people is needed.

1. Demonstrate knowledge of and ability to think about the relationship among events:

   a. Group significant individuals by broadly defined historical eras.
   b. Utilize multiple-tier time lines.

Items addressing this learning outcome refer to the significance of individuals or historical events in the context of other individuals or events and various time periods. Significance is not limited to famous individuals, but can reflect the contributions of ordinary people as well. Information about significant individuals is included as part of the test items.

The ability to identify broadly defined historical eras, as called for, is important for developing a sense of chronology using periodization. The criteria defining historical eras will be included as part of the test items. Students could be asked to examine a brief narrative, time line, or list of events and select individuals or groups of individuals that fit in a particular era. Students could also be asked to identify what era encompassed the activities of particular individuals or groups.

Some items for 1a and all of the items for 1b will require students to use multiple-tier time lines. A multiple-tier time line is a time line that utilizes two or more rows of events, each row representing a different set of subjects or topics occurring during the period under study. An example would be a time line that associated the reigns of French kings with advances in arts and sciences throughout France. Time lines use B.C. and/or A.D. dates.

Items for 1b could ask the students to place significant individuals or events on a time line. Students could be asked to identify which individuals and/or events would be appropriate to include on a given time line. Students could also be asked to explain connections between events on a time line.

Examples:

1. The period from 1400 to 1600 was called the Renaissance Period. This period, which began in Italy, was one of many advances in the fine arts and in learning. Artists began to study anatomy and began to sculpt and paint the human figure much more realistically. Rulers supported the work of the artists and builders by spending vast amounts of money for paintings, sculptures, and buildings.

   Which of the following was representative of the Renaissance period?

   A. The Parthenon, a Greek shrine, was built between the years 447 and 432 B.C.
   B. Colosseum, a building designed for the entertainment of large numbers of people, was built in Rome between the years 72 and 80 A.D.
   C. The statue of David was created between 1430 and 1432 by Michelangelo, a great Italian sculptor.
   D. Pablo Picasso, who has been called the greatest artist of the 20th century, created over 20,000 works of art.

Analysis:
The Parthenon was built between the years 447 and 432 B.C and the Colosseum was built between the years 72 and 80 A.D. Both of these were constructed far before the Renaissance, which took place during the 1400's and the 1500's. Pablo Picasso lived during the 20th century, long after the Renaissance period. Therefore, the only correct answer can be "C." The statue of David was created between 1430 and 1432 by Michelangelo, a great Italian sculptor."

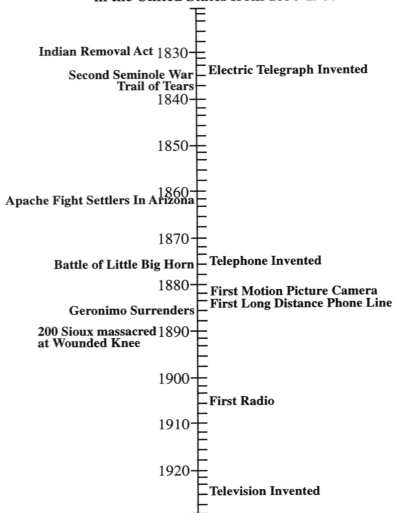

**Indian Developments and the Advancement of Communication
in the United States from 1830-1960**

2. Which of the following events occurred in the history of the Native Americans during the time that the telegraph was invented?

A. 200 Sioux were massacred at Wounded Knee

B. Second Seminole War

C. Battle of Little Big Horn

D. Indian Removal Act

Analysis:
The student should use the same method as mentioned in the above question. The only one of the choices given which is positioned opposite the invention of the electric telegraph is the Second Seminole War. The correct response is choice "B."

2. Utilize a variety of resources to consider information from different perspectives about North America:

   a. Identify the central idea an historical narrative attempts to address.
   b. Inquire into the relative credibility of sources.

Students need to know how to analyze information from a variety of sources. Source materials could include both primary and secondary materials. Primary materials consist of firsthand accounts created by people who were present at the time an event took place. Secondary materials are accounts created after an event has taken place by people who were not present at the time of the event.

Items for 2a require students to distinguish the main idea of a passage. Items for 2b require students to analyze the reliability of views contained in different statements or documents.

Examples:

   3. The years from 1095 to 1492 have been called The Age of Conquerors. It was during this time period that the Mongul tribes conquered areas from central Asia to Europe. In the year 1095, the Pope encouraged European knights to travel to Jerusalem to capture the city from the hands of the Muslims and place it under control of the Christians. The 100 Years War was the result of the English attempting to conquer France. In the Americas, the Incas and the Mayas were building vast empires by conquering neighboring tribes.

   Which of the following is the main idea of the passage given above?

   A. The years from 1095 to 1492 have been called The Age of Conquerors.
   B. It was during this time period that the Mongul tribes conquered areas from central Asia to Europe.
   C. In the Americas, the Incas and the Mayas were building vast empires by conquering neighboring tribes.
   D. The Pope encouraged European knights to travel to Jerusalem to capture the city from the hands of the Muslims and place it under control of the Christians.

Analysis:
In determining the main idea, the students should remember that every sentence in the passage talks about the main idea. The first sentence in the passage is the only sentence which fits this requirement. Notice that all the answer choices are excerpts from the passage. Usually the main idea can be determined by reading the first and last sentence of a paragraph is written properly. The correct answer is "A," "The years from 1095 to 1492 have been called The Age of Conquerors."

4. Several people have given reports of the crash of the Hindenburg, a dirigible in which many people were killed. In the days following the crash, reporters interviewed people who had witnessed it and reported what the witnesses had seen. One radio announcer gave a live, eyewitness account as the crash was occurring.

Which is the most reliable of the reports relating to the crash of the Hindenburgh, the reporters who interviewed witnesses in the days following the crash or the radio announcer who gave the live, eyewitness account? Explain your answer.

4.

_____

_____

_____

_____

_____

_____

_____

_____

_____

_____

Analysis:
Answers may vary. Students should have mentioned that the live, eyewitness account as the crash was occurring was the most reliable because the announcer was stating exactly what he saw happening as it was happening. Some students might mention that this announcers report is a "primary source" and that the reports taken from witnesses in the days following the crash are "secondary sources." Some students might have mentioned that witnesses interviewed in the days following the crash might have forgotten or changed their vision of the event.

5. The decade of the 60's was one of struggle for equality for the African-Americans in the United States. In 1961, "The Freedom Riders", a group of African-American students, traveled by bus across the southern part of the country in an attempt to desegregate waiting rooms. James Meredith became the first black to be admitted to the University of Mississippi in 1962. The year 1963 was the year that Medger Evers, a black activist, was murdered in Mississippi and Martin Luther King, Jr. led the March on Washington. In spite of the Civil Rights Bill passed by Congress in 1964, there was rioting in Harlem. The following year Malcolm X, a civil rights leader was assassinated.

The second half of the decade continued the struggle for equality. In 1965, the Voting Rights Act was passed, ensuring that all eligible blacks were able to vote. The same year rioting erupted in the Watts area of Los Angeles. In 1966, James Meredith was shot while on a protest walk in Tennessee and there was rioting of the blacks in Detroit. On April 4, 1968, Dr. Martin Luther King, Jr. was assassinated.

What is the main idea of the reading selection shown above?

A. The Civil Rights Bill

B. The assassination of Martin Luther King, Jr.

C. African-Americans struggle for equality

D. The Riots

Analysis:
The main idea of the reading selection is about the decade of the 60's being one of struggle for equality among the blacks. The Civil Rights Bill, the assassination of Martin Luther King, Jr. and the riots are all mentioned but are not what the selection is mainly about. The best answer is "C."

✔ **3. Identify significant individuals from the past in North America and explain their contributions to the cultural heritage of the United States.**

As explained for the first student outcome, significance is not limited to famous individuals, but can reflect the contributions of ordinary people as well. Relevant information about significant individuals is included as part of the test items. Students will be provided passages containing information about people from North America. They could be asked to explain how specific individuals have affected the way in which the American people live today or to select a given contribution that is supported by the information provided.

Examples:

6. Vicente Lobalzo immigrated to the United States from his native Italy. Although he was not a highly educated man, he was a wonderful cook. He opened a small Italian restaurant in the neighborhood in which most of the Italian residents in Cleveland resided. As news of the wonderful meals that he served spread, people from other areas of the city came to try these Italian foods. The restaurant grew and prospered, and Vicente and his family became members of the great American melting pot. Which of the following show the way that Vicente helped affect the way in which Americans live today?

   A. He spoke only Italian and helped spread that language in the U.S.

   B. He helped introduce Italian foods to the American people.

   C. He voted in all of the elections and encouraged all people to vote.

   D. He started a trend to immigrate to the United States.

Analysis:
Although we can assume that Vincente spoke Italian, we do not know if he also spoke English. So, Choice "A" can not be the answer. Nothing is mentioned about voting in the paragraph, so "C" can not be the correct answer. Answer choice "D" can not be supported by the passage and is incorrect. The correct answer is that Vincente helped introduce Italian foods to the American people, Choice "B."

7. Thomas Jefferson, born to a wealthy family from Virginia, believed that the American colonies should be free from the rule of England. In June of 1776, the Declaration of Independence, which was written mainly by Jefferson, was presented to and accepted by the Second Continental Congress. Thomas Jefferson was elected President of the United States in 1800 and this led to his second greatest achievement, the Louisiana Purchase.

   What two achievements of Thomas Jefferson affected the way in which American people live today?

   7.

   1)_____

   _____

   2)_____

   _____

Analysis:

Answers may vary. Students should have mentioned that he was one of the writers of the Declaration of Independence, and that as a result of his efforts and those of others, we are free of British rule. His second contribution which affected the way Americans live was the Louisiana Purchase. This greatly increased the size of our country and added to our natural resources and wealth. Some of the students might mention that Jefferson served as President of the United States and therefore helped the American people by leading the country.

8. Susan B. Anthony had a life-long desire to see the women of America have the right to vote. She spoke out in favor of equal rights for women in the areas of voting and education, as well as in the workplace. In 1869 Susan and a friend formed the National Woman Suffrage Association, an organization to promote the right of women to vote. Although she did not live long enough to see women voting in the United States, she influenced many people with her ideas.

Explain how the ideas and actions of Susan B. Anthony have affected the way Americans live today.

8.
_____
_____
_____
_____
_____
_____
_____
_____
_____
_____

Analysis:

Answers may vary. Students could mention that American women today have the right to vote. They also might state that American women have more educational and career opportunities.

4. Identify a significant individual from a region of the world other than North America and discuss cause-and-effect relationships surrounding a major event in the individual's life.

Students are asked to identify cause-and-effect relationships by using information found in a narrative. Students could be asked to explain what a particular cause-and-effect relationship is or to select a given relationship that is supported by the information provided. Relevant information about significant individuals is included as part of the test items.

Examples:

9. In 1804, Napoleon Bonaparte, who was a power-hungry man, crowned himself emperor of France. He then began to work toward achieving his goal of conquering the world. He had defeated most of the countries of Europe by the time he attacked Russia in 1812. He defeated the Russian troops, but the Russians refused to surrender. As the French troops marched across Russia on their return to France, the bitter Russian winter began. The troops did not have enough food or clothing to keep themselves warm. Thousands of French troops died. As a result, Napoleon was forced to give up his power in 1814.

   What was the cause of the Napoleon being forced to give up his power in 1814?

   A. His power-hungry attitude

   B. He defeated the Russian troops

   C. He ran out of food and clothing

   D. Thousands of French troops died because of him

Analysis:
The main cause of Napoleon being forced to give up his power was the death of thousands of French troops. It is true that Napoleon had a power-hungry attitude and that he defeated the Russian troops. But the best answer is still "D" because the French were angry over the unnecessary the deaths of so many men.

10. Louis Pasteur, a French scientist, discovered that many diseases are caused by germs. He also found that, by destroying microorganisms, the spoilage of perishable substances can be delayed. These discoveries led to the development of the process of pasteurization, a rapid heating and cooling of milk and other substances to kill the germs.

Which of the following is the effect of his discovery that, by destroying microorganisms, the spoilage of perishable substances can be delayed?

A. Louis Pasteur became a scientist.

B. He discovered that many diseases are caused by germs.

C. He discovered a field of grass and clover.

D. He developed the process of pasteurization.

Analysis:
Both "A" and "B" have to be incorrect because Pasteur had both become a scientist and discovered that germs cause many diseases before he discovered that spoilage of substances could be delayed by destroying organisms. There is no mention of fields of grass and clover therefore "C" is incorrect. Therefore, the only possible choice is "D".

11. Mahatma Gandhi was born in Porbandar, India in the year 1869 and was trained as a lawyer in England. At the age of twenty-three he moved to South Africa. In South Africa he experienced prejudice, which affected his feelings and beliefs for the remainder of his life. After returning to his homeland, these feelings led him to fight for the poorest members of the Indian society, the people who were called the "untouchables."

What event in his life caused Mahatma Gandhi to fight for the "untouchables" in India?

11.

_____

_____

_____

_____

Analysis:
Answers will vary. Students should have mentioned something about Gandhi's experience with prejudice while living in South Africa.

Teaching Tips for Strand 1

Students at this age may not have enough of a sense of time and place. By creating a large bulletin board which contains both time lines and a map of the world, the teacher can refer to these throughout the entire year. As a new subject comes up, you can ask the students to locate the event on the map and on the time line. You can even have the students fill out index cards to be stapled on the bulletin board and connected to the correct locations on the map and time line by string.

Historically, students have had more problems with nonfiction sections of the Ohio Proficiency Tests then they have had with the fiction sections. Since some of the questions on the test contain the needed information within the context of the question itself, students need to spend more time with nonfiction selections in the classroom.

The use of magazines and newspaper articles, letters, and documents in the classroom can be helpful. If you have access to the Internet, there are wonderful materials which can be printed and used in your classroom. Examples of this are letters from a Civil War soldier, biographies of anarchists, and information on special interest groups.

In teaching main ideas, students should select a sentence which tells what every sentence in the paragraph talks about. Students should be aware that the main idea is usually stated by the author. If the teacher reminds that students that the main idea is called the topic sentence during the writing process, it may help some of them locate this sentence. If the main idea is not stated in the selection, the student must create one. After arriving at his choice of a main idea, the student should reread the selection and check to make sure that every sentence in the selection addresses that main idea.

Have students evaluate the credibility of materials as they are presented. Ask them to determine whether the writer was actually at the event about which he is writing (primary source). They should also evaluate whether he is slanting the material because of his own beliefs or because of monetary gain.

Remember to use questioning techniques which require students to use higher-order thinking skills.

As material is presented, have the students study time lines to see if they can arrive at any cause and effect relationships.

Strand II - People in Societies

Items in the People in Societies strand ask questions pertaining to cultural groups. The phrase cultural group refers to a number of individuals sharing unique characteristics (e.g. race, ethnicity, national origin, and religion). The items pertain to the attributes, experiences, and contributions of such groups.

5. Compare the gender roles, religious ideas or class structures in two societies.

In pursuing this outcome students will be presented with information to examine concerning gender roles, religious ideas, and class structures in various world societies, both past and present. Students could be asked to identify similarities or differences in characteristics of different societies. They could be asked to explain situations based upon characteristics of different societies. Students could also be presented with characteristics in one society and asked to identify an analogous set of roles, ideas, or structures in another society.

Examples:

The aborigines of the Arctic region are the Inuit, which have also been called "the Eskimo." Traditionally they were hunters and gathers, living mainly from seal, walrus, and other animals and fish which they hunted. In the Inuit society the roles of the men and the women are separate and distinct. The men hunt, fish, and build houses. It is the job of the women to cook, make the clothing, and prepare animal skins for use. Traditionally the Inuit believed that all living and nonliving things have a spirit. All events occur because of the influence of the spirits. Although the spirits affect people's lives, they can be controlled through magic charms. In the traditional Inuit society, there are many taboos related to the fear of upsetting the spirits.

The aborigines of Australia were also hunters and gathers. They divided the labor so that the men were responsible for making tribal laws and hunting, while women were to gather the remainder of the food, get water and firewood, and maintain the camp. In the traditional religion, the Aborigines believe that spirits formed the land and established all life.

This time of the formation of the land and the establishment of life is called "the Dreaming." Many land forms are sacred to these people because they represent the spirits who formed them and everything in the world during the Dreaming.

Use the reading selection above to answer the following two questions.

12. In both the Inuit and Aborigine religions, the people believe in the existence of which of the following?

　A. That all men are created equal

　B. Only one god

　C. Many spirits

　D. Farming is sacred

Analysis:
The reading selections don't say anything about their beliefs relating to the equality of man. We can therefore eliminate choice "A." Likewise, nothing is mentioned about the belief in only one god. We can also eliminate choice"B." Although land is mention is the passage "D" is not the correct answer. The reading does mention that the Inuit believe that everything has a spirit, and the Aborigines believe that the spirits formed the land and established life. Choice"C" is the correct answer.

13. Saudi Arabia, one of the most conservative nations in the world has been resistant to change. The government follows the laws of the Islamic religion exactly. Under Islamic law, liquor, gambling, movies, and dancing are forbidden. The women are not permitted to wear Western clothing, travel unaccompanied, or drive. Because the Islamic religion forbids much mixing between the sexes, the educated women are only permitted to work as teachers, nurses or to participate in work in social agencies.

Explain three ways in which the lives of Saudi women and those of American women differ.

13.

1)＿＿＿＿＿＿＿＿＿＿＿＿＿＿＿＿＿＿＿＿＿＿＿＿＿＿＿

＿＿＿＿＿＿＿＿＿＿＿＿＿＿＿＿＿＿＿＿＿＿＿＿＿＿＿

2)＿＿＿＿＿＿＿＿＿＿＿＿＿＿＿＿＿＿＿＿＿＿＿＿＿＿＿

＿＿＿＿＿＿＿＿＿＿＿＿＿＿＿＿＿＿＿＿＿＿＿＿＿＿＿

---

13. continued.

3)_____

_____

Analysis:
Answers will vary. Students might mention that the Saudis are not permitted to drink liquor, gamble, dance or attend movies, and American women are permitted to do all of these. They might say that in Saudi Arabia the women can not drive, wear Western clothing or travel alone. American women can do all of these things. In the United States, women may choose whatever profession they wish to enter, but the Saudi women are very limited in their choices.

6. Draw inferences about the experiences, problems, and opportunities that cultural groups have encountered in the past.

Items addressing this learning outcome require students to examine past experiences of various cultural groups. These groups include groups such as Asian, ethnic groups such as Eskimo, nationalities such as Italian, and religious groups such as Baptist. The items will contain information for students to interpret. Students will need to apply general background knowledge concerning cultural groups to the situations described in the items. The students could be presented with a set of choices or could be asked to explain what inferences they draw from the information presented in an item.

Examples:

14. African Americans have served our country bravely since the time of the Revolutionary War. In spite of this, this they were not permitted to officially join the Army until 1866. At that time a law was passed allowing African Americans to join special units. The African Americans who joined did so for the money, to find a better life, and to get an education. In those early years after the formation of the special African American units in the U.S. Army, they were given the most unpleasant assignments. The Native Americans began to call them "buffalo soldiers," probably because of their courage and spirit. The African American soldiers worked hard and had very few deserters compared with other units in the military. Today the descendent of these "buffalo soldiers" are proud of their heritage and contributions to the United States.

Name one fact from the above reading selection that implies that the United States Army discriminated against African Americans?

14.

_____

_____

_____

_____

Analysis:
Answers will vary. The students might state that the African Americans were not permitted to officially join the Army until 1866. Another possible answer is that the African Americans were permitted to join special units, perhaps because they were not permitted in the same units with the whites. The students might have stated that the special African American units were given the most unpleasant assignments.

15. During World War II, the Japanese Americans had a very difficult time. Although the Japanese Americans donated blood to the Red Cross and volunteered to help during air raids, others pleaded for the government to do something about the Japanese. Many people did not believe that there was a difference between an enemy Japanese soldier and a Japanese American. Beginning in 1942, the Japanese Americans living on the West Coast were ordered into "relocation camps." These relocation camps were permanent detention centers. In 1945, the Japanese Americans were finally released from the camps and permitted to return to their homes on the West Coast.

Which of the following is the reason that Americans wanted the Japanese Americans to be placed into relocation camps?

A. Many Americans feared the Japanese Americans and thought that they would help the enemy.

B. Many Americans thought that the Japanese Americans dressed in a strange way and they did not like it.

C. Many Americans thought that the Japanese food tasted strange and they were afraid that it, like Italian food, would become popular in this country.

D. Many Americans thought that they should be protected in camps.

Analysis:

Japanese Americans were American citizens and many of them dressed as other Americans dress. Therefore, choice "B" is incorrect. Choice "C" is incorrect because people do not place others in relocation camps just because they do like a certain type of food. Answer choice "D" is incorrect. The country of Japan had attacked the United States in the bombing of Pearl Harbor. Americans were angry and afraid. It was because they feared the Japanese and thought that the Japanese Americans would help the enemy, Japan. Answer choice "A" is correct.

✔ **7. Describe ow the customs and traditions of immigrant and other groups have shaped American life.**

Many cultural groups have contributed to the nature of the American culture. Items for this outcome explore some of the ways life in the United States has been impacted by the customs and traditions of various groups. Students could be asked to identify or explain how life in the United States has been affected by different groups. Students could also be asked to identify a group that made a specific contribution to American life.

Examples:

16. In the grocery stores of the United States, people are purchasing tortillas, salsa, refried beans, and enchiladas. Restaurants such as Taco Bell and ChiChis are offering tacos, chimichangas, and burritos. All of these foods were introduced by which of the following immigrant groups into the United States?

   A. Mexican

   B. Germans

   C. Japanese

   D. Texan

Analysis:

The correct answer is "A," Mexican. Tacos and enchiladas are the clues that the students may have recognized. Both of these foods are Mexican.

17. The Cajuns are a group of descendent of the French-Canadians who immigrated into the fertile lands of southern Louisiana from Acadia, an region of colonial Canada. Today most of the Cajuns still live in small, isolated communities in the bayous along the Gulf of Mexico. They work as farmers, raising cattle and growing crops. They speak a distinct language which is a mixture of words from French, Spanish, English, and German, as well as words from former slaves and Native Americans. Although they are set apart from their neighbors by their customs and language, their music and foods have traveled to various parts of the United States to be appreciated by many other Americans.

Name the two most important contributions that the Cajuns have made to American society?

17.

1)_____

_____

2)_____

_____

Analysis:
Answers will vary. The answer is given in the last sentence of the passage. ("their music and foods have traveled to various parts of the United States to be appreciated by many other Americans." The best response to the question is 1) food, and 2) music. The may have responded the their contrivution to farming the the work force.

Teaching Tips for Strand II
Students should be taught to use Venn diagrams to compare and contrast information. Shown below is a Venn diagram which could be used to compare apples and oranges. The attributes of only the apple or only the orange belong in the outer portion of the respective circles. Students should place the attributes which are shared by both in the middle of the diagram where the circles intersect.

APPLES   ORANGES

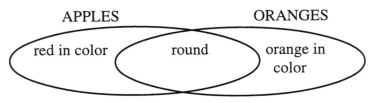

red in color   round   orange in color

More Teaching Tips for Strand II

As students read and discuss material, have them interact with the material by evaluating what their own feelings and reactions would be to the events. This should help them to draw inferences related to the material.

Although the students by this time are aware that various groups have made contributions to our society, the teacher should emphasize these contributions at each opportunity.

Strand III - World Interactions

The World Interactions strand focuses on the student's understanding and use of maps, charts, and graphs. Items present information in a variety of forms for students to analyze and interpret.

8. Utilize map skills

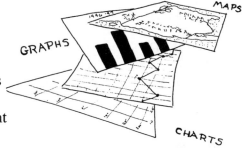

a. Apply latitude and longitude to locate points on maps and globes.
b. Distinguish between relevant and irrelevant information on a map for a specific task.

Citizens interpret information on maps for a variety of purposes. This outcome focuses on the use of maps.

Items for 8a require students to make use of latitude and longitude. The items could ask students to locate bodies of water or land areas on a map. Items for 8b could ask student to identify what parts or features of a map (e.g. title, index, key) are needed to supply necessary information for some purpose. The students could also be asked to explain how to use different parts or features of a map to accomplish a given task.

See the examples and maps that begin on the next page.

Examples:

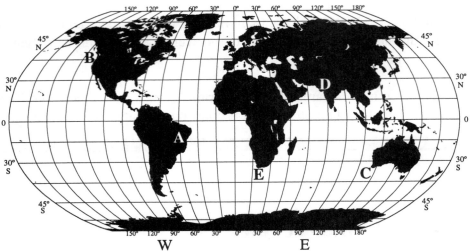

Use the map shown above to answer the following questions.

18. Brasilia is located at 16°S and 48°W. Which of the following letters correctly shows the position of Brasilia?

A. A

B. D

C. C

D. B

Analysis:
*The correct answer is choice "A." The student must find 16° in the southern hemisphere and locate 48° in the western hemisphere. If the student chooses the location labeled **D** on the map they have made the mistake of looking in the northern hemisphere instead of the southern hemisphere. Answer choices "B," "C," and "D" are incorrect locations on the map. Students need to be very careful of all the details.*

19. Refer to the map of the hemisphere above to find the letter that represents each city listed by using the coordinates. Complete the table by filling in the correct letter for each city.

19.	City	Coordinates	Letter
	Cape Town	34°South, 18°East	E
	Vancouver	39°North, 123°West	
	Brasilia	15° South, 50° West	
	Perth	30° South, 115° East	

Analysis:
The correct letter for Cape Town is given as an example. The rest of the answers are
Vancouver = B, Brasilia = A, and Perth = C.

Annual Rainfall in Inches

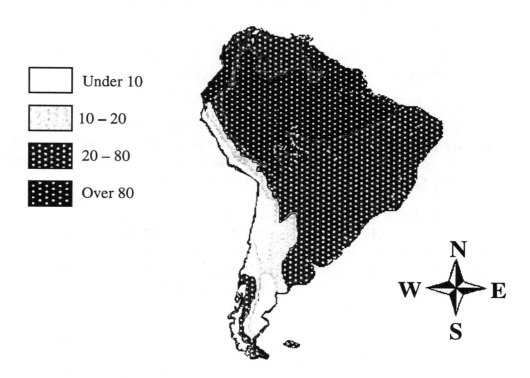

Under 10

10 – 20

20 – 80

Over 80

Use the map shown above to answer the following question.

20. What part of the map would you need to use to find out what areas have
the lowest rainfall in South America?

A. The title of the map: "Annual Rainfall in Inches"

B. The compass rose

C. The key or legend

D. The continent of South America

Analysis:
Answer choice "A" is incorrect, the title of the map only tells that subject of the map is
annual rainfall. Answer choice "B" is incorrect, the compass rose tells us which direction
is north, south, east, and west. The key or legend gives the information to help
understand the colors and patterns on the map. This will in turn allow us to find the areas
in which rainfall is lowest. Choice "C" is the correct answer. The continent is South
America but, this is not the correct answer.

9. Interpret and analyze maps, charts, or graphs to formulate geographic ideas:

a. Utilize time zones to compute differences in time and to describe their impact on human activities.

b. Determine and explain relationships among resources, economic activities, and population distribution.

Maps, charts, and graphs are increasingly used by the media to convey information. Citizens need to be able to understand information that is presented in a variety of formats.

Items for 9a require the student to use the world's 24 time zones to understand concerns involving worldwide travel and communication. Students could be asked to calculate the difference in time across time zones. Students could also be asked to determine how time zones impact planning for travel, sending a FAX, or other similar situations.

Items for 9b use maps, charts, or graphs to illustrate climatic regions, resource distribution, population data, cultural patterns, and other types of information. Students will be provided with information to interpret. They could be asked to identify a relationship that exists based on the information provided. Students could also be asked to interpret a relationship between any of the factors portrayed on maps, charts, or graphs.

Examples:

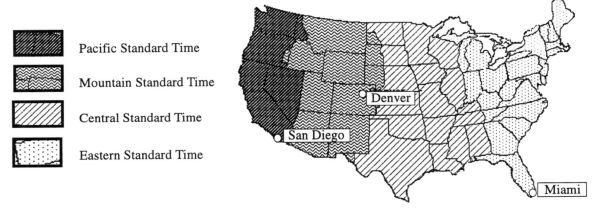

Pacific Standard Time

Mountain Standard Time

Central Standard Time

Eastern Standard Time

Use the map shown above to answer the following question.

21. Jenny Roush, who lives in Denver, Colorado, wanted to place a conference call to her two best friends. These friends are Debbie Church, who lives in Miami, Florida, and Michelle Klein, who lives in San Diego, California. She knew that she and her friends were very busy people and were only able to talk on the phone between 5:00 P.M. and 10:00 P.M. in their respective time zones.

What is the earliest time that she can place the conference call?

21.

_____

_____

_____

_____

Analysis:

Jenny lives in Mountain Standard Time, so the earliest that she can place the call is 7:00 P.M. Mountain Standard Time. At that time, it is 6:00 P.M. Pacific Standard Time, (San Diego) and it is 9:00 P.M. Eastern Standard Time (Miami). Students need to know how to work with time zone maps and understand the time differences between each zone.

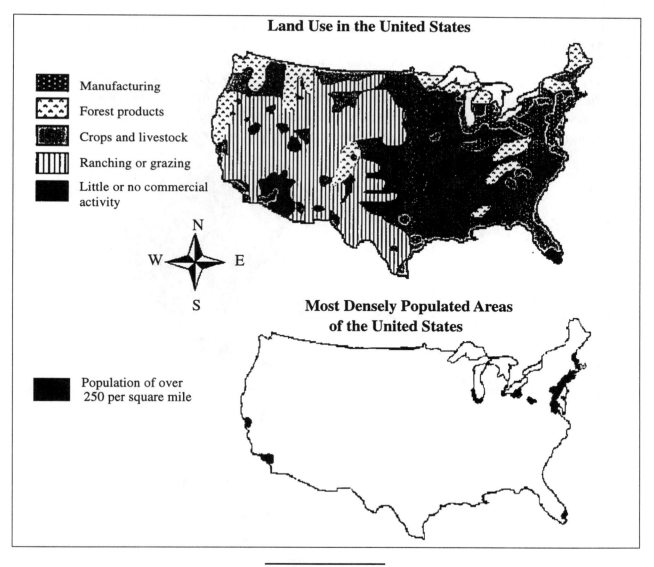

Land Use in the United States

Manufacturing

Forest products

Crops and livestock

Ranching or grazing

Little or no commercial activity

N
W — E
S

Population of over 250 per square mile

Most Densely Populated Areas of the United States

Examples:

Use the two maps labeled **Land Use in the United States** and **Most Densely Populated Areas of the United States** on the previous page to answer the following question.

> **22.** After looking at the two maps of the United States Land Use and Most Densely Populated Areas, what is the major occupation of the people living in the most densely populated areas of the United States?

22.

_____

_____

_____

_____

Analysis:

The students needed to look at each area shaded in black on the population map. Then they needed to find the equivalent areas on the "Land Use in the United States" map. These areas on the land use map are in the black areas with white dots. These areas, according to the legend, are mainly used for manufacturing and trade. The students should have mentioned manufacturing and trade in their answers.

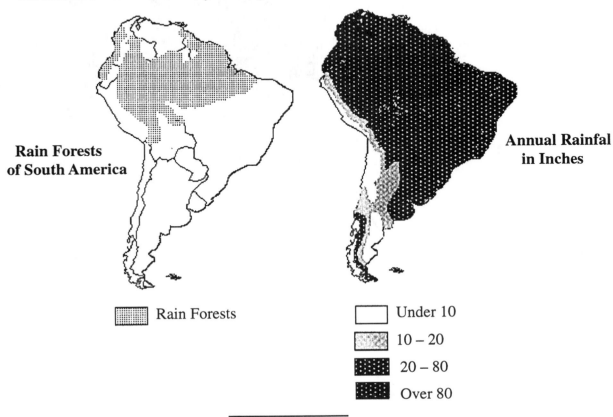

Rain Forests of South America

Annual Rainfal in Inches

▦ Rain Forests

☐ Under 10
▨ 10 – 20
▩ 20 – 80
▦ Over 80

23. Refer to the maps of South American Rainforests and Annual Rainfall to draw a conclusion about what kind of relationship exists between rainfall and the presence of rain forests.

> **23.**
> _____
> _____
> _____
> _____
> _____

Analysis:
Students should be able to describe that the area that is rain forests on one map is the area with the most rainfall in inches.

10. Use maps of North America or the world to identify physical and cultural regions and to show relationships among regions.

This learner outcome examines physical and cultural regions of the world. A physical region is an area characterized by common natural features of the Earth's surface which gives a measure of unity and makes it different from surrounding areas (e.g. a coastal plain or desert). A cultural region is an area characterized by common human features or traits which give a measure of unity and make it different from surrounding areas (e.g. a political unit or land use area).

Students could be asked to identify regions using a map key. They could be asked to use information to describe the characteristics that define a region. Students could also be asked to identify or explain the connections that exist between different regions (physical and/or cultural).

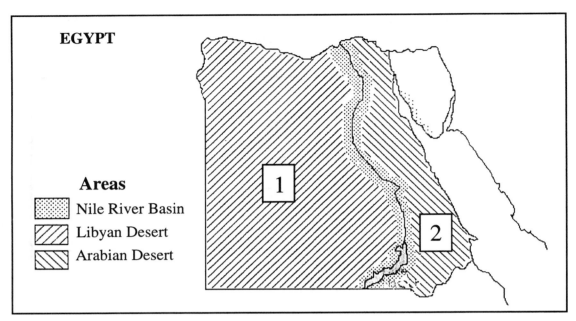

EGYPT

Areas
- Nile River Basin
- Libyan Desert
- Arabian Desert

1

2

24. On the map shown above, how are the regions labeled "1" and "2" alike?

A. Both are part of the Nile River Basin

B. Region "1" is used for growing crops and region "2" is not

C. Both are deserts

D. Both are land locked

Analysis:
By using the key, the students should first locate the striped areas. Both of the striped areas are desert areas. Choice "C" states that both region "1" and region "2" are deserts. Choice "C" is correct.

25. On the map of Egypt shown above, which area of the three different regions would be the most likely place to find farming? Explain why you chose that area?

> **25.**
> _____
> _____
> _____

Analysis:
Answers will vary. Because regions 1 and 2 are both deserts, they are not well-suited for farming. The Nile River provides the water needed for crops. "Nile River Basin" is the most likely place for farming.

✔ **11. Examine instances of contact between people of different regions of the world and determine the reasons for these contacts.**

Increasingly, people from various countries interact with one another because of such factors as trade, politics, religion, and tourism. Items for this outcome ask students to analyze examples of contacts among various groups, societies, and nations. Students could be asked to identify or explain the reasons for contacts between peoples of the world.

Examples:

26. The islands of the Caribbean are beautiful, warm and sunny throughout the entire year. The beaches are sandy and often lined with palm trees and other tropical vegetation. Many Americans travel to these islands during their vacations to enjoy the different cultures as well as the warm climate.

   Which of the following is the reason that Americans and the citizens of these tropical islands have contact with each other?

   A. Politics

   B. Religion

   C. Pessimism

   D. Tourism

Analysis:
Americans visit other places during their vacations for enjoyment, not politics. Therefore, choice "A" is incorrect. As a result of freedom of religion in the United States, Americans have many different religions. The people of the Caribbean islands also have different religions. Choice "B" is also incorrect. Answer choice "C," pessimism, does not make sense here and is incorrect. Choice "D", tourism, is the correct answer.

27. Read the following passage and answer the question that follows:

   Lourdes is a city at the foot of the Pyrenees Mountains in France. Lourdes is famous for its grotto, a small cave where Saint Bernadette claimed to have seen the Virgin Mary several times. Because many people believe that the water in the underground spring has the power to heal, millions of people visit the grotto each year. These pilgrims to the grotto worship in the underground and use the water in hopes that they will be healed.

   People from various countries generally have contact with one another because of trade, politics, religion, or tourism. Which of these is the reason that the people of Lourdes have contact with people from all over the world?

27.

_____

_____

_____

_____

_____

Analysis:
Answers will vary. There are certain key words which the students can use to lead them to the correct answer in this question. These key words are Virgin Mary, pilgrims, and worship. The students should have mentioned religion in their answers.

Teaching Tips for Strand III
After teaching the class how to use latitude and longitude, give them coordinates of a country or major city. Use peer tutoring so that each student learns the skill as quickly as possible.

Have students compare different types of maps to determine a relationship between them. For example, a rainfall map and a map showing forest areas of the world could be used to lead the student to realize that the amount of rainfall is important in the growth of forests. Rainfall and population maps can be compared also. Areas of the world which have very little precipitation also have very low population density.

Using maps of the United States or a specific country, lead students to the realization that most of the major cities are located near bodies of water. Have them determine why this is so. Why are there so few major cities high in the mountains?

Practice using maps showing time zones. Show the students how to determine the difference in time zones between two different cities in the United States. Next, use the same information related to the time zones of the world. Ask students hypothetical questions related to airline arrivals, calling to place catalog orders, calling a relative or friend living in a different time zone. As you discuss different areas, have the students tell what time it is right then in that location.

There are many fun and beneficial ways to teach map reading to student. Have fun!

Strand IV - Decision Making and Resources

Items in the Decision Making and Resources strand assess the students' understanding of factors of production, economic decisions, competition, and trade.

NATURAL RESOURCES

✍ **12. Describe the role of each factor of production in producing a specific good or service and suggest alternative uses for the resources involved.**

This learning outcome requires students to identify how the four basic factors of production (land, labor, capital, and entrepreneurship) are used to produce goods and services. A thorough understanding of the factors of production is required. Land refers to productive resources occurring in nature such as water, soil, trees, and minerals. Labor consists of the talents, training, and skills of people that contribute to the production of goods and services. Capital refers to productive resources made by past human efforts and includes resources such as building, machinery, vehicles, and tools. Entrepreneurship consists of the activities of profit-seeking decision makers who make decisions about which economic activities to undertake and how they should be undertaken.

Test items require students to identify the various uses that can be made of certain resources. Students need to recognize that any given resource can be used in a variety of ways. Students could be asked to provide examples of a given factor or to categorize a set of examples by the factor of production they represent. They could be asked to identify factors of production based on descriptions of the factors. Students could also be asked to suggest a use for a specific factor of production and to provide examples of alternative uses for a factor of production.

Examples:

28. In the manufacture of bubble gum, large mixers are used to combine the rubber, flavorings, sweeteners, and other ingredients. This mixture is then run through a large strainer to remove any impurities. The ingredients are cooked in large vats and then they are rolled out and cut into pieces. All of the various machines used in the manufacture of the bubble gum are examples of which of the following factors of production?

A. Land

B. Labor

C. Capital

D. Government

Analysis:
The correct response is "C" because the "capital" factor of production consists of manufactured items such as buildings, machinery, vehicles, and tools. Land refers to natural resources, or things found in nature. Since machines are not found in nature, "land" can not be the correct response. "Labor "refers to people. Machines are not people. "Labor" is incorrect.

29. Trees are an example of the "land" factor of production. They are used to provide lumber for the construction of our homes. List three alternative uses of the trees.

> **29.**
>
> 1)_____
>
> 2)_____
>
> 3)_____

Analysis:
Answers will vary. The student might have listed items such as paper, pencils, tissues, toilet paper, paper towels, wood carvings, furniture, or other items made from wood. All answers are acceptable as long as the items are made of wood.

✔ **13. Identify the factors that influence:**

  a. Consumer decisions to demand goods or services.
  b. Producer decisions to supply goods or services.

Consumers are people who purchase or use goods and services to satisfy wants or needs. Items for 13a require that the student be able to recognize elements that influence the making of consumer decisions (e.g. price advertising, quality, packaging. Test items could describe a situation and ask students to determine the factor which influenced a consumer decision. Students could also be asked to explain how a particular factor influenced a consumer decision.

Producers are people who are involved in combining land and capital to provide goods and services. Items for 13b require that the student be able to recognize elements that influence the making of producer decisions (e.g. demand, competition, available resources). Test items could describe a situation and ask students to determine the factor which influenced a producer decision. Students could also be asked to explain how a particular factor influenced a producer decision.

Examples:

30. The owner of a local business-supply store was aware that the cost of wood was going to increase within the next year. He realized that that would also lead to an increase in the cost of paper.. He decided that it would be a smart idea to purchase a supply of copier and computer paper before the prices went up.

What factor influenced his decision to purchase the paper now?

A. Holiday and seasonal demands

B. Changes in the cost of materials

C. Fads

D. Lack of rain caused a drought

Analysis:
The paragraph does not mention that the increase in the cost of the wood was related to any seasons or holidays therefore, answer choice "A" is not the appropriate response. Paper is not a fad, so answer choice "C" is also incorrect. We are not given any information of the amount of rain causing a drought, therefore "D" is also incorrect. The cost of the wood would affect the cost of the manufacturing the paper, so choice "B" is correct.

31. Sarah Jackson was interested in purchasing a new·electric skillet for her mother's birthday present. She read advertisements in the newspaper and visited different stores. She found a blue skillet with white flowers for $35.00, a white skillet of a different brand for $29.95, and a silver one made by a third company for $33.95. All of the skillets were the same size and shape. Although she thought that the blue skillet was the prettiest, she decided to buy the white one.

Name two factors Sarah considered before making her purchase.

31.

1)_____

_____

2)_____

_____

Analysis:
Since the skillets were the same size and shape, they were not considered. The correct answers are price and color.

32. Eric Davidson was interested in purchasing a new television set for his living room. He went to the library and read consumer magazines which had tested the different models and brands of televisions sets. Based upon the information he found, he decided to purchase the television with the clearest picture even though it was far more expensive than the other brands.

   Which of the following factors did Eric Davidson use to determine which of the televisions to purchase?

   A. Quality

   B. Price

   C. Packaging

   D. Brand Name

Analysis:
Since Eric chose a television which was far more expensive than the other brands, choice "B," price, is incorrect. Nothing was mentioned about the packaging of the televisions, so the student should not have chosen "C." Although Eric did look at many different brand, he did not choose because the television was a certain brand, so choice "D" is incorrect, too. The paragraph states that "he decided to purchase the television with the clearest picture." This refers to the quality of the television. The correct answer is "A."

14. Identify the factors that determine the degree of competition in a market and describe the impact of competition on a market:

   a. Identify advantages and disadvantages of competition in the marketplace.
   b. Explain the general relationship between supply, demand, and price in a competitive market.

Competition refers to the rivalry between businesses for customers. Such competition has both advantages and disadvantages to both the buyer and the seller, which the student must be able to recognize in items for 14a. Items could present the students with a description of competition in a marketplace and ask them to select a particular advantage or disadvantage of the competition. Students could also be asked to explain the

There is a flow to a competitive market economy in which the connection between the supply of a good, the demand for a good, and the price of that good are closely related. Students could be asked to examine an economic activity and to indicate how the activity affects the relationship between supply, demand, and price.

Examples:

33. A large computer manufacturer developed and began producing a computer which could use any type of computer software and which was faster than any other computer on the market. Immediately, schools and businesses began purchasing the new computer, and people also wanted them for in their homes.

   Explain what happened to the price of these new computers since this was the only company which was manufacturing them.

33.

Analysis:
Answers will vary. Students should mention that the company can set the prices of the computers as high as they want to because no one else is making them and the people want to own them. When only one company produces something that people want, the company is said to have a monopoly on the market. Prices will come down once other companies begin making similar computers and create competition.

34. Village Video, a video rental store in a small town in northeastern Ohio, had been the only place for the residents to rent videos for two years. Then, within a period of only two months, a new video store opened and the local grocery store began renting videos.

What probably happened to the prices of the video rental?

A. The prices went up

B. The prices stayed the same

C. Village Video went out of business

D. The prices went down.

Analysis:
Students should be aware that the prices would go down because the three video rental businesses would have to compete for the business. Competition inspires stores to beat each others price and discount to attrack customers to their store. Answer choice "D" is correct.

15. Use information about global resource distribution to make generalizations about why nations engage in international trade.

Productive resources are unevenly distributed around the world. While one country may have an abundance of a particular resource, another country may be lacking that resource. Trade may develop between the countries involved in this type of situation.

Items for this learning outcome ask students to analyze actual relationships between countries. Students could be asked to recognize the nature of a trading relationship. Students could be asked to explain how nations can resolve a specific problem involving a disparity in resources.

Examples:

35. The coffee which is grown in the country of Colombia, South America is famous throughout the world for its rich flavor. The country also is a producer of petroleum, coal, bananas, and fresh-cut flowers. Unfortunately, the country does not have the capability to manufacture industrial equipment, transportation equipment, or chemicals.

The countries of Europe have combined into a group called the European Union to eliminate trade barriers for the member countries. The members of the European Union export manufactured goods such as machinery and vehicles. They import mostly raw materials and unprocessed goods, including foods. Ecuador is a country in northern South America. Its neighbors are Peru and Colombia. Ecuador's main exports are oil and bananas. They import industrial equipment, transportation equipment, and chemicals.

Of the European Union and the country of Ecuador, with which would Colombia be most likely to trade? Explain your reasoning for the answer that you have chosen.

35.

Analysis:
Answers will vary. Students should mention that Ecuador has the same goods that Colombia has and needs the same manufactured goods and chemicals that Colombia needs. The European Union needs the raw materials that Colombia has, and produces the manufactured goods and chemicals that Colombia needs. Therefore, Colombia would trade with the European Union, not the country of Ecuador.

36. The country of Kuwait, in the Middle East, has vast petroleum deposits. As a result of these deposits, it is a very wealthy country. Unfortunately, it does not have many factories to manufacture electronic products.

The United States produces a little less than half of the petroleum it needs. On the other hand, the United States has the technology and facilities to manufacture many electronic devices.

What can these two countries do to ensure that they will have the goods that they need?

A. They can build more factories

B. They can sell oil to each other

C. They can trade with each other

D. They can sell to other countries

Analysis:
Kuwait has petroleum and needs manufactured electronic goods. The United States has electronic goods, but needs petroleum. Since each has what the other needs, the two countries should trade the goods that they have for the goods which they need. Answer choice "C" is the best and correct answer.

Teaching Tips for Strand IV
Bring to the attention of the students that the four factors of production can be divided into the two which are people (labor and entrepreneurship) and the two which are things (land and capital).

Give the students word sorts and ask them to group them into the four factors of production.

Have the students cut out or draw a product, such as a truck or an item of clothing. After they place this in the center of a large sheet of paper, have them label each of the four corners of the paper with a factor of production. They should then write as many of the four factors needed for the manufacture of that product as possible.

One area in which children, and often even adults, do not have enough knowledge is in the area of alternative uses for resources. It is a valuable use of class time to go over the various uses of resources such as petroleum and wood.

More Teaching Tips for Strand IV

The use of ads is critical in the study of economics. One possible source of ads is the newspaper. Grocery and drug stores often have advertising flyers available to the customers just as you enter the store. Both of these sources are readily available and very inexpensive (or even free!)

Use advertising flyers to compare prices. This is a wonderful way to integrate social studies and math. Conduct a discussion related to the differences in prices and the reasons for the differences. This is a good place to study quality and packaging and their effects upon consumer decisions. Also discuss seasonal and holiday goods and services which appear throughout the year. How do these affect both consumer and producer decisions? How do supply and demand affect consumer and producer decisions?

Combine map studies with shortages and surpluses to lead the students into a discussion of the effect of supply and demand in the marketplace. Teachers who relate the prices of baseball, basketball, and football cards to supply and demand will find that the students will grasp the concept very quickly. This is because so many of them have purchased, sold, and traded cards.

A discussion of students trading books which they have read, CD's, cards, and other items will be a natural introduction into a discussion of nations engaged in international trade. Again, map studies should be included in the discussion. Natural resource maps are particularly important here.

Strand V - Democratic Processes

Items in the Democratic Processes strand assess the student's understanding of the functions and activities of the national government's three branches as well as key characteristics of American democracy. The items will also address the different types of government that exist throughout the world.

✍ **16. Identify the main functions of the executive, legislative, and judicial branches of the United States national government and cite activities related to these functions.**

This learning outcome focuses on the relationship between the activities and functions of branches of the national government. The main function of the legislative branch is to make laws. Items addressing this outcome could use other expressions such as federal legislature or Congress as well as legislative branch. The primary function of the executive branch is to enforce the laws. Items could use other terms such as President or executive agencies as well as executive branch. The primary functions of the judicial branch are to interpret the meaning of the laws and to apply the laws in specific cases. Items could use other expressions such as federal courts or federal court system as well as judicial branch.

There are many activities related to the main functions of the branches of government. Some of these activities include:

- legislative branch - writing proposed legislation and holding committee hearings;

- executive branch - appointing officials and coordinating work of agencies; and

- judicial branch - conducting trials and sentencing convicted persons.

Test items could ask students to identify a main function of a branch of the federal government. Students could be asked to investigate descriptions of activities and identify the branch involved or link the activities with a main function of the branch. Students could also be asked to describe the functions of the branches and to provide examples of related activities.

Examples:

37. What is the function of the judicial branch of government?

    A. Enforce the laws

    B. Interpret the laws

    C. Make the laws

    D. Vote for the laws

Analysis:
Students should be aware that the function of the judicial branch of government is to interpret the meaning of the laws and to apply the laws in specific cases. They should be able to picture the courts conducting trials and/or sentencing people. The correct answer is "B."

38. Writing proposed legislation and holding committee hearings are both activities related the which of the following branches of government?

    A. Legislative

    B. Executive

    C. Judicial

    D. Official

Analysis:
The activities of the executive branch of government include appointing officials and coordinating the work of agencies. The activities of the judicial branch include conducting trials and sentencing convicted persons. Official is not a branch of government. The legislative branch of government is responsible for passing laws. The words "writing proposed legislation" relates to the passing of laws. Answer choice "A" is the correct answer.

17. Interpret how examples of political activity illustrate characteristics of American democracy.

Democracy, as practiced in the United States of America, has certain characteristics. These characteristic include:

- the people serve as the source of the government's authority;
- all citizens have the right and responsibility to vote and influence the decisions of the government;
- the people run the government directly or through elected representatives;
- the powers of government are limited by law; and
- all people have basic rights guaranteed to them by the Constitution.

Items for this outcome will require students to examine applications of these characteristics of American democracy. Students could be presented with an example of a political activity and asked what characteristic of American democracy is being illustrated. They could also be asked to explain how information that is presented relates to the characteristics of American democracy.

Examples:

39. A group of citizens has decided to publish a newspaper to persuade others that the driving age throughout the United States should be raised to twenty-one.

Explain whether they will be permitted to publish the newspaper and how this activity relates to the characteristics of American democracy.

39.

_____

_____

_____

_____

_____

_____

_____

_____

_____

_____

Analysis:
Answers will vary. The student should realize that the group of citizens will be permitted to publish the newspaper because of their right of freedom of speech, one of the basic rights guaranteed to them by the Constitution. They might also state that the power of government is limited, and that the government does not have the right to stop them or pass any laws preventing them from publishing their newspaper.

40. The Congress of the United States can not forbid a person from worshiping according to the religion of his/her choice. Which of the following characteristics of American democracy protects the right of the American people to worship as they choose?

    A. All citizens have the right and responsibility to vote and influence the decisions of the government

    B. The people run the government directly or through elected representatives

    C. All people have basic rights guaranteed to them by the Constitution

    D. The Declaration of Independence grants us many freedoms

Analysis:
Choice "A" does not have anything to do with the right of a person to worship as he/she chooses; it is not the correct response. Choice "B" is NOT a correct answer because the question does not refer to voting or elections. According to the first Amendment of the United States Constitution, the people of the United States are granted freedom of religion. This is one of the basic right guaranteed to the people by the Constitution. The correct answer is "C." The Declaration of Independence gave us freedom from English rule, answer choice "D" is incorrect.

✍ **18. Classify characteristics of government that are typical of a monarchal, democratic, or dictatorial type of government.**

A monarchal type of government is headed by a single leader (a king or queen) whose title is usually hereditary. A democratic type of government is one in which the people hold the power to govern and the rights of the people are guaranteed by law. A dictatorial type of government is headed by one person or a small group of persons holding total power with little responsibility to the people. Power is usually acquired by force or through election in which the people have no choice.

Students could be asked to examine a description of a government and to classify the type of government described. Students could also be asked to identify types of government and to illustrate each type by indicating appropriate characteristics.

Examples:

41. Swaziland, a country in southern Africa, is governed by King Mswati, who followed his father as king. This is an example of which of the following forms of government?

   A. Minority

   B. Dictatorship

   C. Monarchy

   D. Democracy

Analysis:
A monarchal type of government is headed by a single leader, as a king or queen, whose title is usually hereditary. Because the question refers to the title "king" and the position was passed down from the father to the son, the correct answer must be "C."

42. The constitution of Mexico was adopted in 1917. It divides the powers of the government between three branches: the legislative, executive, and judicial. The president and members of the legislature are elected by the people, and the rights of the people are stated in the constitution and the laws.

   The government of Mexico is an example of what type of government?

   42.

   _____

   _____

   _____

Analysis:
The correct response is "democratic" or "democracy". The students should recognize that a government is which the rights of the citizens are guaranteed in the laws and in which the leaders are elected by the people is a democracy.

Teaching Tips for Strand V

The best way to get students to understand the branches of government is to actually have them become involved. Since this is difficult outside of the classroom, set up a government within the class. Although this can be very threatening to the average classroom teacher, it is a valuable learning tool for the children. To carry this out follow these steps:

1. Discuss the need for rules and laws within any setting. This includes home, school, and government.
2. Read the Preamble to the Constitution. Break the class into groups and have each group discuss the meaning of a part of the Preamble and relate that meaning to the class.
3. Discuss purposes for schools. Working together as a whole class, rewrite the Preamble to the Constitution as a Preamble to the Class Constitution.
4. Study the branches of government and the functions of each in the U.S. Constitution. Have the students compare this constitutional government with a dictatorship and a monarchy. Which type of government would they prefer for their class and why?
5. Have the class modify the Constitution to meet the needs of the class. The number of members of Congress and the length of terms are examples of changes which will have to be made. Remind the students that they must always refer back to the purpose of school as stated in the Preamble to the Class Constitution.
6. Study the Bill of Rights. Have the students modify it to meet the needs of the class.
7. Ratify the Constitution and hold elections.
8. As the need for new laws becomes apparent, have the students go through the same procedure as the U.S. government.

This can become as elaborate or as simplistic as you want, but it is a very powerful tool. Remember, you are always in control! You have the ultimate power of veto!

Strand VI - Citizenship Rights and Responsibilities

Analyzing information, examining alternative ways to achieve civic goals, and resolving conflicts are aspects of participatory citizenship that are subjects for this strand. These civic activities help prepare students for their roles as adult citizens. Items in this strand assess the student's understanding of civic issues and goals, conflict resolution, and citizen participation.

19. Analyze information on civic issues by organizing key ideas with their supporting facts.

Citizens need to be able to identify the main idea of a public issue. Items addressing this learning outcome often use statements like those found in local news sources. Students will be asked to examine information and identify the main ideas and/or the supporting facts that are supplied.

Examples:

43. Because a large percentage of the money that Medicare uses for the elderly is spent on nursing homes, the state of Ohio has started a program to help some senior citizens. This program is called PASSPORT, which stands for "Pre-Admission Screening System Providing Options and Resources Today." It costs an average of $28,000.00 each year for a senior citizen to remain in a nursing home. This is about three times what it would cost to keep a person at home, using the PASSPORT program. The purpose of the program is to help senior citizens remain independent and in their homes while, at the same time, saving the state money.

    What is the main idea of the reading selection?

43.

Analysis:
Answers may vary. Every sentence in the paragraph should talk about the main idea. In this reading selection, the first sentence is also the main idea. This sentence states, "Because a large percentage of the money that Medicare uses for the elderly is spent on nursing homes, the state of Ohio has started a new program to help some senior citizens."

44. For years the citizens of the Ohio have been involved in a battle over casino gambling. Those in favor of it say that it will bring in many jobs and millions of dollars in additional tax money. They claim that the majority of the extra money that would come from these taxes would help pay for education. The remainder of the tax money would go to the local government in the area in which the casino is located. Those groups opposed to casino gambling contend that it will damage our families and communities.

   Which of the following is the main idea of the reading selection?

   A. Groups are opposed to casino gambling because it will damage our families and communities

   B. Casino gambling will bring in many jobs and millions of dollars in additional tax money

   C. The citizens of the Ohio have been involved in a battle over the pros and cons of casino gambling for many years

   D. Using casino gambling profits to fund education

Analysis:
Both the sentences given for choice "A" and choice "B" are detail sentences. The student must find the topic which both of those sentences tell about. Answer choice "D" is mentioned in the selection but is not the main idea. In this reading selection, the author is discussing the battle over casino gambling in Ohio. Therefore, the correct answer is choice "C."

45. Farmers in Ohio and many other states are very concerned about urban sprawl, the spreading of cities. They, along with many urban planners, would like for the growth of cities to be controlled. The farmers fear that the cities are attempting to escape the problems of the inner-city by moving industrial and commercial enterprises to the suburbs.

As these changes occur, the percentage of farm land decreases. Eventually, this may endanger the food supply of the United States. They feel that growth should only be permitted in certain predetermined areas around the present cities. One plan calls for the states to legislate land use around cities. Another plan calls for state money to be used to pay farmers to not sell their farm lands to developers. Although, several different solutions are being considered, no decision has been made about how to control this urban sprawl.

Give two detail sentences that support the main idea that Ohio farmers are concerned about urban sprawl.

45.

1) _____

_____

_____

2) _____

_____

_____

Analysis:
Answers will vary. Since the first sentence of the reading selection states the main idea and all of the other sentences are supporting details, any of the sentences except the first can be used as the examples of detail sentences.

20. Identify and analyze alternatives through which civic goals can be achieved and select an appropriate alternative based upon a set of criteria.

A democratic republic depends upon its citizens making reasoned choices when presented with various alternatives to meet civic goals. Items addressing this learning outcome explore ways in which local public issues (e.g. fire hydrant repair, use of public buildings, recycling programs) may be resolved.

Students could be asked to identify an appropriate course of action given a particular set of criteria. The items could ask students to explain how a particular course of action meets a given set of criteria. The items could also ask students to assess the advantages and/or disadvantages of different strategies that could be used to achieve a civic goal.

Examples:

46. The senior citizens in the city of Lemoore were having great difficulty because so many of them were too old and ill to drive. They were not able to get to the grocery store, the drug store, or even to the doctor.

    Realizing the problem, the Lemoore City Council decided to place a levy on the ballot in the next election to pay vans and drivers to transport the citizens.

    Name one advantage and one disadvantage to this solution to the problem.

46.

advantage_____

_____

_____

disadvantage_____

_____

_____

Analysis:
Acceptable responses for advantages can be that everyone will help pay for the cost of the transportation or that the senior citizens will be happier and healthier if this occurs. Acceptable responses for disadvantages might be the fact that many people can not afford higher taxes to pay for the transportation or that the senior citizens are not the only people who need transportation and you could bee discriminating against younger people. All answer responses along these lines are acceptable.

47. A group of citizens was concerned about the children in their public schools not having enough training in computers. They realized that almost all of the jobs of the future would require the use of computers in some way. Fearing that their children would not be prepared for the job market when they finished their education, the citizens decided that some action must be taken. They did some investigating and discovered that the public schools did not have money to purchase any computers or software. They also discovered that because of the speed and power of the new computers which were being manufactured, many businesses and individuals were replacing their old computers with the new models.

The citizen group decided to ask the businesses and individuals to donate their old, slower computers and software to the schools to enable the children to learn computer skills. They also asked for individuals who had computer skills to teach these computer skills to the teachers and to volunteer to help the children with the computers.

Evaluate this strategy to determine whether you feel that it will solve the problem. Make sure that you state your reasons for your answer.

47.

Analysis:
An acceptable response should state that the solution is one that will work because it will not cost the schools any money and the people are getting rid of their old computers and would be willing to give them to the schools to help the children. Other students might state that the proposed solution will not work because people will not want to give their old computers to the schools when they could sell them and use the money themselves. Either response is acceptable as long as the student logically states the reason for the answer.

48. The homeowners on Anna Mae Drive were very upset because of the large potholes on their street. They knew that the street was the responsibility of the local township and not the county or the state. They wished to take some action to have the road repaired. Which of the following would be the best action for the residents to take?

   A. They should write a letter with their concerns to the local government and request that the road be repaired.

   B. They should write to the President and demand that he do something about the problem or they will not vote for him again.

   C. They should build a toll both at the end of the street and charge people who wish to drive down the street. This will generate money for the repair of the street.

   D. They should hire a local paving company to repair the potholes and then send the bill to the township.

Analysis:
Choice "A" is the correct answer. They should write a letter with their concerns to the local government and request that the road be repaired" is the only possible answer. The second choice would be ineffective because the President has nothing to do with local roads and their repair. The third choice is wrong because the residents do not have the legal right to charge a toll on a public street. Answer choice "D" is incorrect. The homeowners can not hire someone to fix something without the permission of the township, city or state that was responsible for it.

21. Identify ways to resolve private and public conflicts based on principles of fairness and justice.

Fairness and justice are basic elements in the civic society of the United States of America and are characteristics of good citizenship. Fairness emphasizes impartially and honesty in dealing with others. Justice stresses following a standard of what is right and proper. Together they enhance the ability of people to respect and to get along with each other.

Items addressing this outcome explore applications of fairness and justice in private and public setting. Students could be given an example of a conflict and asked to identify a fair or just solution. Students could also be asked to explain how a proposed solution to a conflict is either fair or just.

Examples:

49. Woodstock Local School District was running out of money, and the tax-payers had defeated the school levy in the last election. As a result, the board of education decided to cut some athletic programs. They chose to cut cheerleading and girls' basketball. The football team and the boys' basketball team were not affected by the cuts.

Was this a fair and just solution to the problem?
Explain your reasoning as to whether or not it is a fair and just solution.

49.

Analysis:
Answers will vary. If the student stated that the solution is unfair, they might have mentioned that all of the programs which were cut are programs for girls, and that the programs which were not affected are programs for boys. This is gender discrimination. On the other hand, the student might state that the solution is fair because the programs which were cut are programs which cost a lot of money and do not pay for themselves. If the student chose the second answer, and the reasoning is adequate, the student would be given credit.

50. Sam Monroe likes to work on old cars. He often has two or three of them sitting in his drive, but now he has one sitting on the strip of land between his drive and the neighbors drive. Unfortunately, this strip of land belongs to the neighbor, Louise Day. Louise is very upset because the car is sitting on the area where she planted new flower seeds. Louise has asked Sam to move his car to his own property, but he has not done it.

Which of the following would be the best action for Louise to take to resolve this conflict?

A. She should shoot the tires on Sam's car so that Sam knows that she means business.

B. She should offer to pay him $100.00 to move the car so that her flowers will grow.

C. She should ask him to move the car again, and explain that his car was damaging her plants. She should also explain to him that, if he did not move the car, she would have to take legal action against him.

D. She should hire a towing company and have it towed down town.

Analysis:
If Louise shoots the tires on Sam's car, she may be breaking the law. Also, Sam will become angry and the problem will increase rather than be solved. Choice "A" is a poor choice. She should not offer to pay him to move the car because he does not have the right to park the car on her property. This may encourage him to impose on her rights in other ways so that she will pay him once again. Choice "B" is not correct. This leaves choice "C," which is the correct answer.

22. Identify examples of citizen participation in political systems around the world.

The international political scene is composed of monarchies, dictatorships, and democracies-all of which have their unique attributes. Items for this outcome will present scenarios of political activities in various countries (e.g. Great Britain, Uganda, Argentina). Students could be asked to identify or characterize how people participate in the political system of another country.

Examples:

51. In the streets of Baghdad, Iraq, two women are trying to find buyers for the few household goods that they have remaining so that they can have enough money to purchase food. Down the street, a man is robbing his neighbor's house for the same reason. Because the soldiers on the corner are armed and appear to be unfriendly, the venders in the bazaar are afraid. They are aware that one of men who had been selling fruit the week before had been arrested for making comments about the country's leader, Saddam Hussein. They knew that they would never see their friend again; he was now dead. They also realized that if they did or said anything that the government did not like, they would be killed too. So the people remained quiet, except for the growling of their hungry stomachs.

    Which of the following most accurately describes the way in which the people of Iraq participate in the government under the leadership of Saddam Hussein?

    A. The people have no voice in the government. They are not permitted to speak against the government.

    B. The people have the right to vote for all of the government officials and are free to speak against the government.

    C. The people are rich and enjoy good food and beautiful homes. This is because they have voted and helped to make the decisions and laws of Saddam Hussein's government.

    D. The people can only make comments about their leader in private.

Analysis:
The reading selection states that the people of Iraq are afraid of Saddam Hussein's soldiers. They are aware that those who speak against the government are arrested and killed. "B" is incorrect. The selection also tells how people are stealing in order to get money for food. This and the fact that the people are afraid to speak out against the government show that choice "C" is also incorrect. Choice "A" is the only possible answer.

52. As John Bender looked at the billboards along the highway from the airport to his hotel in downtown Mexico City, he instantly realized that a presidential election was approaching. Pictures of the candidate for the Institutional Revolutionary Party, the main political party in Mexico, smiled down at him from the several of the billboards. In his broken Spanish, John asked his taxi driver if he was going to vote in the election.

"Si, senor," replied the driver. "Everyone is Mexico who is eighteen or older is required to vote. We are proud to vote and be a part of the decision-making in this great country."

John thought about this response and wished that everyone in his own country were as concerned with helping to keep the democracy strong by voting.

Explain how the citizens of Mexico participate in the political system of their country.

52.

_____

_____

_____

_____

_____

_____

_____

_____

_____

_____

Analysis:
Answers will vary. Basically, the students should state that the citizens vote and help make decisions for the country. The billboards and the comments of the taxi driver are the keys to the answer.

Teaching Tips for Strand VI

The formation of a class government as presented in the Teaching Tips for Strand V will also help the students meet the objectives in this strand. Discuss why citizen participation is important in the student government.

Studies of local, state, national, and international current events is critical in meeting the objectives for this strand. This can be accomplished through articles in new magazines and the newspapers as well as news programs such as Newsdepth and CNN Headline News. Remember, though, that the news presented on the television will not improve skills in nonfiction reading.

Science

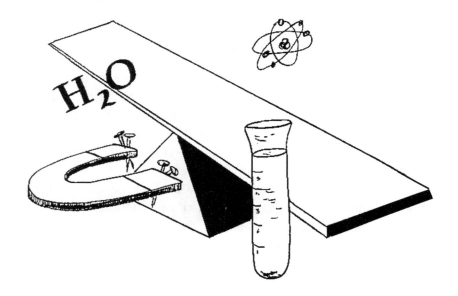

Sixth Grade Proficiency Test: Science

Introduction: Strand and Learning Outcomes

The Sixth Grade Proficiency Test in Science is defined by seventeen learning outcomes which are based on Ohio's Model Competency-Based Science Program. The outcomes were developed by committees made up of Ohio educators and business members through a consensus-building process. These learning outcomes have been identified from the four strands in the State Board adopted model curriculum.

Each form of the proficiency tests includes some embedded field test items. There are five field test items embedded in the science test, making a total of 5 items, only 46 of which are counted to obtain the students' science scores. These field test items give the Ohio Department of Education the potential to continue adding to the item bank for future test forms.

Each form will contain 34 multiple-choice items, 10 short-answer items, and 2 extended-response items. Altogether, the 34 multiple-choice items are worth 34 points, the 10 short-answer items are worth 20 points, and the 2 extended-response items are worth 8 points, making a total of 62 points. In all, the multiple-choice items account for about 55 percent of the total score; short-answer items, 32 percent; and extended-response items, 13 percent.

Science Test Distributions

Type	Number of Items	Total Points	Total Percent
Multiple Choice	34	34	55
Short Answer	10	20	32
Extended Response	2	8	13
TOTAL	46	62	100

Short-answer items might ask students to provide an explanation for an answer they have chosen or a conclusion they have made; make and justify predictions; propose a procedure to resolve an investigation; interpret information from a chart, graph, paragraph, or drawing; explain simple cause-and-effect relationships; provide examples; or explain the cause of certain natural phenomena or observations.

Extended-response items might ask students to evaluate a procedure and point out its flaws and/or suggest improvements; make and justify predictions or conclusions; describe natural processes or interactions among the components of a biological or physical system; make and use inferences in resolving an investigation; and interpret information from a chart, graph, paragraph, or drawing.

Each strand has at least one short-answer or one extended-response item. Since credit for answers is usually based on demonstrated understanding of concepts, students should be encouraged always to explain their answers, when asked to do so. The more understanding that a student demonstrates, the more credit may be assigned.

Science Item Distributions

Strands	Multiple Choice	Short Answer	Extended Response	Totals
I. Nature of Science (5)	8–12	1–3	0–1	9–16
II. Physical Science (5)	8–12	1–3	0–1	9–16
III. Earth and Space Science (3)	5–9	1–3	0–1	6–13
IV. Life Science (4)	6–10	1–3	0–1	7–14
Total Number of Items	34	10	2	46
Total Number of Points	34	20	8	62

( ) = number of learning outcomes

A sixth-grade level of competency in science requires an understanding of scientific processes and inquiry, and application of knowledge, skills, and concepts to problem-solving situations. Test items assess the learning outcomes at one of three levels of science processes. These requirements are: Acquiring Scientific Knowledge, Processing Scientific Knowledge, and Extending Scientific Knowledge.

Acquiring Scientific Knowledge (approximately 30% of the items on the test)
Items in this category test students' proficiency at recalling, observing, collecting, and recording data and information from a variety of sources and representations and performing operations and making measurements to obtain data. This includes the ability to read graphs and tables; take measurements and/or make observations or identifications from graphs, keys, tables, or drawings; and recall fundamental facts, concepts, or relationships.

Processing Scientific Knowledge (approximately 45% of the items on the test)
Items in this category test students' proficiency at organizing, interpreting, manipulating, verifying, summarizing, and reformulating observations and data. This includes the ability to interpret data or information from text, graphs, tables, or drawings; recognize and infer relationships, structure, and/or function among objects or organisms from text, tables, or drawings; and recognize procedures appropriate to a given investigation.

Extending Scientific Knowledge (approximately 25% of the items on the test)
Items in this category test students' proficiency at evaluating, applying, formulating, transforming, and communicating ideas and hypotheses in various contexts. This includes the ability to propose solutions or conclusions based on data from graphs, tables or drawings; determine and/or explain the effectiveness of a procedure; and use spatial, inductive, or deductive reasoning in problem solving.

What are the sixth-grade learning outcomes in science, and what do they mean to students and teacher?
The leaning outcomes define the proficiencies that sixth-grade students are expected to possess and apply as a result of their learning experiences from kindergarten through February of the sixth-grade year. There are seventeen learning outcomes that are grouped into four strands:

- Nature of Science
- Physical Science
- Earth and Space Science
- Life Science

The learning outcomes and related information about test content are provided on the next page and in more detail in the pages that follow.

Science Strands and Learning Outcomes

I. Nature of Science

1. Use a simple key to classify objects, organisms, and/or phenomena.
2. Identify the potential hazards and/or precautions involved in scientific investigations.
3. Make inferences from observation of phenomena and/or events.
4. Identify the positive and/or negative impacts of technology on human activity.
5. Evaluate conclusions based on scientific data.

II. Physical Science

6. Recognize the advantages and/or disadvantages used in the operation of simple technological devices.
7. Predict the influence of the motion of some objects on other objects.
8. Propose and/or evaluate an investigation of simple physical and/or chemical changes.
9. Provide examples of transformation and/or conservation of matter and energy in simple physical systems.
10. Identify simple patterns in physical phenomena.

III. Earth and Space Science

11. Describe simple cycles of the earth, sun, and moon.
12. Identify characteristics and/or patterns in rocks and soil.
13. Demonstrate an understanding of the cycling of resources on earth, such as carbon, nitrogen, and/or water.

IV. Life Science

14. Trace the transmission of energy in a small, simple ecosystem and/or identify the roles of organisms in the energy movement in an ecosystem.
15. Compare and/or contrast the diversity of ways in which living things meet their needs.
16. Analyze behaviors and/or activities that positively or negatively influence human health.
17. Analyze the impacts of human activity on the ecosystems of the earth.

How the Tests are Scored

Each multiple-choice item on the test is worth one point; each short-answer item is worth two points; and each extended-response item is worth four points. Altogether, the thirty-four multiple-choice items are worth 34 points; the ten short-answer items are worth 20 points and the two extended-response items are worth 8 points. The total score is 62 points.

Conventions of writing (sentence structure, word choice, usage, grammar, spelling, and mechanics) will not affect the scoring of short-answer or extended-response items, unless there is interference with the clear communication of ideas.

Short-answer items will be scored on a 2-point scale based on these general guidelines:

A 2-point response shows complete understanding of the concept or task, logical reasoning and conclusions, and correct set-up.

A 1-point response contains minor flaws in reasoning or neglects to address some aspect of the concept or task, or contains a conceptual error.

A 0 is assigned if the response indicates no scientific understanding of the concept or task.

Extended-response items will be scored on a 4-point scale based on these general guidelines:

A 4-point response contains an effective solution. It shows complete understanding of the concept or task and thoroughly addresses the points relevant to the solution. It contains logical reasoning and valid conclusions, communicates effectively and clearly through writing and/or diagrams, and includes adequate and correct set-up when required. It may go beyond the requirements of the item.

A 3-point response contains minor flaws. Although it indicates an understanding of the concept or task, communicates adequately through writing and/or diagrams, and generally reaches some conclusions, it contains minor flaws in reasoning and/or knowledge, or neglects to address some aspect of the item.

A 2-point response indicates gaps in understanding and/or execution. It contains some combination of the following flaws: an incomplete understanding of the concept or task, failure to address some points relevant to the solution, faulty reasoning, weak conclusions, unclear communication in writing and/or diagrams, or a poor understanding of relevant scientific procedures or concepts.

A 1-point response indicates gaps in understanding and/or execution. It contains some combination of the following flaws: little understanding of the concept or task, failure to address most aspects of the item or solution, major flaws in reasoning that led to invalid conclusions, a definite lack of understanding of relevant scientific procedures or concepts, or it omits significant parts of the item and solution or response.

0 Points - This score is assigned if the response indicates no understanding of the concept or task.

Facts from the Sixth Grade Proficiency Field Test

Test items based on the science learning outcomes were field tested. While the number of students responding to each test item was limited, some general observations regarding student achievement can be made. The summary below is based upon review of student performance on multiple-choice items only.

- Student performance was highest on multiple-choice items measuring outcomes 2, 5, 7, and 16. Throughout this chapter, the symbol, "✔," will represent these learning outcomes.
- Student performance was lowest on multiple-choice items measuring outcomes 9, 10,11, and 13. Throughout this chapter, the symbol, "✍," will represent these learning outcomes.

> **Key:**
> ✍ = Learning outcomes where student performance was LOW on field testing
> ✔ = Learning outcomes where student performance was HIGH on field testing

Additional Information Concerning the Learning Outcomes

In general, the science portion of the sixth-grade proficiency tests is designed to assess long-term student learning-problem solving and thinking skills and is not limited to rote knowledge and facts.

This type of learning, according to the State Board adopted model program, is best achieved through hands-on experience, the use of authentic science text, and long-term activities during which students ask questions, collect and analyze data, and make and explain decisions. In this view of science, students' reasons and processes to find answers are more important than their memory of facts. The more experience students have with collecting and analyzing data and information, and justifying their answers, the better prepared students will be.

The learning outcomes reflect the world view of science as both a body of knowledge and a process for producing or obtaining knowledge; they also reflect the "hands-on, minds-on, inquiry-based" approach to science. Though manipulatives are not part of the science test, items with pictorial representations are frequent, and outcomes are assessed in multiple formats that address different learning styles.

About the Science Learning Outcomes

The following pages will review all the Strands and present simulated proficiency test questions as samples. The student workbook has the same sample test questions.

Strand I - Nature of Science

Built into this science test is an
assessment of students' abilities and
thinking habits in investigating science
ideas. The five outcomes in this strand
overlap traditional science units and
each other and should therefore be
reinforced throughout the science
curriculum – that is, should be taught
in context – at every grade level.

1. Use a simple key to classify objects, organisms, and/or phenomena.

This outcome tests students' ability to classify or identify things using a simple identification key (dichotomous key, flow chart, key in table or chart format). This can mean using a key to identify which one of a set of objects can be identified by name or as belonging to a particular group; using a key or flow chart to separate large groups of objects into smaller groups; or analyzing a key to determine what characteristic always distinguishes one group, organism, or object from another. Dichotomous keys have two divisions or choices at each step and are typically based on an "either - or" classification system – either something has a particular characteristic or it doesn't.

The use of a dichotomous key relies on the student's ability to make clear observations and follow a logical sequence. Students should know how to proceed through a dichotomous key step-by-step, from the beginning, to identify a single unknown object or organism. Students should also be able to go to an object or organism identified in the key, and proceed "backward" thoroughly, step-by-step, to gather or identify all distinguishing characteristics of an object or organism. Important to such processes are practice in following written directions and in reading keys such as those found in many plant and animal "field guide" series.

Any illustrations in test items will clearly display all relevant key characteristics needed to distinguish groups or objects from one another.

Simulated proficiency test items that cover this learning outcome are in the examples on the next page.

Examples:

```
■■■■■■■■■■■■■■■■■■■■■■■■
■           What Animal Is It?        ■
■  1. If only the toes and the center pad of  ■
■     the paw shows, go to number 3.      ■
■  2. If the entire paw shows, go to number 5. ■
■  3. If the claws can be seen at the front of ■
■     the toe pads, go to number 8.       ■
■  4. If no claws can be seen at the front of  ■
■     the toe pads, go to number 7.       ■
■  5. If the claws can be seen at the front of ■
■     the toe pads, go to number 9.       ■
■  6. If no claws can be seen at the front of  ■
■     the toe pads and there are marks between ■
■     the toes of the back feet, go to number 10.■
■  7. This animal is a weasel.            ■
■  8. This animal is a red fox.           ■
■  9. This animal is a red squirrel.      ■
■ 10. This animal is a beaver.            ■
■■■■■■■■■■■■■■■■■■■■■■■■
```

1. Eric found the tracks shown above in a field near his house. Use the key to determine what animal made the tracks. Which of the following animals made the tracks?

   A. Weasel

   B. Red fox

   C. Red squirrel

   D. Beaver

Analysis:
Since the entire paw shows, the student should have then gone to number 5. Number 5 indicates that, if the claws show, the student is to go to number 9. Since the claws do show, the student should read in number 9 that the animal is a red squirrel or "C."

Cold-Blooded Animals

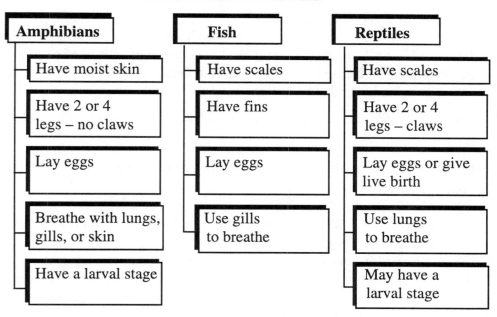

Amphibians	Fish	Reptiles
Have moist skin	Have scales	Have scales
Have 2 or 4 legs – no claws	Have fins	Have 2 or 4 legs – claws
Lay eggs	Lay eggs	Lay eggs or give live birth
Breathe with lungs, gills, or skin	Use gills to breathe	Use lungs to breathe
Have a larval stage		May have a larval stage

2. The chart above shows the characteristics of cold-blooded animals.

First, name two characteristics of reptiles?

Second, compare and contrast fish and amphibians.

2.

1) _____

_____

2) _____

_____

_____

Analysis:
1) By finding the section of the chart which has the heading "reptiles," the student merely has to read the information below the heading. Any two of the following are acceptable answers: they have scales, they have two to four legs with claws, they lay eggs or give live birth, they use lungs to breathe, and they may have a larval stage.
2) Answers will vary. Students might mention that fish and amphibians are alike because they both are cold-blooded and lay eggs. They are sometimes alike because some amphibians breathe through gills like fish. Amphibians are different than fish because fish have scales and amphibians have moist skin.

> **Teaching Tips for Learning Outcome #1**
> As the students learn new information, have them both read and create keys, flow charts, tables or charts. Flow charts and tables do not have to be limited to scientific subjects. They can also be used to help children understand how to use possessives or how to perform a mathematical operation.

✔ **2. Identify the potential hazards and/or precautions involved in scientific investigations.**

This outcome focuses on identifying basic safety measures (or precautions); explaining the reasons for existing precautions or safety measures; identifying possible dangers to human safety (hazards), equipment or materials, and/or natural ecosystems; and predicting potential hazards or bad results from circumstances. Safety measures addressed in items may include the following: fire, glassware, eye and face, chemical, electrical, and sharps safety; dress code; and clean-up.

Examples:

3. When using chemicals during scientific investigations, one should always do which of the following:

   A. Wear safety goggles

   B. Chill the chemicals before conducting the investigation

   C. Put a small piece of chalk into the chemicals to see what will happen

   D. Make sure that the lids are on the bottles at all times

Analysis:
The correct response is choice "A" because of the fact that chemicals could splash into one's eyes if they are not protected. The other answer choices are not necessarily something that should always be done.

4. During their study of electricity, the students in Mrs. McArthy's fifth-grade class were each given three wires, two dry cell batteries, and two light bulbs and told to use only the materials which they had been given to investigate the way to make the light bulbs light up with the brightest light. Todd was not satisfied with the light that he was getting from his equipment. He decided that he would stick one of the wires into the wall socket instead of using the second battery. Explain what safety rules Todd broke.

4.

_____

_____

_____

_____

_____

_____

_____

_____

_____

Analysis:
Answers will vary. Students should have mentioned that Todd should have followed the teacher's instructions. Next, they should have stated that nothing should ever be inserted into electrical sockets except plugs which are designed for those sockets. They might also have mentioned that if Todd wished to try something different, he should have spoken with the teacher first.

Teaching Tip for Learning Outcome #2

Discuss safety precautions at the beginning of each investigation or class. During the class, reinforce safety rules which are being practiced and correct those which are not. "You have the right of choice, but not of consequence." This statement, which is the motto of the Tough Love organization, is one which we should teach each and every child. Students should be taught to consider the possible results of each of their actions. If they are trained to consider possible outcomes, safety precautions will become a priority.

3. Make inferences from observation of phenomena and/or events.

Students should be able to identify inferences that are consistent with data or observations; use known characteristics of plants or animals or their remains to infer or extrapolate other characteristics of those plants or animals (or remains); and use inductive and deductive reasoning with visual representations, charts, text, or graphs in items, to make or identify correct inferences. For instance, if an adult animal has gills, an inference can be made that the animal lives in an aquatic environment.

By the sixth grade, students should clearly understand the difference between an inference and an observation, and should be making inferences about the meaning of observations they (or others) have made, as well as using these inferences to design questions and simple tests to verify their inferences.

Examples:

5. Sherry Gill observed hummingbirds flying around the red flowers at the side of her house. She also noticed that he hummingbird feeders in the local garden store were all red.

   What inferences could she make about hummingbirds?

   5.
   _____
   _____
   _____
   _____
   _____

Analysis:
Answers will vary. Students may answer that the hummingbirds are attracted to red or that they like the color red.

6. An important skill which scientists must use is the ability to distinguish between observations and inferences. Which of the following is an inference?

   A. The spider was wrapping silk around the insect.

   B. The frog is a bright orange color, so it must be poisonous.

   C. The elephant used its trunk to pick up clumps of hay.

   D. The bee had a yellow powder on its wings.

Analysis:
Answer choices "A," "C," and "D" are descriptions of what the person sees. Answer choice "B" takes the description one further step and states that since the frog is bright orange, it must be poisonous. This is an inference. "B" is the correct answer.

7. In a local park scientists have found limestone deposits containing fossils of life forms which had fins and gills. Dating of the rock layers indicated that the fossils were thousands of years old. In the layers of the sedimentary rock they also found traces of shells which appeared to be similar to those found along the ocean today.

   What inference can be made about what the area was like thousands of years ago? Explain your answer.

   7.
   _____
   _____
   _____
   _____
   _____
   _____
   _____
   _____
   _____
   _____

Analysis:
Answers will vary. The student should have inferred that the area was once part of a body of water, perhaps a river, lake, or ocean. The clues in the reading selection were the mention of fossils of life forms which had fins and gills and the traces of shells. The sedimentary rock is another clue because sedimentary rocks are formed in water.

Teaching Tips for Learning Outcome #3

During the course of the students' investigations, have them list their observations. Discuss with them the difference between an observation and an inference.

---

4. Identify the positive and/or negative impacts of technology on human activity.

Technology is defined as the application or use of scientific knowledge or inventions; human activity is interpreted to mean "human life activities" broadly, so topics addressed range from health tests and regulations to environmental regulations and issues that impact humans, to procurement of "crucial resources" such as water, food, shelter, etc. Students should be able to identify or deduce from text and/or prior knowledge the positive or negative impacts of a particular technology on human life activities.

Students should be aware that there are few human activities in which impacts are entirely positive or entirely negative. In their explorations and asking of questions, students should have frequent experience in discussing both sides of human activities. From these discussions and explorations, students should be able to make decisions and provide written justification of their decisions.

Examples:

8. In 1928 Sir Alexander Fleming, a British scientist, was conducting re-search on influenza when he noticed that mold in one of his culture plates was killing the bacteria. This led to his development of penicillin, a drug which is still used today to fight bacteria. Which of the following is one of the impacts of the use of penicillin today?

   A. All of the bacteria in the world is dead

   B. More people are dying

   C. Fewer people are dying

   D. Influenza is killing the bacteria

Analysis:
Choice "A" is incorrect, because there is still much bacteria throughout the world today. Therefore, students should be able to eliminate "A" right away. Since choices "B" and "C" are opposites, one of them is probably the wrong answer. Choice "B" is incorrect because penicillin generally helps people get well, not die. Answer choice "D" is also incorrect because the question states that the "mold . . . was killing the bacteria." Therefore "D" can be eliminated. The correct choice is "C" because penicillin is a commonly used medicine which is used to destroy bacteria. If the student did not know the answer, he could have figured it out through a process of elimination.

9. The development of the combustion engine has greatly improved transportation throughout the world. Trucks can move raw materials to market faster, and the finished produced can be rushed to the consumer. People are able to travel longer distances in shorter periods of time, and are able to see more of the world. These are some of the advantages of the use of combustion engines. What are some disadvantages?

9.

Analysis:
Answers will vary. Sample responses might include: The combustion engine uses gasoline and this is using up the worlds supply of oil. The exhaust from the cars, trucks, and other machines which use the engine is causing air pollution. The increasing search for and finding of oil have caused petroleum spills which have destroyed many plants and animals, as well as cause damage to the environment. The drilling of wells and petroleum platforms in the oceans can cause damage to the land or sea and can catch fire which would cause a waste of the oil and, because of the danger, could take lives.

10. John Wesley Hyatt invented the first plastic around 1860 when a com pany which manufactured billiard and pool balls offered a $10,000 prize for a substitute for natural ivory. Since that time, the plastics industry has grown tremendously. Although plastics are difficult to dispose of in an environmently-friendly manner, they have many advantages.

Name two advantages of the use of plastics in the manufacture of various products.

10.

1)_____

_____

2)_____

_____

Analysis:
Answers will vary. Among the acceptable answers are that plastics are strong, lightweight, waterproof, inexpensive, durable, and sometimes recyclable.

Teaching Tips for Learning Outcome #4

Very few events are totally positive or totally negative. Challenge students to look at various events taken from the news, the school, their own lives, or hypothetical situations. They should be able to come up with a positive outcome for negative events and a negative outcome for positive events.

Create a large bulletin board which contains both a double-tier time line and a map of the world. As students learn new material, have them relate it to the time line and the map. Ask the students to brainstorm ways in which these events affected the world.

Create T-charts with the students, showing positive and negative effects of various forms of technology.

✔ **5. Evaluate conclusions based on scientific data.**

This outcome tests students' abilities to identify or evaluate conclusions from graphs, tables, charts, and/or text information; make conclusions about relationships from data; summarize or identify summaries of data from charts, tables, or graphs; and analyze whether conclusions about test results can be made based on previous test results and known changes to a test set-up. Since scientific data are often presented in graph or table format, items include maps, graphs, or tables (and keys) of data for analysis; item content can range from weather data to physical characteristics of substances (melting point, boiling point) to statistics about populations or natural disasters.

Students should be able to interpret data and make conclusions and decisions based on the data that are critical. Also, since learning in science is often linked to finding flaws in data or conclusions, students should be practiced in relying on their own data (or others' data) and examining their conclusions for flaws, as well as in examining data for flaws. Students should be practiced in making observations about data, and in distinguishing inferences from observations.

Examples:

	Fertilized Plants		**Unfertilized Plants**	
	Height	Appearance	Height	Appearance
Day 6	2 cm	Plants are just coming through soil	2 cm	Plants are just coming through soil
Day 12	8 cm	Plants appear to be green and healthy	8 cm	Plants are green, but not as dark as the other group
Day 20	20 cm	Plants appear to be green and healthy	20 cm	Plants have a purple cast
Day 26	50 cm	Plants appear to be green and healthy	65 cm	Color is pale green with a purple cast
Day 32	65 cm	Plants appear to be green and healthy	65 cm	Color is pale yellow-green; looks sickly

11. Sam North wanted to conduct an experiment on the effects of fertilizer on corn. He purchased a bag of potting soil at a local garden store and placed soil into six identical pots. He then planted a corn seeds into each pot. He placed the six pots under growing lights, watered them. He then added 12-12-12 fertilizer to three of the pots. After six days, the plants began to emerge from the soil. Every several days he observed and measured the height of the plants and recorded the data in his scientific journal. The table which he made to show the height of the plants is shown above.

How did the fertilizer affect the corn plants?

11.

_____

_____

_____

_____

_____

_____

_____

_____

Analysis:
Answers will vary. The students should have referred to the table to arrive at their answer. The table shows that the height of the plants was the same for each day that they were observed. By comparing the columns labeled "Appearance" the students should see that the plants which were fertilized remained green and healthy. The unfertilized plants began to get a purple cast, were not as deep green, and eventually turned a yellow-green. They also began to look sickly. Using this information, the students should have concluded that the fertilizer helped the corn.

	Group 1	Group 2	Group 3
Trial 1	55 cm	83 cm	56 cm
Trial 2	54 cm	95 cm	54 cm
Trial 3	55 cm	91 cm	55 cm
Average	54.6 cm	89.7 cm	55 cm

12. Three groups of students in Mr. Wood's sixth-grade Science class were conducting an investigation to determine the relationship between the height of a ramp and the distance which a small toy car would travel from the top of the the ramp until coming to rest. Mr. Wood gave each group identical materials to use for the ramps, identical toy cars and centimeter rulers. The classroom floor was sectioned off so that each group had adequate room in which to conduct their investigation. After three trials with the ramp elevated to five centimeters on one side, the students were repeat the experiment, each time raising the end of the ramp five centimeters and conducting three trials at that height.

The results of each group's trials with the end of the ramp elevated to five centimeters are shown above.

   a) Based upon the data given, what you would conclude about whether the investigation is flawed or not?

   b) State your reasons for your conclusion.

12.

a) _____

b) _____

_____

_____

_____

Analysis:

Answers will vary. The students should recognize that the investigation is flawed. Sample responses for the reasons could be: The measurements for group two are very different from those given for groups one and three. Since all of the materials used by the students in conducting the investigation were identical, the measurements should have been quite close to each other. Group 2 had measurements that were much higher.

13. Dr. Johnson, a researcher for a drug company, was conducting experiments on a new drug which was supposed to prevent breast cancer. He took twenty-one mice and divided them into three groups. After injecting them with breast cancer cells, he placed all of the mice in identical environments. He gave the first group of mice no medication at all. He gave the second group a medication which looked identical to the cancer medication yet was designed to have no affect on the mice or the cancer. The third group of mice received the cancer medication. The assistants who were giving the medications did not know which animals were actually receiving the cancer medication.

Which of the following is a true statement about the experiment?

A. The experiment is flawed because all of the mice should have been given the same medication

B. The experiment is flawed because the assistants should have been told which animal was being given the cancer medication

C. The mice were not given enough medicine

D. The experiment is not flawed

Analysis:
The correct answer is "D." The well-designed experiment should have both a control group and an experimental group. The assistants were not told which of the mice were receiving the cancer medication so that they could not unconsciously treat the mice differently or do anything which would affect the outcome of the experiment.

Teaching Tips for Learning Outcome #5

This outcome relates to higher-order thinking skills. As the students work through material or investigations, ask them to draw conclusions and state reasons for their conclusions.

Look for topics in the news which you can bring into the classroom for students to discuss. The topics may or may not be related to science. The importance of this outcome is having children learn to use observations, facts, and reasoning.

Strand II - Physical Science

Commonly thought of as physics and chemistry, physical science for this level is limited to physical principles that can be observed and explored, and the inferences that can be made, based on concrete experiences that can be observed without complicated instrumentation or theories.

6. Recognize the advantages and/or disadvantages used in the operation of simple technological devices.

Advantages and/or disadvantages to the user refers broadly to a device's mechanical advantage, or the ratio of the output force produced by a machine to the applied input force. The concept of mechanical advantage, rather that the term itself, is tested. For instance, an item might test student's ability to recognize an advantage of using a ramp to slide a heavy box into a truck (less force is needed to move the object) in comparison with lifting the box straight up off the ground, as well as a disadvantage of using a ramp (the box must be moved through a greater distance). Simple technological devices are straightforward, mostly one-function devices that are real-life application of the six basic simple machines (lever, wedge, pulley, wheel and axle, inclined plane, and screw): ramps, pliers, scissors, wheelbarrows, etc.

Students should understand that simple machines do not reduce work, but they commonly make an action less effort for people. Students should also know that the principle "you don't get something for nothing" applies to simple machines: when a machine is used and the effort gets easier, something else (like speed, or the distance of the effort) is sacrificed. Students should be practiced at discussing the advantages and disadvantages of any simple technological device as they explore its functions and uses in a real-world context.

Examples:

14. Jason Walthum use the wheelbarrow shown above to move a heavy box from his garage to the barn behind his house. Which of the following is a true statement about what is occurring as he uses the wheelbarrow to move the box?

A. The wheelbarrow is a simple machine that reduces work

B. The wheelbarrow is a simple machine that reduces the effort for the person using it

C. The wheelbarrow is a simple machine that is made of a lever and a pulley

D. The wheelbarrow is a complex machine that is very complicated to use

Analysis:
A simple machine does not reduce work. Choice "A" is incorrect, but could be a commonly picked wrong answer. There is no pulley in the wheelbarrow, so choice "C" is incorrect. The wheelbarrow is not a complex machine, so answer choice "D" is incorrect. The wheelbarrow is a simple machine that reduces the effort to complete an action. Choice "B" is the correct answer choice.

15. Michael Allen's mother was getting older, and he could not be in Georgia, where she lived, to help her with her yard work. He purchased the hose reel shown on the previous page as a gift for her, but he was concerned that the handle would be too difficult for her to turn. He decided to adapt the length of the handle so that it would be easier for her to turn.

Should he make the handle longer or shorter to make it easier for her to turn? Explain how you arrived at your answer.

15.

_____

_____

_____

_____

_____

_____

_____

_____

_____

_____

Analysis:
Answers will vary. For the first part of the question, the student should have stated that he should make the handle longer. For the second part of the question, the student should state that the shorter the handle is, the harder it is to turn.

Teaching Tips for Learning Outcome #6
For this outcome, students need hands-on experiences with simple machines. As they use and study the machines, discuss with the students what disadvantages there are with the use of each machine.

Encarta Multimedia Encyclopedia has animations which show how some simple machines work. These are clearly understood by the students.

More Teaching Tips for Learning Outcome #6

Allowing the children to use the tools will help them to see how they work. A ruler, a block and a book will make a lever and fulcrum. A board can be used as an inclined plane. A small pulley can be purchased very inexpensively at a hardware store.

After the students have learned about each of the simple machines, challenge them to find the simple machines that are part of other things. For example, a bicycle is made of several simple machines. The wheel and axle are obvious to most of the children, but the lever on the hand brakes may not be so obvious.

David Macaulay's book, The Way Things Work, and the coordinating CD-ROM from Dorling Kindersley both show how simple machines are a part of most of the more complex items which we use today.

✔ **7. Predict the influence of the motion of some objects on other objects.**

Students should have a practical understanding of Newton's laws of motion: (1) an object will remain at rest or in uniform motion unless acted on by an outside force; (2) when a force acts on an object, it changes the momentum of that object, and this change is proportional to the applied force and the time that it acts on the object; and (3) every action (force) is accompanied by an equal and opposite reaction (force). Students should be able to predict the motion of objects thrown or released by people who are in motion; identify or describe how the motion of one object can affect the motion of other objects; and identify or describe the apparent forces or impacts people can feel as a result of a change in an object's motion. For instance, when an elevator begins descending rapidly, the people in it will have a slight " floating" sensation, and their feet will press more lightly against the elevator floor (since people were at rest, their bodies tend to remain at rest even when the car moves downward). Another example would be when a rowboat is traveling from north directly south, a strong wind from the west would tend to change the boat's direction to the southeast.

Among the fundamental concepts students should understand are that things move only when something moves them; they keep moving until something stops them; the harder something is pushed, the faster it goes; and the more massive something is, the harder it is to move. Students who can best apply those concepts are those who have observed many moving things and investigated why they moved and why they may have stopped.

Examples:

16. Monica was riding her bike down a long hill when suddenly her tire hit a large stone. As the bike slowed, she went over the handlebars of the bike and landed on the street. Which of the following caused her to go over the handlebars?

A. The stone was bigger than the bike

B. The hill was so steep that it caused her to go over the handlebars

C. Her body had more weight on the top so that she tended to go over the handlebars when she rode on hills

D. Her body was traveling at a constant speed until the bike hit the stone. Although the bike slowed, her body tended to stay at that constant speed, throwing her over the handlebars

Analysis:
Answer choice "A" is incorrect, the question states that the stone was large but doesn't say it was bigger than the bike. Choice "B" is a poor choice because the steepness of the hill would not have caused her to go over the handlebars. Choice "C" is also incorrect because a person being top-heavy would not have caused them to go over the handlebars. This question is about the application of Newton's law of motion which states that when an object will remain at rest or in uniform motion unless another force acts upon it. Choice "D" is correct.

17. Mrs. Church's sixth-grade class was conducting an investigation on the relationship between certain surfaces and the distance which a small rubber ball would travel from the top of a ramp until coming to rest.

What would explain the difference in the distance that the ball travels over each surface?

17.

_____

_____

_____

_____

_____

Analysis:

Answers will vary. Students might state that the surfaces which are the smoothest allow the ball to travel the farthest. The most sophisticated answer, and one which would earn the maximum number of points, would mention that a force, friction, is acting on the ball and slowing its movement.

18. Four-year-old Jennifer Yerkey wanted to hold the balloon that her father was blowing up for her. As she tried to take the balloon from his hand, the balloon escaped.

a) Where did the balloon go?

b) What caused the balloon to move in that direction?

18.

a)_____

_____

b)_____

_____

Analysis:

Answers will vary. In the first part of the question, the students should state that the balloon will go straight up. In the second part of the question, the students should state that for every action there is an equal and opposite reaction. As the air goes out of the balloon, the balloon goes in the opposite direction.

Teaching Tips For Learning Outcome #7

Once again, the students learn this best if they actually use hands-on activities. Have the students make "sleds" from manila folders or other light-weight cardboard. Tell them to make the sleds go without touching or using anything else to touch them. Through guided questioning techniques, have them arrive at the conclusion that something has to make them begin their movement. Next, have the students propel the sled by using air pressure (an inflated balloon or an air pump would work) over various surfaces and have them record the distances. Ask them to compare the distances and determine why the sled traveled farther over some surfaces than others. For another activity the students could place small objects into the sled to determine whether the distance is affected.

Teach the students the game of marbles and have them guess where the marble which they hit will go. This can also be combined with interesting information about the popularity of the game of marbles in the United States years ago.

8. Propose and/or evaluate an investigation of simple physical and/or chemical changes.

This outcome tests students' abilities to distinguish between or identify changes that are physical changes only and changes that involve chemical changes; identify or describe procedures that would resolve investigations of physical and/or chemical changes, identify or describe the rate or nature of physical and/or chemical changes that are taking place; and evaluate how well a particular investigation or procedure measures physical and/or chemical changes. For test purposes, simple means observable. A physical change involves a change in the size, shape (configuration), or state of matter of a substance, without its producing or becoming a new substance, whereas a chemical change results in a permanent change in properties.

Simple chemical changes are very difficult to reverse, involve some kind of change in the properties of the material, and often give off heat on their own. Simple physical changes are more easily reversible and do not involve permanent changes in the properties of a material. Students should examine the characteristics of something before and after an event and use this type of analysis to decide whether a change is chemical or physical. Many common devices such as chemical "cold packs" or "heat packs" are in the range of student experience for this outcome, as are the effects of physical changes caused by water and chemical changes involving water and other common elements.

Examples:

19. Both physical and chemical changes occur during erosion. Which of the following is an example of a chemical change?

    A. During periods of extreme heat, the top layers of rock expands and cracks away from the layers underneath

    B. Fluctuating changes in temperatures from heat and cold crack rocks

    C. The pressure created by trees growing and putting pressure on rocks breaks the rock

    D. Acid rain falls on granite and changes it into clay

Analysis:
Students must be able to find the answer choice which discribes a chemical change as well as a physical change. Only answer choice "D" has both. The granite and the acid rain react together to form a new substance. In the other examples, the rocks are broken but new, chemically different substances are not formed. The correct answer is "D".

20. Chastity Freeman decided to make a snack to take to the football game on Friday night. She mixed corn cereal, peanuts and pretzels in a large bowl.

    Is this an example of a physical or chemical change?

20.

Analysis:
Students need to understand that physical change involves a change in the size, shape, or state of matter of a substance, without its producing or becoming a new substance, whereas a chemical change results in a permanent change in properties. The snack did not form a chemically different substance because each of the individual ingredients can still be seen in the snack after they have been mixed together. Simple physical changes are more easily reversible and do not involve permanent changes in the properties of a material. Since it is possible to separate each of the ingredients, the correct answer is "physical change."

21. Logs burning is an example of a chemical change. Give an example of a way that logs could undergo physical change.

21.

_____

_____

_____

_____

_____

Analysis:
Answers will vary. Among the possible answers, students might have mentioned splitting the logs, carving, sawing, chipping, or nailing them together. Also correct would be making the logs into lumber.

Teaching Tips for Learning Outcome #8

A demonstration by the teacher of a match burning will show the class the classic example of a chemical change. Have the students study the match and write their observations before and after the burning.

Cooking is an excellent way of showing physical and chemical changes. It can be as simple as pouring peanuts and M & M's together for an example of physical change or making cookies as an example of chemical change.

9. Provide examples of transformation and/or conservation of matter and energy in simple physical systems

Students should be able to identify what type of energy transformation is occurring in a situation; identify or give an example (situation) of energy being transformed from one specific form to another; describe or identify something that performs a particular transformation of energy; and identify or describe how energy is conserved in a situation, or how matter can be converted into other matter plus energy (e.g., combustion), or how energy can be used in converting matter (e.g., photosynthesis). Students should have a basic understanding of potential and kinetic energy; the five main forms of energy (electrical, mechanical, chemical, thermal [heat], and nuclear); various types of energy conversions, one form to another; conversions of matter to energy, and energy to matter; and the laws of conservation of matter and energy.

In any system, energy must be accounted for, and students should be practiced in explaining how the energy in a given system has changed through an event. Because energy can be a difficult and abstract concept for students, students should be accustomed to discussing and describing familiar energy movements in their surroundings, such as those involved with a light bulb or a cup of hot tea. Specific names for the types of energy are learned as students use them in discussions and explanations.

Examples:

22. Green plants convert the heat energy of the sun into this type of energy.

   A. Chemical

   B. Electrical

   C. Nuclear

   D. Physical

Analysis:
"A" is the right answer. The sun's energy is chemically altered during the process of photosynthesis. In this process water and carbon dioxide combine to form glucose. The sun's energy is changed into the chemical bonds in the glucose. Thus, the heat energy is converted into chemical energy. Neither electrical nor nuclear energy are a part of this process.

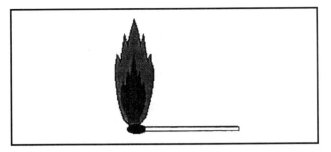

23. The picture shown above shows a match burning. In this illustration, the energy in the match is changing from potential energy into two other forms of energy. Name the two types of energy forms after lighting the match.

23.

    (1) _____ Energy, and

    (2) _____ Energy.

Analysis:
Before burning, the match has chemicals on the end which store chemical energy. When the match is lit, the student can feel the heat given off and see the light. Therefore, the correct answers are light energy and heat energy.

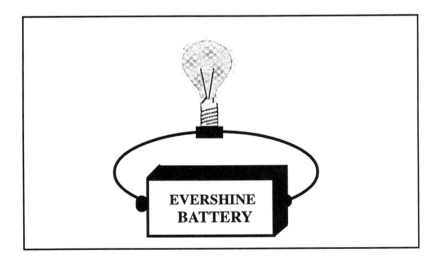

24. In the illustration shown above, energy is stored and converted. Describe the picture. Then, explain how and where the energy is stored and converted.

24.

_____

_____

_____

_____

_____

_____

_____

_____

Analysis:

Answers will vary. Students should mention the following facts. Chemical energy is being stored in the battery. When the wires are connected and the circuit is complete, the chemical energy in the battery is converted into electrical energy. In the light bulb it is converted into light energy and heat energy.

Teaching Tips for Learning Outcome #9

As the children study energy, demonstrate to them how the chemical energy which is stored in a match tip is converted to light energy and heat energy when the match is lit.

Brainstorm with the students different ways in which energy is transformed from one form to another.

Reinforce this concept of conservation of energy during the study of plants. Explain to the students that the heat and light energy from the sun is converted into chemical energy in the plants through the process of photosynthesis.

✍ 10. Identify simple patterns in physical phenomena.

Simple patterns in physical phenomena includes such things as reflection and refraction of light and waves (e.g. in water); properties of waves (e.g. light and sound); production of high-pitched and low-pitched sounds (vibrating columns of air); elasticity and/or compressibility of materials; seasonal patterns (e.g. light and shadows) due to orientation of sun and earth; daily or seasonal temperature patterns of land and/or water; and movement of heat in a system and/or factors affecting heat movement (e.g. surface area). Students should be able to identify, deduce, and/or explain simple patterns and relationships from text, graphs, charts, drawings, or prior knowledge.

Patterns can also be the generalities that students infer from a broad range of observations; students should understand that while there may be some irregularities in events or phenomena they experience, an underlying pattern can often be found.

Examples:

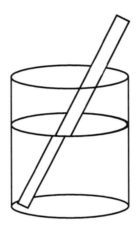

25. In the illustration above, the straw which has been placed in the glass appears to be bent. Which of the following explains the reason for this.

    A. Reflection

    B. Refraction

    C. Amplitude

    D. Camouflage

Analysis:
Reflection of light refers to the bouncing of light off of a surface. This illustration does not show reflection. Choice "A" is incorrect. Amplitude refers to sound. The question has nothing to do with sound. Choice "C" is incorrect. Camouflage refers to the blending into your environment, so "D" is incorrect. Refraction means the bending of light as it passes from one substance to another. The light in the illustration is passing through the water and the air. The bending of the light causes the straw to appear to bend. "B" is correct.

26. A hot air balloon rises. The temperature near the ceiling of a room is higher than the temperature near the floor. What conclusion can you arrive at about warm and cold air?

26.

_____

_____

_____

Analysis:
Answers will vary. Students might say that warm air rises or that warm air is lighter than cold air. They might also state that the molecules are more compressed in cold air than in warm air. The correct answer is "B."

27. As a race car approaches, the sound of the engine appears to have a higher pitch than after the car has passed. Yet, the sound of the engine remains at a constant pitch for the race car driver.

What causes the change of pitch for the person watching the race car?

A. The person watching hears better out the left ear than the right ear

B. The engines revelations per minute are greater as the car approaches

C. The sound waves created by the engine compress as the car approaches

D. The pitch varies with the speed of the car

Analysis:
In answer "A," the change is pitch is not caused by bad hearing since everyone with good hearing hears the same change in pitch. In answer choice "B," the engine is running at a constant pitch and the revelations has nothing to do with the change in pitch. Although true, answer choice "D" is incorrect because it does not answer the question being asked. The change in pitch is actually caused by the Doppler effect, in that as the race car approaches, the sound waves are more compressed causing the high pitch. After the car has passed, the sound waves are stretched, causing a lower pitch. The correct answer is "C."

Teaching Tips for Learning Outcome #10

Experiencing these concepts make it easier for students to actually understand them.

Give students mirrors and flashlights. Ask them to shine the flashlight toward the mirror at different angles and predict where the reflected light will shine. Allow them to work together with more than one mirror to change the angle of the light.

Using flashlights, have the students investigate the position of the light and the length of the shadow of an object. This can also be expanded with a study of the time of day, the position of the sun, and the length of the shadows of objects. Make sure that you have the students guess how long the shadow will be at a later time and see how close they come.

Take a pebble and drop it into a bowl of water, the students will see the rings which move away from where the pebble was dropped. This will help them understand that sound waves travel in a similar way.

Have the students stack a few books on top of a ruler which is hanging out over the edge of the desk. Have them hit the end of the ruler so that it vibrates. After they have recorded their observations, have them move the ruler so that more of it is hanging over the edge of the desk, and record their observations once again. How did the length of the part of the ruler which was sticking out affect the amount of vibration and the sound of the ruler?

Strand III - Earth and Space Science

Earth and space science at the sixth-grade level generally involves events or phenomena that students can witness either directly in their surroundings or indirectly through television or film. Collected observations and inferences made based on collected evidence are also topics for consideration.

11. Describe simple cycles of the earth, sun, and moon.

This outcome tests students' abilities to describe or identify arrangements of earth, sun, and moon that produce eclipses (solar and lunar), a new moon, high and/or low tides, seasons, phases of the moon (crescent to full), etc. Students should have a basic understanding of the relationship between the earth's tilt and the seasons; the relationship between hemispheric location and seasonal temperatures or cycles (e.g. amount of sunlight); the revolution of the earth around the sun and the moon around the earth;

phases of the moon and their relationship to the moon's position near the earth; tides; and changing daylight/darkness hours. Particularly important is that students not retain common misconceptions regarding cycles or phenomena (e.g. the misconception that the earth's distance from the sun causes the seasons, or that a crescent moon is the result of the earth's shadow on the moon).

Since arrangements of the sun, earth, and moon are often simulated using models, students should be aware of and able to discuss limitations of such models. Students should also be able to discuss the concepts and phenomena reinforced by such models.

Examples:

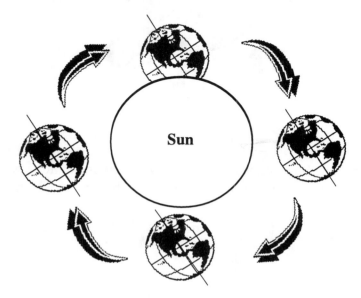

28. The revolution of the earth around the sun, as shown in the illustration above, affects the earth. Which of the following does this revolution affect?

   A. The tides

   B. The mantle layer

   C. The seasons

   D. The height of the mountains near the equator

Analysis:
The tides are caused by the movement of the moon, so choice "A" is not correct. The mantle layer of the earth is not shown in the illustration, so choice "B" is also incorrect. Choice "D" is incorrect because the revolution of the earth does not affect the mountains. The correct answer is "C" is the answer. As the earth revolves around the sun, the tilt of the earth remains consistent, so that at different times the northern hemisphere is closer to the sun than the southern hemisphere and receives more direct sunlight. This creates the changing of the seasons.

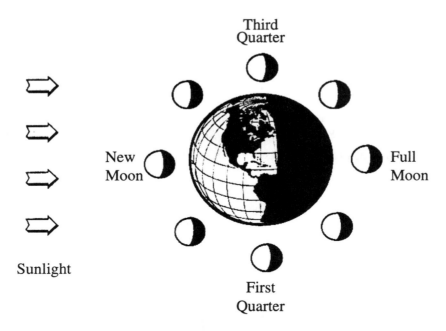

29. The illustration above shows the phases of the moon. Which phase occurs when the whole lighted half of the moon is visible from the earth?

    A. New Moon

    B. Third Quarter

    C. Full Moon

    D. First Quarter

Analysis:
If the students did not already know the corect answer to this question, they could look at the illustration. The sun's rays are hitting the side of the moon closest to the sun. Since the moon on the far right of the picture is the only one in which the entire light side is facing the earth, this must be the correct answer. The correct answer is full moon, or answer choice "C."

30. When Tim was on a family vacation in Florida he spent a lot of time on the beach. He learned a lot about the sea life, shells, and the ocean tides. Describe a beach at high tide and low tide and explain what causes the tides to change.

30.

_____

_____

_____

_____

_____

_____

_____

_____

_____

Analysis:

Answers will vary. Students should have mentioned that the gravitational forces of the sun and the moon pull on the oceans of the Earth. When the sun and moon line up with the earth, the gravitational pull is greatest along that imaginary line. This causes the tides to be highest on the oceans which are along that imaginary line and lowest at the farthest points from the line. When the moon and sun are not lined up, the tides are not at their highest or lowest.

Teaching Tips for Learning Outcome #11

To help the children learn about eclipses, have them position a flashlight (sun), a globe (earth), and a ball (moon) and move the moon to see how the shadow is affected. By using the materials mentioned above, the objects can be moved in such a way that the students can see how the light and shadows cause the phases of the moon. The illustrations below will help students with their understanding of the relationship between the tides and the moon.

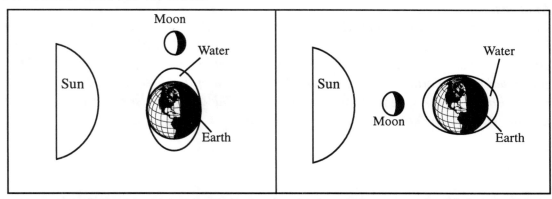

12. Identify characteristics and/or patterns in rocks and soil.

This outcome tests students' abilities to identify the relative hardness of a mineral using scratch tests and the Mohs scale of hardness; recognize or describe in comparative terms (e.g. oldest, youngest) the age of disturbed or undisturbed rock layers; identify or describe characteristics and/or patterns caused by various natural phenomena (e.g. glaciers, earthquakes, rivers, wind); identify land features from a contour map; and analyze data about rock or soil types and identify the following: steps in the formation of rock types (igneous, sedimentary, and metamorphic), water-holding capacity, and factors affecting the development of soil (e.g. climate, plants and animals, land surface features, time, type of parent material).

Students should be familiar with those characteristics or patterns of rocks and soil that can be directly observed or tested; erosion, weathering, layering, hardness testing, and scratch testing are things with which students should have direct experience.

Examples:

31. The students in Mr. Symon's sixth-grade class were conducting scratch tests to help identify various minerals. Jamelle found that his mineral could be scratched with a copper penny, Sherry could scratch her mineral with her fingernail, and James could scratch his with a steel file. Which of the three students had the softest mineral?

    A. Jamelle

    B. Sherry

    C. James

    D. Mr. Symon

Analysis:
Jamelle's mineral was scratched with a copper penny, which is harder than a fingernail but not as hard as a steel file. Therefore, answer choice "A" could not be the correct answer. The steel file that James used indicated that his mineral was very hard. Sherry scratched her mineral with her fingernail, the softest of the three items, therefore, her mineral must be the softest of the three minerals. The question asked for a student name not the teacher. The correct answer is choice "B."

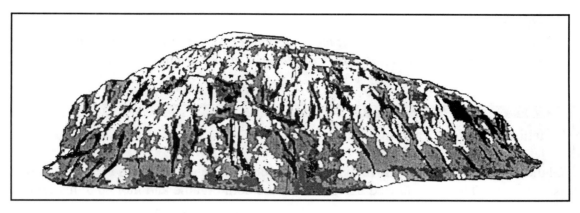

32. Observe the hill pictured above which shows the effects of erosion. What was the cause of this erosion?

    A. Sun

    B. Wind

    C. Chemicals

    D. Water

Analysis:
Students should be aware that weathering is caused by wind, water, and chemicals. The distinctive vertical lines in the side of the hill in the picture above are caused by water. The water moves to the lowest part of the hill. The effects of gravity continue to pull the water down, forming streams and eroding the hillside. The correct answer is "D."

33. Pumice is an igneous rock which has tiny holes from which gases escaped during the formation of the rock. Because it is the lightest of all rocks, it is often used on movie sets when rocks are needed in the film. How are igneous rocks formed?

33.

Analysis:
Answers will vary. Students should mention that igneous rocks are formed from molten rock. They may also mention that they are formed in and around volcanoes.

Teaching Tips for Learning Outcome #12

Gather various soil types. Have the students examine them with a hand lens to see what is in the soil. They should find that soil contains both organic and inorganic material.

Place some soil in a plastic dishpan and tilt it on one end. Slowly pour water over the soil to demonstrate erosion by water. Have students write a description of the process, the patterns formed in the soil from the erosion, and the effects of this process in the world.

Give students various rock samples (available from Carolina Biological Supply and other companies). Number the rocks so that you will be able to tell the students what they are. Have the students work together to describe and compare the rocks. If you give the students sedimentary rocks first, then igneous, and finally metamorphic, they can compare the characteristics of each group of rocks.

---

13. Demonstrate an understanding of the cycling of resources on earth, such as carbon, nitrogen, and/or water.

Students should be able to identify major steps or processes in the carbon, nitrogen, and water cycles (e.g. respiration, combustion, photosynthesis, decomposition, evaporation, condensation, precipitation); identify or describe organisms or pathways through which these processes occur; identify or describe physical or biological factors that affect these processes; and identify where organisms get the nutrients or gases they need in the cycle, and/or how they make those nutrients or gases available to other organisms. Understanding of cycling of resources, plants' importance to all these processes, and environmental results of deforestation are important to this outcome.

Students should be practiced in thinking about the cycling of resources as an accounting of things as they change form, similar to how one can think of the conservation of mass or energy. Students should also be experienced in discussing and explaining what can account for changes in matter or the way resources can and cannot be cycled.

Examples:

34. A group of students securely fastened a plastic bag around a small house plant so that no moisture could enter or escape. The following day they observed that small drops of water had formed on the inside of the plastic bag. Which of the following did the students observe?

A. Decomposition

B. Precipitation

C. Transpiration

D. Conduction

Analysis:
Decomposition is the breaking down of dead organisms by other organisms such as bacteria. Precipitation is any form of water which falls to the surface of the earth. Conduction is the movement of heat or electricity through an object. None of these definitions are applicable. Transpiration is the process of plants giving off water vapor through their leaves. Choice "C" is correct.

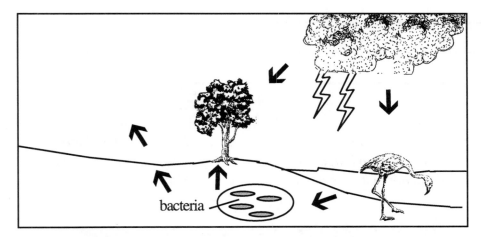

35. The illustration above shows how bacteria and lightning change nitrogen into a form which can be used by plants. Animals get this element by eating plants. The nitrogen is returned to the soil through the waste products of the animals and through the decaying bodies of dead animals.

What is the name of this cycle?

A. carbon cycle

B. water cycle

C. life cycle

D. nitrogen cycle

Analysis:
The three cycles which the students should know are the carbon cycle, the water cycle, and the nitrogen cycle. As the student reads the question, the clue to the answer is the mention of the word "nitrogen." Life cycle is not a correct response. This diagram and the related question refer to the nitrogen cycle, answer choice "D."

36. The destruction of the rain forests of the world may have a major impact upon the world's oxygen supply. Explain why rain forests are so important to us.

36.

_____

_____

_____

_____

_____

_____

Analysis:
Answers will vary. The students should mention that plants take in carbon dioxide and give off oxygen. If the rain forests of the world are destroyed, the plants located there will be destroyed and will no longer be able to give off oxygen. This will diminish the oxygen supply in proportion with the numbers of plants destroyed.

Teaching Tips for Learning Outcome #13

To demonstrate evaporation, place a dish of water on the windowsill of the classroom and have the students observe the water level each day until the dish is dry.

Demonstrate condensation by bring a glass of ice water into the class. Water droplets will form on the outside of the glass as condensation occurs.

Place a small potted plant inside a plastic bag and seal the bag so that no moisture can enter or escape. After a day or so, the inside of the bag will have droplets of water from the plant transpiring.

Strand IV - Life Science

This program emphasizes life science concepts that can be directly observed or explored by students, while minimizing the need to acquire terminology.

14. Trace the transmission of energy in a small, simple ecosystem and/or identify the roles of organisms in the energy movement in an ecosystem.

Items will test students' abilities to analyze food chains and/or food webs and trace the energy transfer among organisms or the level of dependence of groups/organisms on one another; analyze or identify food pyramids for correct representation of energy available at various levels; identify the roles of organisms in a food chain, web, or small ecosystem (producer, consumer, decomposer, predator, prey, scavenger, etc.); identify the primary producers in an ecosystem; identify the relative amount (most, least) of energy from producers that is available to an organism or group of organisms in a food chain or web and describe types of relationships organisms have with one another (parasitic, predator-prey, etc.). Students should recognize that food-chain arrows are drawn from organisms that are eaten to the organisms that eat them.

Students should be accustomed to accounting for the conservation of energy in living systems, just as they are in simple physical systems. Students should understand that organisms ultimately lose energy as heat and gain energy, directly or indirectly, from the sun. Energy can be stored in chemical bonds and passed on as organisms consume this food; and some energy is lost every time energy is transferred. Terms commonly used in discussion (such as producer, consumer, decomposer) should have strong experiential association for students.

Examples:

37. In the forest, grass and other plants are eaten by rabbits. Rabbits, in turn, are eaten by bears. After the bears have died, bacteria consumes the bear.

    Which of the following organisms is a decomposer?

    A. The grass and other plants

    B. The bear

    C. The bacteria

    D. The rabbits

Analysis:
Students should recognize and be able to define the term "decomposer." The decomposer acts as the recycler of nature by breaking down the bodies of dead organisms. Since the only dead organism mentioned in the reading selection is the bear, it can not be the decomposer. The body of the bear was consumed by the bacteria, so the bacteria must be the decomposer. Choice "C" is correct.

38. Plants called strangler figs grow in the canopy layer of the rain forest. As their seeds germinate, the plants grow downward and entwine around the host tree. Eventually, the strangler fig kills the host tree on which it is living.

What type of relationship do the strangler figs and the trees on which they live have? Explain your answer.

38.
_____
_____
_____

Analysis:
Answers will vary. The strangler fig lives on the tree and eventually kills the tree. The student should mention that the relationship is parasitic. They also might say that the strangler fig is a parasite and the tree is the host. Either answer is acceptable.

39. In the food chain, what do we call the organisms which change the energy from the sun into chemical energy?

    A. Entrepreneurs

    B. Primary consumers

    C. Decomposers

    D. Producers

Analysis:
Entrepreneurs are one of the four factors of production. This does not relate to science. Choice "A" is wrong. The primary consumers are animals which eat the plants; they do not have the ability to change energy from the sun into chemical energy. Choice "B" is incorrect. Decomposers are not able to change the sun's energy into chemical energy, therefore answer choice "C" is incorrect. The producers are the plants, which change the sun's energy into chemical energy through the process of photosynthesis. Plants are producers. Therefore, answer choice "D" is the correct answer.

Teaching Tips for Learning Outcome #14

Give students names of animals which are high on the food chain and have them make flow charts of the foods that each one eats down to the plants which produce food by using the energy from the sun. Make sure that you emphasize that the consumers and the decomposers are not able to change the energy from the sun into other forms of energy as plants can. Follow the path of the energy from the sun to the producers, consumers, and decomposers.

On index cards place the names of various examples of producers, consumers, and decomposers. Have the students determine which group each belongs to and state why. Next have the students attach their cards to the bulletin board or chalk board. Have them draw arrows showing the relationships between the organisms. Since a consumer may eat many different organisms, the relationships will become quite complex. Explain to the students that these various relationships are a diagram of a food web.

15. Compare and/or contrast the diversity of ways in which living things meet their needs.

Ways in which living things meet their needs includes both physical characteristics and behaviors by which organisms meet basic needs: energy and/or nutrients for growth; water; shelter and protection or escape from other organisms; thermoregulation or reactions (e.g. migration, hibernation) to climate or other environmental stresses; elimination of wastes; reproduction; and growth and maturation. Items will test students' abilities to identify what need is being met by a particular characteristic or action; identify what characteristic or action would meet a particular need; compare the advantages and/or disadvantages of characteristics or actions that meet the same or similar needs; and analyze an animal's physical characteristics and tell how that animal would react to a particular stress. Items that require analysis of physical characteristics will be clearly illustrated.

Students must be familiar not only with the basic needs of living things, but with characteristics and behaviors through which those needs are met. Since the environments that provide basic needs often change with the seasons, students should be familiar with those changes, with organisms' responses to those changes, and with the effects those responses have. Students should have experiences of growing something or keeping something alive at home or in the classroom, or observations that provide similar understanding.

Examples:

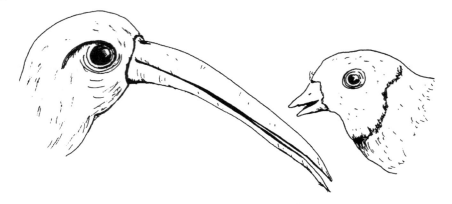

40. Shown above are the heads of two different types of birds. Explain how the difference in the beaks would affect the birds' eating habits.

```
┌─────────────────────────────────────────────────────────┐
│ 40.                                                       │
│                                                           │
│ _____      │
│                                                           │
│ _____      │
│                                                           │
│ _____      │
│                                                           │
│ _____      │
│                                                           │
│ _____      │
│                                                           │
│ _____      │
│                                                           │
│ _____      │
│                                                           │
│ _____      │
│                                                           │
│ _____      │
│                                                           │
│ _____      │
└─────────────────────────────────────────────────────────┘
```

Analysis:
Answers will vary. The student will probably mention that the shape of the beak of each bird would determine the type of food that it would eat. The bird on the right is a seed-eater. The long beak of the bird on the left would allow it to reach into deep, hard-to-reach areas, such as lakes or into flowers. The bird on the left probably eats fish or nectar.

41. Animals such as owls, raccoons, skunks, and bats are nocturnal. Which of the following is an advantage for animals to be active at night?

    A. To help their skin breathe

    B. To keep warmer at night

    C. To allow them to avoid mosquito bites

    D. To keep from being seen by predators

Analysis:
The correct answer is "A." All of the other choices are true statements.

Teaching Tips for Learning Outcome #15
Children are almost universally interested in animals. Since large numbers of them have had experience with pets, draw from their experiences.

Have students work in cooperative groups to compare and contrast two animals. Make sure that you guide them in this to ensure that they focus on the tested objectives. Have them begin by creating a Venn diagram, and then have them write their compare/contrast paper in paragraph form. This will help them strengthen their writing and reading skills as well as the learning outcomes for science.

Provide the students with the opportunity to grow plants in the classroom. Seeds can be purchased very inexpensively at grocery stores, discount stores, and garden stores. Potting soil, fertilizer, and plastic cups are also needed. Many parents are more than willing to provide some of these items if they are aware that the materials are needed.

Have the students conduct investigations using plants in the classroom. Examples are the effect of sunlight on the plants. Make sure that the investigation is carried out using the scientific process. Have students observe, measure, and record data.

✔ **16. Analyze behaviors and/or activities that positively or negatively influence human health.**

Students should be able to analyze and/or identify behaviors or activities that will have the most beneficial effects on human health in a given situation; identify the reasons for such effects, and identify actions to take in situations where there is potential for harm to human health. Topics or areas covered include exercise plans and precautions; food preparation and/or diet; public and personal health and hygiene; accident prevention with materials or equipment at home or in classrooms; basic first aid responses or measures; and safety measures in outdoor activities.

Clear advantages and disadvantages to human health are the focus of this outcome, and students should be practiced in explaining the science and logic behind their evaluations of the behaviors or activities in question. Class-determined safety rules for activities are helpful references in students' learning of the principles of this type of decision-making.

Examples:

42. The sixth grade class of Jackson Middle School was having a class picnic at a nearby park. The students brought fried chicken, potato salad, baked beans, chips, and containers of lemonade to school. The food was kept on a table in the class until it was time to go to the park. At the park, the students placed all of the food on a picnic table while they played baseball, took a hike in the woods, and had relay races. Because it was such a hot day, the food was warm when they finally sat down to eat, but they all enjoyed the meal. In the afternoon, most of the children became very ill.

Explain what the students and teachers should have done to prevent the illness which the students experienced.

42.

_____

_____

_____

_____

_____

_____

Analysis:
Answers will vary. The students should know that cold foods should be kept refrigerated and that warm foods should be kept warm to prevent spoilage. They should have mentioned something about storage of the foods to prevent their becoming spoiled.

43. Deshon, a sixth grade student, wants to become a video-game designer when he is an adult. Each day after school he reads about video games and plays video games. He also practices his keyboarding skills by using a computer program designed to improve those skills. Unfortunately, Deshon has a big problem. None of his classmates want him on their sports teams in physical education class or during their free time at school. The students say that he is too fat and that he can not run fast enough. Deshon feels hurt and lonely. What changes should he make to help correct his problem?

A. Start to play baseball, football, and basketball video games.

B. Begin a diet plan and an exercise program and which will help him lose weight and become physically fit.

C. Tell the teachers at his school to make the other students let him play on the team he wants.

D. Tell his parents to phone the other parents to ask them to make their children let him play.

Analysis:
The correct response is "B". Playing sports-related video games will not help him run faster or lose weight, therefore, choice "A" is not correct. Choices "C" and "D" are incorrect because, even if the teachers do tell the other students to allow him to play, he will still be too fat and he will still not run fast enough. The students will still not want him to play on their teams. This choice would probably increase the problem by causing resentment among the their students.

44. Jeremy knew that his mother wanted a table refinished. He decided that he would surprise her by removing the finish while she was at work. He took the table to the basement and began using the paint remover on the table. After a few minutes, he began to get a headache and feel dizzy. What probably caused his headache and dizziness?

Explain what Jeremy could have done differently to prevent his feeling ill.

44.

_____

_____

_____

_____

_____

_____

Analysis:

Answers will vary. For the first part of the question, the students should have said that the remover caused him to feel ill. For the second part, the students could have said that Jeremy should have read the instructions on the side of the container of remover, that Jeremy should not have used the remover without his mother's approval and supervision, or that he should have opened the windows before using the remover to provide adequate ventilation.

Teaching Tips for Learning Outcome #16

Learning Outcome #16 is an excellent place to also work on nonfiction reading and cause and effect. Bring in newspaper and magazine articles which relate to this outcome, and have the students read them for main idea, detail and cause and effect.

17. Analyze the impacts of human activity on the ecosystems of the earth.

This outcome tests students' abilities to analyze, describe, or identify how human actions or activities can affect the earth's ecosystems and its plant and animal species, in terms of pollution (air, soil, water); conservation of natural resources (including preservation of land, plant and animals species); change or maintenance of habitats for particular plant or animal species; erosion; soil fertility; and effects associated with the use and/or production of different forms of energy.

Students should understand that human activity can have certain effects on the environment, just as the characteristics of an environment can have certain effects or limits on human activity. There are advantages and disadvantages to any activity, and students should be able to identify or discuss these from multiple viewpoints.

45. Dr. Frederick M. Bukowski purchased a two-acre lot on which he wished to build a house. Because the back of the lot was low and very wet, he chose to fill it in and plant grass. How did his actions affect the plant and animal species already existing in the back of the property?

    A. The plants and animals would be much happier because their habitat would not be so wet.

    B. The plants and animals would begin to reproduce at a much faster rate because they would have more room.

    C. The plants and animals would lose their habitat and would die or be forced to find new habitats.

    D. The plants and animals would get more sunlight and grow larger.

Analysis:
Choices "A," "B," and "D" are incorrect because the habitat would be destroyed. The plants and animals would either die or have to find a new habitat after the destruction of the habitat. Choice "C" is correct.

46. Give one cause of air and water pollution and one possible solution for each.

46.	Cause	Possible Solution
Air pollution	(a1)	(a2)
Water pollution	(b1)	(b2)

Analysis:
Answers will vary. Students may have mentioned any of the following causes of air pollution: factories, cars, buses, trucks, or fires. Among the acceptable solutions for air pollution are stronger laws to regulate emissions from factories and vehicles and use of cleaner energy sources. The causes of water pollution are chemicals seeping into the water from the ground, and the dumping of garbage and chemicals directly into the water. Among the acceptable solutions are strong laws to control the dumping of substances into the water, enforcement of existing laws relating to environmental concerns, and use of

alternative methods of pest control and fertilization in place of chemicals. Students may have used other acceptable answers which have not been mentioned here.

Teaching Tips for Learning Outcome #17

Once again, newspapers and magazine articles are an excellent learning tool for this outcome. Make sure that you also use the objectives for reading (nonfiction) and writing also.

Acknowledgments

E & A Publishing wishes to acknowledge their appreciation to the people below for their contributions to the *Show What You Know*® material in this book and the student workbook that is an accompaniment to this teacher edition.

Cindi Englefield Arnold for her talents in graphic designs and layout.

Judi L. Jemson for her effort in assisting in the production of this book. Her endless hours dedicated to seeing the book through the stages of writing, editing, layout, sales, and marketing are truly appreciated.

Angela Mesarchik for her timely, efficient, and superior proof reading and editing on this project.

About the Writers

Jolie S. Brams, Ph.D. is a clinical child and family psychologist who has been in private practice in the Columbus, Ohio area for 11 years. She received her doctorate in clinical psychology at Michigan State University in 1981. Dr. Brams has been a professor at two medical schools, and a pediatric psychologist at several major hospitals. In addition to her practice duties, she teaches medical students and residents at The Ohio State University. She dedicates a large portion of her clinical work for forensic psychology; the relationship between psychology and the court. Dr. Brams is the contributing writer for the Test-Taking Strategies and Test Anxiety chapters in this book.

Joan Schrader has been an educator for 20 years and is currently a teacher at Jennings Middle School in the Akron Public School District. She holds a Master of Science degree from Kent State University in Curriculum and Instruction. She has received two Impact II Awards and two Impact II Adaptor Grants for innovative and creative teaching. She is currently piloting the STEM mathematics program in her classroom, which has an emphasis on the use of manipulatives, problem solving and cooperative learning. She lives in Suffield, Ohio. She is the mother of 4 children, 3 sons and a daughter. She has traveled world wide for 14 years. Joan is the contributing writer for the Mathematics chapter of this book.

Patricia Nay earned a B.A. degree in Spanish and an M.A. in Elementary Administration from the University of Akron. She has been a teacher in the Akron Public Schools for 23 years. She began her career as an elementary and secondary Spanish teacher and then became an elementary teacher in grades 3 through 5. Pat resides in Mogadore, near Akron, with her three sons, Frank, Chris, and Ricky, and a Golden Retriever. She loves to read and travel and has lived in Columbia, South America and Mexico City. Patricia is the contributing writer for the Citizenship and Science chapters of this book.

Deborah Tong has taught and tutored both English and Writing at the middle and upper school levels. Her background in education and writing includes experience as a museum education coordinator, and as a published writer. In 1994, Deborah received an Educational Press Award for a children's magazine article on gardening. She graduated from Middlebury College, VT. She has lived in New England, California, North Carolina, and Ohio. She is married to Kyle, and is the mother of Conor and Emily. Deborah owns her own writing and editing business where she resides in Gahanna, near Columbus, Ohio. Deborah is the contributing writer of the Reading and Writing chapters of this book.

About the Illustrator

Cindy Kerr was born and raised in America's Midwest. She attended Wilmington College. She graduated from The Ohio State University with a Bachelor of Arts degree in Education in 1975. She has taught art to elementary school children and travelled America with her husband's medical training. She is the program coordinator for The Arts Castle, of the Delaware County Cultural Arts Center. She is trying to remain sane and creative while raising five children and a dog in Powell, near Columbus, Ohio. Cindy's talent is evident with her beautiful illustrations found throughout this book.

NOTES

NOTES

NOTES

Prepare for Ohio's Proficiency Tests!
WITH...
Test Preparation Material Specifically Designed for The Ohio Fourth, Sixth, and Ninth Grade Proficiency Tests

Test Preparation Books - designed to help students succeed on the proficiency tests. Written by Ohio teachers, administrators, and psychologists for Ohio's teachers and their students.

Grade	Item #	Title of Book/Description	ISBN#	Price *
9	900	Passing the Ohio Ninth Grade Proficiency Test	1884183-06-9	$15.95
6	601	Show What You Know™, Teacher's Edition	1884183-04-2	15.95
6	602	Show What You Know™, Student Workbook	1884183-05-0	9.95
6	603	Show What You Know ™, Answer Key**	1884183-11-5	2.00
4	401	Show What You Know ™, Teacher's Edition	1884183-08-5	15.95
4	402	Show What You Know ™, Student Workbook	1884183-09-3	9.95
4	403	Show What You Know ™, Answer Key**	1884183-10-7	2.00

* Plus Tax & Shipping   ** Answer Key is a booklet that lists the answers for easy grading of student workbooks

Black Line Masters - Master templates for pattern tiles, transformations, 100 grid blocks, and polyhedras. For Ohio's 6th Grade Mathematics Proficiency Test.

Grade	Item #	Title	ISBN#	Price*
6	604	Show What You Know™ Math Masters - Grd 6	1884183-26-3	$29.95

* Plus Tax & Shipping

Flash Cards - 98 flash cards that cover all of Ohio's 4th, 6th, and 9th grade Mathematics, Citizenship, and Science learning outcomes. The cards tell students why correct answers are correct and why incorrect answers are incorrect.

Grade	Item #	Title of Flash Cards/Subject***	ISBN#	Price *
9	912	Pass In A Flash™, Math flash cards	1884183-07-7	$ 9.95
9	913	Pass In A Flash™, Citizenship flash cards	1884183-12-3	9.95
9	914	Pass In A Flash™, Science flash cards	1884183-15-8	9.95
9	915	Pass In A Flash™, Reading/Writing flash cards	1884183-23-9	9.95
6	612	Show What You Know™, Math flash cards	1884183-19-0	9.95
6	613	Show What You Know™, Citizenship cards	1884183-20-4	9.95
6	614	Show What You Know ™, Science flash cards	1884183-21-2	9.95
6	615	Show What You Know ™, Reading/Writing cards	1884183-25-5	9.95
4	412	Show What You Know ™, Math flash cards	1884183-16-6	9.95
4	413	Show What You Know ™, Citizenship cards	1884183-17-4	9.95
4	414	Show What You Know ™, Science flash cards	1884183-18-2	9.95
4	415	Show What You Know ™, Reading/Writing cards	1884183-24-7	9.95

* Plus Tax & Shipping

Software - Interactive Software for Ohio Proficiency Tests available on CD-ROM for IBM and MAC. Students can have fun while working on colorful interactive software. Call or write for a free demo.

Grade	Item #	Title	ISBN#	Price*
9	925	Passing, Ninth Grade Proficiency - CD	-----------------	$39.95
6	625	Show What You Know™ 6th Grade - CD	-----------------	39.95
4	425	Show What You Know™ 4th Grade - CD	-----------------	39.95

* Plus Tax & Shipping   ALSO AVAILABLE: LAB PACKS $149.95 AND SITE LICENSE $599.95

Englefield & Arnold Publishing

2121 Bethel Road, Suite D
Columbus, Ohio 43220-1804
Phone: (614) 459-3994 • 1-800-225-7277
Fax: (614) 459-3995 • Email: EAPublishg@aol.com

Date:

Purchase Order#:

Tax Exempt #:

Ship To:	Bill To:
ATTN:	ATTN:
Company:	Company:
Address:	Address:
City: State: Zip:	City: State: Zip:
Phone: ( )	Phone: ( )

Quantity	Item #	Title/Description	Price	Amount

Credit Card: VISA   M/C   DISCOVER (Circle One)

Credit Card #:

Exp. Date:

Signature:

Subtotal	
Discount	
Tax	
Shipping	
Total Order	

Shipping Rates

Qty	Rate	Qty	Rate
1-2	$4.00	11-15	$8.00
3-5	4.50	16-20	10.00
6-8	5.00	21-29	14.00
9-10	6.00	30+	4%

Quantity Discounts

Qty	Discount
1 – 29	0%
30 – 49	10%
50 – 199	15%
200 or more	20%

Tax add 5.75%

"Publisher of Educational Materials, Specializing in Proficiency Test Preparation Materials"

Call, Mail, Fax, or Email Your Order To:

Mail: Englefield & Arnold Publishing
2121 Bethel Road, Suite D
Columbus, OH 43220-1804

Phone: (614) 459-3994
800-225-7277 (Ohio only)

Fax: (614) 459-3995

Email: EAPublishg@aol.com

Website: www.eapublishing.com

Publishing